VESTAL GOODMAN
with KEN ABRAHAM

VESTAL!
PUBLISHED BY GOODMAN & ASSOCIATES
P.O. Box 158778
Nashville, TN 37215

The authors and publisher extend grateful thanks to Word Publishing for permission to adapt some material in chapter six from *O Happy Day* by Jamie Buckingham, © 1973, Word Publishing, Waco, Tex. All rights reserved. Used by permission.

Also, grateful acknowledgment is extended to the following publishers for permission to reprint lyrics: "I Wouldn't Take Nothin' for My Journey Now," words and music by Charles (Rusty) Goodman; © Journey Music/Word Entertainment. Used by permission. "God Walks the Dark Hills," words and music by Audra Zarnaco; © 1971, First Monday Music. Used by permission. "Who Am I?" words and music by Charles (Rusty) Goodman; © Journey Music. Used by permission. "He Keeps Lifting Me Higher," words and music by Rick Goodman and Johnny Minick; © First Monday Music. Used by permission. "I've Got Leavin' on My Mind," words and music by Charles (Rusty) Goodman; © First Monday Music. Used by permission. "Standing in the Presence of the King," words and music by Charles (Rusty) Goodman; © 1990, Playin' Tag Music. Used by permission. "Until Then," words and music by Stuart Hamblen; © 1958, Stuart Hamblen Music, Co. Used by permission. "The Answer's on the Way," words and music by Charles (Rusty) Goodman; © 1964, Reico Music Publishers, Inc.; Peer Music, New York. Used by permission. "Sweet Hour of Prayer," words by William W. Walford (1772-1850); music by William B. Bradbury (1816-1868); public domain.

Unless otherwise noted, scriptures are taken from the *King James Version* (KJV). Also quoted: *The New American Standard Bible* (NASB) © 1960, 1977, by the Lockman Foundation.

Copyright © 1998 by Vestal Goodman

All rights reserved. No part of this book may be reproduced or transmitted in any form or by any means, electronic or mechanical, including photocopying or recording, or by any information storage and retrieval system, without permission in writing from the publisher.

Printed in the United States of America

2000

*This book is dedicated in loving memory
to my wonderful dad and my loving mother,
Gordy M. and Mae Freeman.*

CONTENTS

My Thanks ix
Foreword xi
1. Caught on Tape 1
2. The Early Days 15
3. Almost Persuaded 25
4. Saved! 37
5. Howard and Vestal 53
6. An Unusual Courtship 63
7. Singing the Message 77
8. A New Voice 83
9. A New Adventure 93
10. Pastor Vestal 101
11. Rusty Returns 109
12. The First Goodman Album 123
13. Signing with Word 139
14. Rough Roads Bring Out the Best 145
15. The Church on the Move 151
16. Give and It Shall Be Given 161
17. Country Friends 167
18. Heart Trouble 179
19. God Can Heal a Heart 189
20. On the Road Again 205

21.	The Unhappy Goodmans	215
22.	The End of the Line	229
23.	This Can't Be Happening!	237
24.	No Problem Is Too Big	247
25.	Miracles Still Happen	257
26.	Life Out of Death	265
27.	A Journey of Faith	277

My Thanks

To Howard, my loving companion and best friend for more than forty-eight years, who fended for himself the past few months while I was writing this book: I love you.

To Rick, Dianne, Travis, Leslie, You are my passion and I love you deeply.

To Sister Willodean Vaughn, Rev. Earl and Betty Sherrick, Linda and Lela Burnett, and Dr. Bob Minnis—my prayer warriors: I know you each have a direct line into the throne room of God.

To Bill and Gloria and the entire family: What a blessing God bestowed on me when he brought all of you into my life. You are all very special to me and I love you.

To Ken Abraham: Thanks for waiting on me all those times I was late getting to the office. God has given you a wonderful talent, and I thank you for the awesome way you have chosen to use it. May God richly bless you.

To Dr. Marvin Gregory, Dr. Drew Gaffney, and Dr. Robert Schwartz: You are more than just great doctors—you are my friends. I love you all.

To my sisters, Bobbie, Fay, Jonnie Bee, and Millie: Thank you for always being there for me. I love you. Notice I did not say who is the oldest! I'm smarter than that.

Foreword

At first I only knew her by her voice, holding its own with three strong male voices in an insistent sound that could stop you in your tracks.

"Who is *that?*" I asked Bill when he put the needle down on the grooves of a new LP album. I had never heard such power.

"That's the Happy Goodman Family," he said as the contagious rhythm of "I Wouldn't Take Nothin' for My Journey Now" filled our family room. Our little nine-month-old daughter, standing on her newly discovered legs beside the coffee table, began to bend her knees to the beat and laugh with glee. I picked her up and held her by the seat of her pants as she bounded up and down on the back of the couch to "though the devil tempt me and try to turn me around . . ."

"Again!" she would shout from then on whenever she heard "her song." I didn't blame her. There was something addictive about that sound and especially about the voice we had come to know as "Miss Vestal."

I would never have guessed then that God had launched our whole family on a journey of our own that would lead to a close and treasured relationship with this family, the Goodmans.

I have learned that the power behind "that voice" is more than vocal energy. It is the power of undaunted trust in God and His faithfulness to do what He said He would do.

I have learned that the "Happy" in Happy Goodman Family is more than a clever marketing label—that this family loves to laugh, play tricks, tell stories, and, yes, have an impromptu party anytime you set foot on their bus or show up at their house.

I have learned that Vestal is a no-nonsense prayer warrior who bosses Satan around like he is a pesky nuisance who is aggravating but powerless to ruin our picnic.

And I have come to treasure Vestal as a friend who is always "on call" for any reason: a broken heart, a bewildering problem, a joyful victory, or simply a reassuring word.

Vestal can outsing any singer, outpreach most clergymen, outendure the most baffling circumstances, and outrun the devil. She can both hug and scold my husband and get away with it, advise my kids and make them listen, and make her presence felt to us all when she's two hundred miles away. She can travel like a trooper, make the most lethargic audience leap from their seats in ovation, and bake the meanest fresh coconut cake you've ever put in your mouth.

I'm not sure I want to go through all she's been through to get where she is, but I pray with all my might that the journey God has for me leaves me with even a tenth of her character and plain old pizzazz.

One thing is for sure: She's one of a kind, and I thank my Lord for dropping her into my life. Reading this book will teach us all a whole lot more about what it means to sing, "If I could, still I wouldn't take nothin' for my journey now." Dance, baby, dance!

—GLORIA GAITHER

Dear Friend,

Life is a journey, and the road often leads through dark valleys. As you read this book, you will quickly come to realize that my life, like yours, hasn't always been filled with mountaintop experiences. I've walked through times of laughter and great rejoicing, but I've also suffered through pain and heartache. Still, I have been determined to give God glory no matter what comes my way, and I'm thankful for all He has done in my life.

Through my testimony of God's faithfulness, I pray you will be encouraged to hold on to Him. Wherever you may be in your journey, look to God. His promises are true, His Word everlasting, and He loves you!

Vestal

"I Wouldn't Take Nothin' for My Journey Now"

I started out trav'lin' for the Lord many years ago.
I've had a lotta heartache, met a lotta grief and woe.
And when I would stumble, then I would humble down,
And there I would say I wouldn't take nothin' for my journey now.

—Charles (Rusty) Goodman

CHAPTER 1

CAUGHT ON TAPE

*A*s I picked up the telephone receiver, I never dreamed this call was going to catapult my husband and me into an entirely new adventure in our lives. In our journey of more than fifty years together, traveling and singing, we had appeared on stages and in churches all across America as members of the Happy Goodman Family. This telephone call, however, in February 1991, was destined to make Howard and Vestal Goodman household names around the world.

The voice on the other end of the line belonged to a good friend of ours, Bill Gaither. Bill is one of the most successful and highly respected men in the music business. Howard and I had known Bill and his wife, Gloria, for more than thirty years, first as the songwriters of such Christian music classics as "He Touched Me" and "Because He Lives," then as a much-sought-after singing group, the Bill Gaither Trio, comprised of Bill, Gloria, and Bill's brother, Danny. More recently, Gloria had focused her attention on her writing while Bill had formed a new gospel group known as the Gaither Vocal Band.

Bill and Gloria had been innovators in Christian music, always willing to incorporate new sounds and formats, constantly developing fresh ways to communicate the Word of God through words and music, but never compromising the message of Jesus Christ. Although they have written more than five hundred published songs, recorded more than forty albums, performed in countless concerts, and won a myriad of music-industry awards, I wasn't surprised when Bill began telling me about his latest idea for another gospel recording project.

"Vestal, I need your help," said Bill in his usual upbeat tone.

"Honey, anything that Howard and I can do to help you and Gloria . . . you know you don't even have to ask," I replied.

"Well, the Vocal Band is recording a new album—I think we're going to call it *Homecoming* or something like that—and we want to include some of the grand old gospel songs. So Gloria and I got to thinking about it, and we said, 'Wouldn't it be fun to invite some of our friends to sing a song—some of the great gospel singers who influenced us when we first started on the journey so many years ago?' We're going to be recording in Nashville, and I'd be thrilled if you and Howard could come and help us out on the song 'Where Could I Go But to the Lord?' We'll probably shoot a video of that song too. You do remember that old song, don't you, Vestal?"

I laughed at Bill's teasing. He knew full well I knew that song. I said, "Why sure, Bill. I used to sing that song as a young girl back home in Alabama. I've been singing it ever since."

"I'm not sure who all is going to show up, but I'm going to ask several other friends, some of the old-timers like Glen Payne and George Younce of the Cathedrals, J. D. Sumner and some members of the Stamps, Jake Hess, Hovie Lister, and who knows who else. We'll just have an old-friends party."

"Bill, that sounds like fun," I said. Howard and I had seen very few of our former music colleagues in recent years. I thought it would be wonderful to see everyone again—sort of like a gospel music reunion. "When are you going to do it?"

Bill gave me the details of the recording session, and I said I'd check our schedule to see if we were available. Howard and I had been singing at a wide variety of churches since leaving the Happy Goodman Family back in the early 1980s. Although the hectic pace of our schedule had slowed somewhat, to the point we actually had some openings on our calendar, we had been keeping comfortably busy. More importantly, the Lord was using us to minister to many congregations. It was not easy for Howard and me to be on the road, traveling from state to state, city to city, singing and preaching from church to church, but we felt that as long as the Lord gave us health and strength, and as long as He used us to encourage and help other people, we'd keep going.

Nevertheless, for many of our friends and fellow gospel singers, things were getting tight. Although some of them were still able to keep their datebooks relatively full, it was obvious that with each passing year, fewer and fewer people remembered groups such as the Happy Goodman Family, the Speers, Blackwoods, Stamps, and others. Many gospel legends were barely eking out a living, as fewer and fewer congregations invited them to sing in their communities.

At least, that's the way it was before Bill's telephone call.

"Yes, Bill. We have that date open. You want to roll tape around one o'clock, right? Okay, Howard and I will be there shortly after noon." I hung up the receiver and thought, *How nice of Bill to include us in such a fun project!* Little did I know this would be the first of many projects we "old friends" would share.

On the day of the recording session, Howard and I prayed before we left our home. "Lord, You know what needs to be done in this session today. You know Bill's desire to use these songs to encourage a lot of people. Give us a good time today, but even more, use us to glorify Your great name. Grant it, O Lord, we pray. Amen." And out the door we went.

The foyer of the Master's Touch studios in Nashville was already abuzz with activity by the time Howard and I arrived, accompanied by our son, Rick, and his wife, Dianne. It was like walking into a class reunion. The room was crowded with friendly faces, people we had loved for years but hadn't seen or talked with for ages. There was Buck Rambo, formerly of the Singing Rambos, another family singing group with whom the Happy Goodmans had frequently shared the stage. Off to one side of the room were our dear friends Rosinell, Mary-Tom, Brock, and Ben Speer, of the Speer Family. The Speers were one of the first professional gospel music groups to sing Bill and Gloria's songs, recording such favorites as "The Family of God," "The King Is Coming," and "There Is Something about That Name" before most of the world had even heard of the Gaithers. It was fitting that they should be here on this special occasion.

In another part of the room was Eva Mae LeFevre, one of the founding members of the LeFevre Family, also one of the most popular singing groups in America for decades. More recently, Eva Mae's son, Mylon LeFevre, had achieved a good measure of fame as a wayward rock 'n roll artist, before finally coming back to the Lord. In the mid-1980s, Mylon had taken the message of Jesus he had learned from his mama and had melded it with the showmanship he had learned as a rock artist. He formed a Christian rock group known as Mylon LeFevre and Broken Heart, which helped thousands of young people establish a genuine relationship with Christ. The LeFevre legacy continues to touch lives for the Lord.

Everywhere I turned in the studio foyer I saw another old friend. There was Hovie Lister, the sensational piano player and leader of the Statesmen, and Glen Payne and George Younce of the Cathedrals, and James Blackwood of the Blackwood Brothers Quartet fame. Jim Hill and J. D. Sumner of the Stamps Quartet, the renown gospel singers who backed up Elvis Presley during the last few years of his life, were there too. It was just as Bill had said it would be—an old-friends reunion. "Youngsters" Mark Lowry, Mike English, and Jim Murray of the Gaither Vocal Band were also there.

Two country music artists, Larry and Rudy Gatlin, were in the studio foyer too. I had known the Gatlins since they were young boys and had watched them achieve superstardom in their chosen field of music. In the 1970s and 1980s, the sound of the Gatlin Brothers' close, family harmonies, along with their brother Steve (and even their sister LaDonna on some of their recordings), was a pleasant reprieve for many music lovers whose ears were being bludgeoned by psychedelic rock and heavy metal and even crossover country music. The Gatlins' rich voices took them around the world to some of the biggest and best music venues of the day. But they never forgot their roots—solidly planted in the gospel music they had grown up listening to.

All in all, it was a well-traveled group of singers assembled at Master's Touch studio that day. If someone could have added up the miles traveled by the people in that room, the number would have reached the tens of millions. Most of these singers had been instrumental in shaping the face of Christian music in the twentieth century. Each of them was a "world changer" in his or her own way, and each person had sung the message of Jesus to thousands and thousands of people.

The atmosphere in the foyer was electric. Everyone was talking and laughing, hugging each other's necks, and saying "Howdy!" Howard and I joined right in with the party.

"What all's been goin' on?"

"Why, where have you been keeping yourself, darlin'?"

We were huggin' and howdyin' everyone in sight! It was so good to see everyone and to catch up on what our friends had been doing. For years, we saw each other regularly at concerts around the country. We worked together so often that most of us knew each other's songs by heart. Often if one group was doing an encore, the other groups on the same program would join them onstage for the finale. Frequently musicians from various groups joined in the fun. It was like one big musical family.

But by now, most of us had lost touch with one another. Some of the men and women in the studio that day hadn't sung a note for several years. It took Bill Gaither to bring us together once again.

The excitement was almost palpable as Bill called the performers into the studio to begin the session. "Let's go in here and sing awhile," said Bill in his inimitable low-key manner, as he motioned toward the studio door. We eased into the room, and when everyone had assembled in the main studio, Bill prayed a brief prayer, thanking God for allowing us to be together, asking God to bless our efforts. We all said "amen," and Bill went to work, positioning the singers at various places in the oak-paneled studio. Overhead microphones were strategically placed throughout the room, allowing most of our old-timers chorus the luxury of remaining seated while singing. Bill had selected several of us, including Michael English, Larry Gatlin, and me, to sing solos at certain points. The three of us gathered around a large Sennheiser microphone near the center of the room. The only instrument in the studio was a grand piano. Bill had already recorded the instrumental tracks, which we could hear in headphones as we sang along with the music. Everyone donned the headphones and waited for the red light to go on in the studio, indicating that we were recording.

It was clear right from the start that Bill's biggest problem was not getting us to sing—his problem was getting anyone to keep quiet! We were so excited to be together and everyone was having such a wonderful time that our enthusiasm just kept overflowing. The singers were professionals; we all knew that under ordinary recording circumstances we were to be quiet before the red light was illuminated as the song began and until the light went out after the song was over, indicating that the recorder in the control room was turned off. And of course we knew that in most recording situations, one was not to give in to any extraneous expression of praise or worship, no matter how spiritually moved a person might become during a song.

But these were *not* ordinary recording circumstances. And it became obvious after about ten minutes that this was *not* going to be an ordinary recording. Everyone could sense the Spirit of the Lord in that studio.

Jake Hess arrived late at the studio, and I nearly cried when I saw him. I had known Jake since I was a teenager and had followed his career both as a friend and a fan. Jake had sung for years with the Statesmen before forming the Imperials, one of gospel music's trendsetting vocal groups. Jake's smooth-as-velvet voice was the lofty standard that aspiring gospel singers of my generation hoped to emulate. Since his retirement in the mid-1980s, I hadn't seen much of Jake and had only talked with him by phone on a few occasions. I had heard that he had been in poor health, so it was extraspecial to see him that day at the studio!

As Jake listened to the music he, too, immediately recognized that something unusual was going on. "Something special is happening here. I have never felt such a strong presence of the Spirit in a room in my entire life," he said reverently.

Michael, Larry, and I sang our parts on "Where Could I Go?" and the chorus joined in. The song was recorded flawlessly. It was one of most beautiful recordings I had ever been part of. But before the bouncing red needles on the recording console had time to lie still, Bill was already saying, "Let's do another take. That's just too good!" It wasn't that we had sung our parts incorrectly or that anyone had made a mistake; I think Bill just wanted to hear it again!

We sang the song again and "stacked" the vocals—singing the song again and again, putting several "layers" of the same singers' voices on tape, making the chorus sound even larger than it was. It was sounding so good! While we were singing, Bill's studio crew was not only recording our voices, they were also videotaping the entire event—including the comments and expressions between takes.

After a few more takes we completed the recording, and there was really no reason to prolong things any further, but nobody wanted to leave! We wanted to stay right there and bask in the Presence that had obviously permeated the studio.

Bill had arranged for a photographer to take a group photo at the close of the session to commemorate our getting together. We thought perhaps Bill wanted to use some pictures for the album project as well. As we gathered around the piano for the photo, Larry Gatlin suggested, "Let's sing something."

Ben Speer moved over to the grand piano and started playing another favorite old gospel song, and without further provocation the group spontaneously joined in. It was beautiful. Then someone called out, "Hey, what about 'I'll Fly Away'?"

So we sang that song.

"Let's do 'The Eastern Gate,'" someone else suggested.

We sang that one too. On and on it went; with no preplanned or orchestrated arrangement of who was going to sing what, or even what song we were going to sing, we moved from one great old gospel song to another.

"Hey, remember that old song . . . let's sing that one!"

"How about that one the Speers used to do? Remember that one?"

"I've got an idea. Let's try this."

Whoever was closest to the piano (and could remember how to play the song) would jump in and begin playing. Sometimes the person who used to sing the solo in concerts stood up next to the piano and did his or her part, just as we might have done it years before. The music still carried an unusual power.

Most of us had no trouble remembering the words to the songs. An amazing reservoir of spiritual truth was resident in the words of those classic gospel songs, and with the slightest tug by the Spirit of the Lord, we were soon reliving old memories while making new ones. We sang the old Stamps-Baxter songs. We sang the old Vaughn Music Company songs. We sang gospel favorites as well as the old hymns. Looking around that studio and reminiscing about the many great songs and the innumerable lives that had been touched by that music, the words of a song Howard's brother Rusty had written came wafting back across the years: "I wouldn't take nothin' for my journey now."

At one point, almost on a whim, Bill asked Howard to recite a reading that he used to do with the Happy Goodman Family. It was a long poem entitled "I Won't Regret a Mile (That I've Traveled for the Lord)." With no advance preparation, Howard movingly recited every word of that poignant poem.

Tears began to flow freely as members of our group recalled the goodness of God and how He had used the words and melodies of our songs to minister to so many people—including us—over the years. One of the singers raised his hand at the end of a song and said, "I want to say something." He then proceeded to give a word of testimony, telling what God had done in his life recently. He admitted his failures and said something like, "I haven't always lived up to what I have sung, but by the grace of God, I want to from now on."

We all understood. None of us claimed to be perfect Christians. It was only the love of God and the grace of God that He put up with any of us. We all could rejoice with our brother. And rejoice we did! We all prayed and praised the Lord and shouted a little—it was a real "hallelujah time!"

All the while, Bill's recording crews kept the audio- and videotape rolling. When someone eventually realized that the tape was on and pointed it out to Bill, he said, "I don't want to do a video of just 'Where Could I Go?' Let's get it all. There's too much good stuff here. Just let the tape roll, guys."

It's doubtful that Bill Gaither knew at the time what he had. I think he just wanted to record us as a souvenir. Bill has always been not only a premier writer and performer of gospel music, he is one of the genre's biggest fans. He loves the music and the people who have performed it over the years, and he is as close to a gospel-music historian as anyone in the field. To have some of his favorites on tape for posterity, whether the group sang well or not, would be a treasure to him. None of us in the studio that day could have imagined just what a role that tape was going to play in all of our lives.

Eva Mae LeFevre sat down at the piano, and we began singing some of the old LeFevre songs. Someone requested a Gaither favorite, so Bill moved to the piano. Next it was Rosinell Speer's turn, as we all joined in singing some classic Speer numbers. Some of the songs were soft and deeply moving. Others were rousing "camp meeting" numbers, the foot-tapping style of songs that we had literally performed in camp meetings and gospel concerts around the country.

We started singing shortly after one o'clock, and several hours later we were still going strong with no signs that anyone wanted to quit. We took a short break to eat though, when from seemingly out of nowhere a few delivery boys showed up with enough fried chicken to feed an army. Apparently Bill had ordered the food for everyone so we could eat right there at the studio and continue singing. Fried-chicken-wielding singers were all over that studio. No doubt the engineers and studio manager were going bonkers worrying that their expensive recording equipment might be the unintentional recipient of a grease job. But nobody said anything. Everyone was having too much fun!

After eating we went back to singing, and the sound and camera boys continued to capture it all on tape. We sang, prayed, and praised the Lord all afternoon. Nobody wanted to go home, as everyone was aware that God was doing something extremely special.

One of the most moving moments came when Michael English sang the old favorite, "I Bowed on My Knees and Cried Holy." By the time Michael got to the emotionally gripping climax of the song, "I want to see Jesus!" tears were flowing freely down the faces of almost everyone in the studio. It was the heart cry of each one of us.

At one point in the day, the Lord's presence in the place was so powerful that Larry Gatlin sat down "Indian style" on the studio floor. As various members of the group shared what this day had meant to them, Larry listened in awe. Finally he spoke up and said, "This is the most amazing experience I have ever had!" He went on to say, "I was sitting here thinking awhile ago, 'Lord, please don't let anything happen to the people in this room, because if it does, I'll lose all my heroes.'"

It was dark outside by the time our troupe finally sang itself out. As we exited the studio, hugging each other and reluctantly calling out our good-byes, we were tired, and our throats were nearly raw from singing so long, but we were exuberant. God's Spirit had been with us in an unusual way all day.

A few days later, when Bill Gaither sat down in the video-editing room to view the videotape we had made, he was mesmerized by the music and the supernatural power, the *anointing*, that seemed to accompany it. Although the music was not technically "tight," with people singing whatever melodies and harmony they wanted, and the camera shots lacked professional variety—we had used only one video camera, after all—Bill nonetheless sensed that we had captured something special on tape. Unwilling to pull his eyes from the screen for a moment, Bill said aloud as he continued to watch, "We've got ahold of something good here. We've got to do this thing right."

Bill showed the video to a few friends, including Stan Moser, then president of Starsong Records in Nashville. Stan was so moved by the contents of the video he insisted that Bill allow him to take it to someone at The Family Channel. At that time the Christian Broadcasting Network was associated with The Family Channel, and Norm Mintle, a producer at CBN, requested permission to air the Gaither tape.

Bill could hardly believe it. "Are you serious?" he asked Norm. The broadcaster assured Bill that his offer to air the video was genuine. Bill and CBN worked out the details, and the rough video—with no overdubs and very few musical edits, except those necessary to fit into the format of an hour-long television show—aired on national television. Almost immediately CBN's telephones began to ring with accolades and requests that the video be repeated. The network replayed the tape several times, sometimes in the wee hours of the morning, and the response was always the same. Their switchboards were inundated with telephone calls asking for more of the same.

Norm Mintle had included a commercial on the video with a toll-free telephone number people could call to order a copy of the spontaneous revival that had been caught on tape. More than seven thousand people called and placed orders.

Always one to know a good thing when he saw it, Bill Gaither was soon on the telephone again, calling the many friends who had performed in the *Homecoming* tape as well as other gospel-music legends who had been unable to participate in the first recording session.

"We've got to do this again," Bill gushed.

In a matter of months, "the old-timers" were gathered in another recording studio, singing more great songs such as "Peace in the Valley," "Farther Along," "Thank God, I Am Free." This time we were more organized—Bill actually had several cameras on hand for this shoot—but the atmosphere was just as informal. Once again, the Spirit of the Lord took over, and His presence in the room was contagious.

We have now done more than forty video recordings, many of which have aired as television specials. Over one hundred gospel legends have appeared on the tapes, as well as "the new kids on the block," younger gospel artists such as Janet Paschal, Lillie Knauls, Guy Penrod, Cynthia Clawson, and one of gospel music's most talented young groups, the Martins. More than four million Gaither videos featuring the good old gospel music have been sold.

In 1995 Bill struck a deal with The Nashville Network to air some of our programs. The first two that were broadcast were the most popular programs on TNN during the weeks they were carried.

On a personal level, the programs reacquainted many people with Howard and me, while introducing us to a worldwide television-and-video audience, many of whom had never heard of the Happy Goodmans. Suddenly Howard and I were receiving invitations to come and sing in churches and auditoriums around the globe. Interestingly, the invitations spanned the spectrum of denominational lines, from overtly Pentecostal groups to Southern Baptists and Methodists, Lutherans, and so-called sophisticated, uptown Presbyterians. Additionally, in 1997 Bill and Gloria put together a *Homecoming Concert Tour,* taking us old-timers to thirty-two cities across America. As part of the *Homecoming* entourage, in one arena after another, Howard and I sang to crowds as large as twenty-four thousand people—enthusiastic, rejoicing crowds who longed to hear the old gospel songs. In Lexington, Kentucky, the *Homecoming Tour* outsold country crooner Travis Tritt by six thousand tickets. In Memphis the *Homecoming Tour* drew a larger crowd than the rock band Aerosmith!

Crisscrossing the nation by jet or private tour bus and singing to huge audiences can be pretty heady stuff. If I didn't know where my roots are, it would be easy to get swept away in a rush. But believe me, it hasn't always been this way. Let me tell you a bit about where I have come from and where I believe, by faith, God is taking me in the days ahead. The journey hasn't always been an easy one.

CHAPTER 2

THE EARLY DAYS

People who are born and raised in the South hardly ever grow up and move to northern cities such as Boston, Cleveland, or Atlantic City. To a true southerner, moving north might mean being transplanted from Alabama to Tennessee, or from South Carolina to North Carolina, but any further migration northward would most certainly result in severe culture shock or worse. For several generations before I was born, my ancestors on both sides were all southerners . . . real southerners, the kind that wouldn't think of eating fried chicken with anything other than their bare fingers.

Mae Bell Hicks (my mama) was born near Carrolton, Georgia, the baby in a family of seven children. Her real daddy died before she got a chance to know him, but her mama eventually married LaFayette McGee, the man my mama called "Daddy." When Mae was barely six years of age, the McGee family moved to Sand Mountain, Alabama, about seventy-five miles north of Birmingham, where her family worked in the cotton fields.

Gordy McKinley Freeman (my daddy) grew up in a large southern family as well, with five brothers and two sisters. Gordy took after his daddy, Charlie Freeman, a saintly man with a sterling reputation who started a church in his home and helped pioneer the Church of God in Alabama. The Freemans were farmers and settled in the small town of Fyffe, Alabama.

Fyffe is a friendly little town, located atop Sand Mountain, about fifteen miles northwest of Fort Payne, nestled in the heart of some of the South's best cotton-growing country. Most all the neighbors know each other by their first names, and most know each other's business. There aren't many secrets in Fyffe. It was that way long before I was born, and it's still that way today. On the other hand, when anyone in Fyffe needs something, the entire town jumps in to help. It is a way of life that has been lost in many parts of America.

Mae Bell Hicks and Gordy Freeman met as children and grew up on neighboring farms. They married in 1920 and set up housekeeping in a sparse, four-room rental house on a tiny parcel of land on Grandpa Freeman's 120-acre property; Daddy was seventeen and Mama was only fifteen. When Grandpa Freeman died, Mama and Daddy purchased the entire property from the remaining family members for twenty-seven hundred dollars. The purchase included 120 acres of land, the original homeplace, the rental house, a barn, a smokehouse, a corncrib, and a well with a shed over it in the middle of the front yard. Two streams flowed through the property, making it easier to keep the pastures watered. Later Mama and Daddy sold 20 acres and the rental house for twenty-five hundred dollars, enough to pay off the mortgage and live there debt free. Daddy and Mama were to raise their family on the same land where two previous generations of Freemans had lived.

Of Irish ethnic background, Mama boasted a full mane of wavy, brunette hair swirling around the finely chiseled features of her incredibly beautiful face. Mama was a slender, petite, five-foot-two-inch beauty on her wedding day. Over the years, especially after having given birth to six children, Mama gradually gained weight, blossoming into a pleasingly plump bundle of energy. She was still beautiful, but Mama didn't see herself that way. She battled her weight most of her life. She'd throw herself into losing a few pounds, diligently watching her diet, then after a while, she would gain the weight right back.

I was the fourth of six children born to Mae and Gordy Freeman. My brother Claris—C. G. for short or simply "Cat" as we called him—

was the oldest. Two sisters, Jonnie B. and Mildred Mary—whom we called Millie—were older than I, and two sisters, Faye and Bobbie, were younger. For some unknown reason, I was the only Freeman baby that Mama and Daddy gave only one name—Vestal, a name that connotes purity and chastity, as in vestal virgins. My parents named me in honor of Mama's best friend, Vestal Robinson, whose daddy had at one time pastored our church. To this day, Mrs. Robinson and I are the only two people I have ever heard of with that first name.

Since it was an unusual name, as a high school student, I was a bit uncomfortable with it. Not that I didn't like the name—quite the contrary—but one of my schoolteachers insisted on calling me Vess-tale, and it nearly drove me up a wall every time she mispronounced my name. One day I got so upset I wrote V-E-S-T-E-L on a piece of paper and marched up to the teacher's desk. I handed the paper to the teacher and said, "From this day forward my name is Vestel, not Vess-tale." Unfortunately, the change of spelling did not produce a change in pronunciation. My teacher continued to call me Vess-tale as long as I was in her class.

Long after high school, however, the spelling change stayed with me. It wasn't until years later, when the Happy Goodmans were traveling overseas and I needed a passport, that I changed it back to the original spelling that Mama and Daddy had given me: V-E-S-T-A-L.

As far back as I can remember, I have always been aware of a calling on my life. I knew that God had something special for me to do. Daddy believed that too. Daddy told me that before I was born, he had often prayed for another son. He was already the father of one boy and two girls so Daddy really wanted a brother for Cat. One day as he was praying for a second son, the Lord spoke to his heart and mind and said, "No, you are not going to have another son. I'm going to give you another daughter, and she is going to carry My gospel."

Daddy loved to tell me that story. He never let me forget that God had a special plan for my life, even before I was born. Daddy and I had a close relationship, and as I was growing up, at every opportunity he'd tell me, "One of these days, baby, you're going to sing, and you're going to be behind a pulpit preaching the gospel."

He told me so frequently that I developed a terrible dislike for women preachers. I had heard a few women preachers in our home church, and I found them distasteful. "Daddy, I am not going to do that," I told him. "I'm not going to preach."

"We'll see," he said with a mischievous smile.

I was always extremely sensitive to whatever Daddy said. Because of his Cherokee Indian heritage, Daddy's features were dark and well defined. Not a large man—he stood about five foot ten inches tall, about 165 pounds—yet Daddy possessed a strong, wiry, athletic build, topped with the prettiest bald head I had ever seen. He lost his hair in his early thirties, so even as a child I had to look at family photographs to recall him with hair.

Ironically, Daddy was a barber, the best in Fyffe, according to what I've been told. His income from farming and growing cotton was not enough to support our large family, so for most of my early life, Daddy worked full-time in his barber shop and part-time on the farm. He got up early in the morning to do his farm chores, then he went and opened the barber shop, where he put in a full day's work before going back out to the fields in the evening. Sometimes he'd go back to the shop after supper, working until nine or ten o'clock at night. Despite his long, grueling workdays, Daddy never complained about having to work so hard to make ends meet.

Daddy's workplace was a strictly male bastion; it was a *barber shop* not a styling salon, as we have nowadays. Surprisingly, some of Daddy's best customers were high school students, many of whom would not allow any other barber to cut their hair. Once when Daddy was sick and had to be hospitalized for two weeks and out of his shop four additional weeks, the boys refused to get their hair cut until he returned.

Daddy loved those students too. He maintained a standing offer to cut the senior boys' hair for free. Sometimes when money was tight (which was most of the time I was growing up), Mama cringed whenever Daddy insisted on cutting the seniors' hair without charging them, but Daddy never reneged on his offer. "Those kids have a lot of expenses during their last year of school," Daddy said. "It don't hurt none for me to give 'em a few haircuts."

Jovial, quick to laugh, Daddy was an easygoing, laid-back man, with an extremely sensitive spirit. Mom was the disciplinarian around our house; she would get a switch off a tree and wear us kids out. But not Daddy; he was usually the peacemaker. He disciplined with his words rather than whippings. Only one time can I recall Daddy whipping one of us . . . and even then, Mama had to talk him into it. On that occasion Millie had done something seriously wrong, and Mama was extremely angry with her. "She needs a good whipping," Mama told Daddy.

"Well, then give it to her," said Daddy.

"No, you give it to her. And give her a strong spanking."

Daddy resisted, but Mama coaxed him until he finally relented. He cut off a twig from a tree and took Millie behind the shed where he gave her a sound thrashing. When Daddy finished whipping Millie, he walked despondently from behind the shed, sat down on the front porch steps, and put his face in his hands. He burst into tears and cried and cried.

"What's the matter?" Mama asked.

"Don't ever ask me to do that again," Daddy said through his tears. "I won't do it. I'll never strike one of our children again." And he didn't.

Mama was frequently in poor health as I was growing up. She was always taking a cold or was about to. If someone had a headache or a pain, Mama had a worse one. How many of Mama's aches and pains were real and how many were imagined is still debated among my family. Regardless, Mama's complaints didn't slow her down any. She worked hard from long before sunup until long after sundown. She helped Daddy with the farm work and in the cotton fields, but mostly she was so busy around the house she had little time left for working outdoors. Besides keeping up with the usual washing and ironing, Mama sewed clothes enough for all six of us kids. She also cooked incredibly delicious meals almost every day. When she wasn't busy working at home, she was pouring herself into working at our church. She organized quilting bees, special times when the women of the church gathered to sew blankets for our missionaries or others who might need them. She also played the organ during many of our church services.

Hard work was a way of life in our family. All of the Freeman kids worked, not because we wanted to, but because we had to. We never thought of ourselves as poor. We wore dresses made from flour sacks, went barefoot a lot of the time, and had to work in the sweltering cotton fields to help support our family . . . but to us that wasn't poor; that was normal!

With no television to dominate our lives—it hadn't been invented yet when I was a little girl—most of our days were occupied by either school or work. Evenings were spent reading, playing our own made-up games, telling stories, singing, or listening to the radio. We loved to pop popcorn and gather around the radio as Mama or Daddy tuned in their favorite programs. Usually Daddy adjusted the dial on the old tube-style radio until he could bring in the voice of some country preacher. Every once in a while, he scanned past a frequency that aired good old gospel or country music. Daddy would smile as our eyes lit up. Ever so slowly, with that mischievous grin on his face, Daddy would turn back to the music. It wasn't that we didn't enjoy preaching, but we heard plenty of good preaching at church. Music, on the other hand, was a special treat. As I listened to the singers on the radio, something triggered a response deep within me. Even as a child, I knew I wanted to be a singer. *Someday,* I thought, *maybe someone will listen to me sing on the radio.*

From the earliest days I can remember, the Lord was the center of our family. A relationship with God wasn't something Mama and Daddy simply talked about. It was something they *lived.* Each evening around nine o'clock, Daddy called us together. "It's time to pray," he'd say. The family gathered in front of the fireplace in the living room; we all knelt, and Daddy led us in prayer. Of course, Daddy liked it better when each of us prayed aloud. He encouraged us to talk straightforwardly to the Lord. "God's got ears," Daddy said frequently. "He can hear every one of you, not just Mama or me. Just tell Him what you want Him to know. Whenever you have a problem that worries you, tell it to the Lord. God is concerned about you."

Everyone at our house knew that we might as well not go to bed until we had gathered to pray. If one of us kids got tired and decided to go to bed ahead of the others, at prayer time Mama or Daddy would simply wake him up. Even in our teens, when we might have thought, *I'm getting a little too old to get on my knees and pray like this*, it was futile to consider that Mama and Daddy might allow us to miss family prayers. Now I'm sure glad they didn't.

Usually before our family prayer time, Daddy read the Bible to us. He and Mama both could read or tell the ageless Scripture stories in such a way that they came alive. I sat in rapt attention as I heard for the umpteenth time about David and Goliath or Daniel in the lions' den. I never got bored with the biblical stories because it was obvious they were so precious to Mama and Daddy. Sometimes as Daddy was reading along, he'd come to a rich passage of Scripture, and suddenly we'd see tears streaming down his face. Daddy loved the Lord, and he loved the Word of God, and he wasn't ashamed to let us know.

My daddy used to have a saying that I repeat to this day. Daddy said, "Read the Scripture, and if it says it, honey, believe it."

A lot of Christians are fond of saying, "God said it, I believe it, and that settles it." Daddy wouldn't have bought that slogan. To Daddy, God said it, and that was it. If you have any sense at all, you'll believe it, but even if you don't, God's Word is still true.

As for Daddy, he believed it, and he modeled it. He taught us kids to believe God's Word. Praying and believing God for practical things such as food and clothing and other basic necessities was a way of life for us.

Mama and Daddy were also excellent models when it came to giving. They took seriously those biblical passages that talk about tithing (giving the first 10 percent of your resources to God) and the giving of offerings (the amount given beyond the first 10 percent). They believed that as they obeyed God's commands to bring the first 10 percent into the "storehouse," God would keep His promise and return blessings upon them (Malachi 3:10-12).

Daddy never had a lot of money, but he and Mama were very conscientious about giving the first portion of whatever they had to the Lord, whether it was cotton, corn, or hay. When Daddy raised hogs, the proceeds from the sale of every tenth pig went to the church. In addition, we had an apple orchard, some pecan trees, and a vegetable garden. Daddy and Mama always gave the first part of the harvest to the church. Mama canned the peas, carrots, green beans, potatoes, and other produce from the garden. As she did, she set aside every tenth jar of vegetables in a special box which she later took to the church to be distributed by the church leaders. Sometimes the food was used to help feed the pastor and his family; sometimes it went to other needy families in the congregation or in the community. The one place it did not go was to the Freeman family. The first 10 percent belonged to the Lord.

Daddy gave the first 10 percent of his income from the barber shop to the church. Since cotton was our main crop, Daddy also made arrangements to give every tenth bale of cotton to the church. Sometimes he'd take the actual bales to the church; sometimes he'd sell the cotton first and take the money to the church. At other times he placed the first 10 percent of the cotton in a cotton "pool," sort of a community warehouse where the cotton was stored until the price went up, and then it was sold to the highest bidder. In any case, the church received the first 10 percent of Daddy's cotton money. Similarly every tenth bushel of corn went to the church.

Daddy and Mama never made a big deal about their giving; they just did it. Nor were they overly concerned about getting a return on their giving. Although they believed the scriptures that promised God would open up the heavens and pour out blessings upon them, they were not "blessing mongers," giving to get. They were giving because they wanted to obey and please God. They left the return up to Him. And God always gave back more than we gave.

Once a pastor told Daddy, "Brother Freeman, I need some corn for my pigs."

Daddy was quick to respond. "I have one corncrib nearly full, and out of that crib, at least fifty bushels of corn will go to the church. Why don't you bring your truck over to the farm any day you want and get fifty bushels."

"Well, thank you kindly, Brother Freeman," the pastor replied. "I'll do just that."

The day the pastor came for the corn, Daddy was not at home. Mama called to me and said, "Vestal, the pastor is out there to get some corn. Please go show him which crib he should get it from."

"Okay, Mama," I answered as I darted out the door. I greeted the pastor and showed him the appropriate corncrib. In the corncrib were two baskets, a one-bushel basket and a three-bushel basket. The pastor picked up the three-bushel basket and began loading the corn on his truck. He loaded one basket full of corn, two baskets, fifteen baskets, sixteen, twenty, and he kept right on loading until he had counted out fifty baskets of corn. Fifty *three*-bushel baskets! One hundred fifty bushels of corn in all. Even a child my age could tell the difference between the baskets. It was obvious that the pastor used the larger basket intentionally. As I watched the pastor plundering our corn supply, I knew what he was doing was wrong, but I was reluctant to say anything. After all, the fellow was a minister of the gospel. Surely he would never cheat my daddy.

That evening when Daddy and I went to the corncrib to get feed for the animals, Daddy took one look at the corn supply, and I saw his face drop. "What in the world happened to our corn?" he exclaimed, the surprise evident in his voice.

"Daddy, I wanted to say something, but I didn't know if you'd want me to or not. I saw the pastor load all that corn, and I knew it was wrong, but I didn't know what to do."

"You did the right thing, Vestal. You didn't need to say anything to the pastor."

"He used the big basket, Daddy."

"Yeah, he did," Daddy said softly. "He got 150 bushels instead of 50."

Suddenly my righteous indignation flared, and I became furious at the pastor who had cheated my daddy. I expected Daddy to get angry, too, but he didn't. Instead, as he stood there looking at our depleted corn supply, he began to cry. The thought that the pastor had stolen from him hurt Daddy deeply.

Daddy turned around and said to me, "Honey, don't mention this. Don't say anything about it to Mama or anyone else."

"Daddy, I'm gonna go tell that pastor what he has done!" I said angrily.

"No, no, no, no," Daddy said as he waved his hand back and forth. "Let it go. God will take care of it." I stood watching as Daddy turned away from the corncrib and walked down through the hollow toward the barn, wiping the tears from his face and praying as he went.

I obeyed Daddy's order, and for years I never told anyone about the missing corn. But I couldn't help noticing that the following year Daddy had the largest corn harvest he had ever had. God restored to him what he had lost plus much more!

Interestingly, a few weeks after the pastor had cheated my daddy, the preacher got into some other trouble, and he was forced to leave our area.

CHAPTER 3

ALMOST PERSUADED

From the time I was a little girl, Mama and Daddy taught me that our heavenly Father could not only save our souls and take us to heaven one of these days, He could take care of our physical bodies during this life as well. Not surprisingly, when one of us kids got sick, Mama and Daddy's first response was not to run to the doctors—there weren't too many within running distance anyway. But when afflictions or problems came, Mama and Daddy always turned to the Lord first.

When I was about nine years old, we owned a wagon that was pulled by two mules. The wagon was used for farm work, hauling cotton bales, and all sorts of other things, but it was also our main means of transportation. We didn't have an automobile, so all of us kids would pile into the back of the wagon while Mama and Daddy perched on the front seat. That was how we went to church. We lived out in the country, and we rode in the wagon about five miles to and from church every service.

One Sunday night coming home from church, our mules spooked. They began jumping violently, backing up toward Mama and Daddy. The wagon was lurching backward and forward, and Daddy was holding on for dear life, trying to get the mules under control, but he wasn't having much success. Mama got scared that the mules were going to get wilder and start kicking her and the kids, so she tried to jump out of the wagon. As she tried to leap from the wagon, however, she slipped and fell, and her foot caught in the spokes of the moving wagon wheel. Lying on the ground, her leg contorted, Mama screamed for Daddy.

Whether it was Mama's screams or something else that caused it, we'll never know, but the mules—thanks be to God—stopped their commotion. They calmed down, and the wagon stopped lurching. Daddy quickly set the brake and jumped off the wagon to help Mama. He freed her leg from the wheel, and as he did, a pained expression crossed his face. "Oh, Lord! Honey, your leg is broken," Daddy said.

Daddy tried to help Mama to her feet, but she grimaced with pain every time she put pressure on her leg. Finally Dad picked her up and gently placed her back on the front seat of the wagon.

They prayed and prayed, "Lord, don't let that leg be broken, but if it is broken, let it be healed." They prayed like that the whole way home. Meanwhile, the older ones of us were praying along with Mama and Daddy, but mostly we were listening as our parents called out to the Lord.

When we got home, Daddy said to Mama, "Now, sit right there, and I will help you out of the wagon."

But before Daddy could even get around to her, Mama stood right up in the front of that clapboard wagon and started praising the Lord. She had been healed! She said, "I don't need to be helped, honey." And she climbed out of the wagon herself and walked on that leg—the same one that Daddy had been certain was broken! When Daddy saw Mama walking toward the house, he started praising the Lord too. We about had "church" right there in the front yard, thanking God and praising Him for His goodness.

Praying for each other and believing God for healing was as natural to my brother and sisters and me as reciting the letters of the alphabet might be to other families. We had seen all kinds of miracles, and we knew many people who had been healed. When one of us got sick, we didn't think it was weird or unusual that we should pray. We just did it.

When I was thirteen years old, my brother, Cat, became seriously ill. At the time, he was traveling and singing with the Melody Masters, a gospel quartet from Birmingham. He had been singing in Nebraska when he developed a bad case of bleeding ulcers. He winced with pain when anything touched his stomach, and he lost so much weight he could hardly move. When he came home, Mom and Dad got him in bed, and then Daddy told me, "Honey, I want you to round up all the church people. We're going to pray for Cat." By then we had a car, and one of my older sisters took me from house to house, to the church people we knew were good prayer warriors. We asked them to come quickly to our house, as we had to pray for Cat since he was bleeding internally. Believers from all around came that night and filled Cat's bedroom. So many people responded it would have been almost impossible to fit anyone else in the room.

Daddy knew there was a more important issue at stake than simply the healing of Cat's body. In his kind, gentle way, Daddy leaned over Cat and said, "Son, you've got to give your life to the Lord, and when you give your life to the Lord, the promises of the Word are more powerful to you."

"Okay, Dad," Cat replied in a weak voice through his pain. "I will."

"Let's do it right now then," Daddy encouraged. "Are you ready to receive Christ, to ask Him into your life and to repent of your sins?"

"Yes, Dad, I am."

I will never forget hearing my brother praying, repenting of his sins and asking the Lord into his life. It was one of the most joyous moments of my life!

Within fifteen minutes, Cat rose up in bed and began to loudly praise the Lord. The believers who had gathered around his bed were already praying loudly, but Cat's voice overpowered them all as he shouted, "Dad, I am healed!"

Before we had prayed, Cat could hardly stand his clothes to touch his stomach. Now Cat started slapping his stomach like he had just eaten a huge meal. "Dad," he cried, "there is no pain." The awesome presence of God was in the room that evening as we all praised God for what He had done—not just healing Cat, but saving his soul, too, which is much more important.

Those early experiences of learning how to trust God for physical healing would literally save my life in later years.

Family was important to the Freemans, not just as a concept, but as a practical way of living. With so many aunts, uncles, and cousins, it was a rare day we didn't have an extra mouth to feed at the supper table. Two of my favorite relatives on my dad's side of the family were Uncle Ernest and Auntie Mary Freeman. When Uncle and Auntie visited, they usually showed up on Sunday mornings in time for church. As soon as I saw them, I managed to wriggle out of my family's front seat and make my way back to Uncle and Auntie. I'd squeeze into their seat, just as close to Uncle as I could get. I was always possessive of him. I didn't want to share him with anyone, sometimes not even Auntie!

Each summer Mama and Daddy allowed me to visit Auntie and Uncle for a few weeks. It was always great fun. Their house was roomy and fresh, and Auntie kept their home immaculate. Both Uncle and Auntie worked at the cotton mill, so during the daytime while they were gone, I'd play with the neighbor children.

One day while Auntie was at work, Ivalee, one of the neighbor girls, and I busied ourselves by making mud pies. We had a grand time all day, playing in the mud, packing it into pans, and pretending we were baking our pies in an outdoor oven. By the time we were done, Ivalee and I were caked in mud. That wouldn't have been so bad, but then we decided to wash our muddy pots and pans . . . in the house. We carried our grimy pots and pans through the house, dropping and tracking mud as we went into the bathroom where we began washing them in the sink. Mud splattered in every direction, all over the room.

When Auntie came home from work, she discovered our mess. "Vestal, what have you done?" Auntie cried.

"Well, Auntie, we had to wash our pots and pans," I answered.

Auntie didn't get angry or yell at me; she simply said, "You mustn't do that again," as she set about cleaning up the mess. Talk about the patience of Job.

If I had to pick a favorite relative on Mama's side of the family, it would probably be Granny McGee. Grandpa McGee died when I was just a little girl, so after Grandpa's death, Granny McGee visited our family often. Millie and I especially enjoyed Granny's visits, because during her stays, Granny slept with us in our room. Lying in our big double bed, with Millie on one side of her and me on the other, Granny loved to tell us bedtime stories. She knew more funny stories than anyone. She'd start telling us a tale, and soon she'd get tickled and fall out laughing. We'd laugh so hard the entire bed would jiggle!

Granny especially loved telling us scary stories at night. As Granny used her voice expertly to dramatize every detail of the story, Millie and I snuggled in that much closer to her. Before long we'd be so petrified we didn't dare move. As frightened as we were, we couldn't get enough of Granny's stories. "Tell us the rest of it, Granny," we'd plead if she even hinted she might not continue.

Granny and Daddy were big buddies when it came to storytelling. Sometimes Granny and Daddy would plot to see who could scare us the most with their stories. Mama played right along with them. She thought the way Granny and Daddy could get to us was hilarious. There was never a dull moment when Granny was around.

Granny was an incredible cook too. She was especially good at baking cakes and cookies. Granny cut towels out of feed sacks, which she washed over and over until they were soft, then dried them in the sun. She used those towels for lots of things, but especially for cooling her baked goods. When Granny was making cookies, she'd take them out of the oven and put her warm cookies in one of those towels. We kids always wanted to know where Granny's towels were.

Her wardrobe included a large apron wrapped around her dress. The pockets of that apron were stuffed full of just about anything we might need throughout the day. "Granny, do you have a pair of scissors?" one of us might ask. Granny would search in her apron, and sure enough, she'd pull out a pair of scissors.

Oddly enough, Granny dipped snuff. While this may seem rather unfeminine to modern women, back then it was common to see a woman with a wad of snuff in her mouth, especially on a hot summer day in the heart of Alabama. The tobacco juice mixed with saliva substituted for having to drink gallons of water and possibly getting sick. Granny was meticulously neat about her snuff dipping. She was always sure to spit the snuff juice in a can and then toss the can in the garbage.

Granny looked as though she enjoyed her snuff so much that we kids begged her to let us dip some snuff too. She never permitted it. Instead Granny made us some chocolate cookies that looked a little like snuff, and we pretended we were dipping the real stuff. No doubt the sugar-filled cookies didn't do our teeth any good, but I guess they did less harm than the tobacco might have done to our mouths.

Mama was the authoritarian in our family, but when a decision concerning the kids could go either way, she often ceded her power to Daddy and allowed him to have the final word.

One day I was giving Mama fits about wanting to go somewhere with my friends.

"No, I don't think that's such a good idea," Mom answered.

I kept on begging, "Please, Mom, can't I go? Everyone else is going. If I don't go, I'm going to be the only one who misses out. Please, I'll be fine, honest."

Mama acquiesced. "Oh, all right. Go ask your daddy. Whatever your daddy says will be okay with me."

Daddy was out plowing the fields, and he reined in his horse and stopped immediately when he saw me running toward him. "Whatcha need, baby?" he called.

Even before I stopped running, I quickly began to pour out my request, telling Daddy what I wanted to do.

Daddy stood behind his plow for a moment, wiped the sweat off his brow, and looked me right in the eyes. He pulled me close to him and hugged me. "Now, baby, you know whether you ought to go. You know what's going to be happening there before you go. And you know I trust you. If you think it's all right, then I think it's all right. I trust your judgment. I know you ain't gonna do anything wrong. If you think it's all right, then go ahead, but if you don't think it's good, don't go."

In my heart, I knew I wasn't about to go.

Years later Howard and I used that same formula with our son, Rick. He responded much the way I did. With our daughter, Vicki, we had to be much more specific, but both of our children knew that their parents trusted them.

Much of my early life revolved around the church. We were there every time the doors were open. We spent a lot of time going to revivals and camp meetings, special series of services designed to deepen the spiritual lives of believers and draw the uncommitted and unbelievers into a relationship with Jesus Christ. Most of the churches in our area held revival services at least twice a year, sometimes more. Usually revivals and camp meetings lasted from a week to ten days. Sometimes though, if God seemed to be moving, which meant that the unconverted were getting "saved" and the believers were being "filled with the Holy Ghost," a revival might go on for several weeks. I can still vividly recall a special outpouring of the Spirit at our church, the Highway Church of God, which lasted more than six weeks. We had church every night, and my sisters and I attended every single service. We never got home before midnight, but Mama and Daddy didn't mind, and neither did we. If God was doing something special, nobody wanted to miss it.

Many folks went from one series of revival services to another, from one church to another; if the Baptists were having revival services, the Methodists attended the services, too, and vice versa. Back then, the church, school, and family all supported each other. Nowadays parents consider themselves blessed if the church and schools can help them teach their children ethics and values. As I was growing up, it was the other way around—the home was the primary place where morals were taught; the church and school merely buttressed the already firm structure that parents built.

Highway Church of God was nestled serenely in the shade of a towering pine grove, about a mile off Alabama's State Road 75, which was the main highway going from Rainesville to Albertville. The church was about five miles from our home and, as I mentioned earlier, we usually traveled there in an open-air wagon. If it looked as if it might rain, we prayed a little harder. We carried quilts to sit on that helped soften the bumpy ride and also prevented our Sunday-best clothing from getting dirty. If it rained while we were on our way to church, the blankets became our umbrellas.

Early on Sunday mornings, long before the service was scheduled to begin, the men and women of our congregation gathered at the church to pray. For their prayer meeting, the men walked deeply into the pine grove behind the church to an area where they had cleared out some trees. The women went to another clearing in the pines behind the sanctuary. Back then, in our congregation men and women did not mix during prayer time on Sunday morning.

Meanwhile the children went into the church and sat quietly, playing or scribbling on whatever paper we could scrounge from our parents or peers. Then just before the service, we could hear the adults coming out of those woods. It was a sound I will never forget: men and women emerging from the pines, singing, shouting, and praising God at the top of their voices. What a sight they were too! The saints were radiant as they entered the sanctuary from both sides of the church.

Once inside the sanctuary the men took their seats on one side of the building, and the women sat on the opposite side. Usually my sisters and I sat with Mama. When we were about ten or twelve years old, Mama allowed us to sit with our friends . . . as long as we behaved properly.

Our worship services were loud and rousing, incorporating not only the organ and piano, but usually several guitars, a French horn, and any other instruments that members could play. An enthusiastic choir sang loudly during each service, followed by the pastor's strong, often hellfire-and-brimstone sermon. The Sunday morning service usually let out shortly after noon.

Members of the congregation who lived a long distance from the church often brought their lunches with them and, between services, had "dinner on the grounds," a sort of family-style picnic. They'd lounge around the church property, some of the adults stretched out on blankets, others relaxing in chairs, while the children amused themselves in the pines or played games on the church lawn. Toward evening the rest of the congregation began to amble in for another preservice prayer meeting in the pines. Sunset was the signal to start the evening service. Once again the congregation gathered for a spirited time of singing, praising God, and preaching. The service did not have a planned closing time; we simply stayed until everyone got tired. Then my family and I piled into our wagon and bumped our way back home.

Beginning around the age of seven and continuing into my teenage years, I became conscious that I needed my own genuine relationship with the Lord, that I needed to be "saved" as folks in our church put it—saved from my sins and saved to live for God. About that time our pastor, T. B. Wesson, and his wife, Ruth, took an interest in me. I especially loved Sister Wesson. She was more than a pastor's wife to me; she was a friend. When I was about ten years old, Sister Wesson asked me kindly but directly, "Vestal, when are you going to get saved?"

"Sometime, Sister Wesson," I replied. "We'll talk about it."

Sister Wesson looked at me with such concern and compassion I felt free to confide in her one of my main fears about committing my life to Christ. "Sister Wesson, I know that when I get saved I'm gonna have to confess that I have been called to preach the gospel. And I'm not ready to do that yet."

Sister Wesson was an extremely wise woman, especially when it came to matters of the Spirit. She did not regard my response as the excuse of a precocious little child. On the contrary, she took my answer very seriously. "I understand, Vestal," she said. "When it's time, you'll know." Throughout my younger years, Sister Wesson continued to pray for me. She kept an eye on me and encouraged me to know the Lord, but she never tried to rush what God was doing in my life. We both knew that eventually God would win out; it was only a matter of time. I went so far as to tell the Lord, "I'll wind up doing this. I'm gonna give You my life, but I'm not ready yet."

At times I wished that I was ready. Our church had a strong emphasis upon the second coming of Christ and being ready spiritually when Jesus returns. The church taught that Jesus could return at any moment, that He would take His people out of this world, and those who were not living clean, godly lives at the time of His coming would be left behind. Antichrist fodder, we considered those who were not ready to meet Christ.

One day I came home from school and went into the house, but nobody was there. In a family our size, that was rare. Our house always seemed to be bustling with people. I quickly ran through the house, shouting as I went, "Mom! Daddy! Millie! Faye? Bobbie? Jonnie! Cat? Anybody!"

No voice answered my calls. Instead, silence and fear wrapped around me. Only one conclusion could be drawn: Jesus had come and had taken my family to heaven. All except me. I had been left behind!

I ran out the back door and raced across the yard to the barn. I got just outside the barn door when I heard a voice—a familiar voice, one of the most beautiful sounds I had ever heard. It was Daddy!

Huffing and puffing, I pulled up short of the barn door and edged closer to hear what Daddy was saying. At the same time, I breathed a huge sigh of relief. If Daddy was still here, I knew Jesus had not come yet, because if He had come, my daddy would have been gone.

I peeked inside the barn and saw Daddy down on his knees. He was talking, but there was nobody else in the barn! Suddenly I realized that Daddy was praying. I listened more closely and heard him call out my name. *What was he saying about me?* I wondered.

I strained to hear Daddy's prayer. "Oh, Lord," he said, "whatever you need to do, please save Vestal. Cause her to turn around, to turn away from sin, and to turn her life over to you."

Almost as a reflex action, I pulled my face away from the barn door. I leaned back against the building and thought, *There is no way out of this but to get saved.*

By the time I regained my composure and walked nonchalantly into the barn, Daddy had finished praying and had gone back to working. "Daddy, I heard you praying," I told him after we had greeted each other. "Don't worry. It's all going to be all right. You don't have to worry about me."

"I know, baby," he said with a smile, as he hugged me tightly. "I gave you to the Lord even before you were born. Someday you are going to sing and preach for Him, and you're gonna carry His gospel to the world."

CHAPTER 4

SAVED!

When I was about ten years old, Mama and Daddy paid for me to take piano lessons. That wasn't going to fly with me. I didn't want to play an instrument . . . I wanted to sing!

I had always wanted to sing. I sang my first solo in public when I was three years old. Naturally it was in church. Daddy was sitting in his favorite spot, on the right side of the congregation, two rows from the front. When the pastor announced that I was going to sing, Daddy encouraged me, "Go on up there, darlin', and sing for us."

I hurried onto the platform, turned around, took one look at the congregation waiting to hear me sing, and got scared. I ran back to where Daddy was sitting.

"Go ahead, baby," Daddy said softly as he wrapped me in his arms. "You can do it. Do it like Daddy taught you. Now go back up there." I would have done anything to please Daddy, so I didn't need a lot of coaxing. I bounded back up the two stairs leading to the platform. I turned around and looked at Daddy. He was beaming. "Help her, Lord; help her," he said aloud.

In my biggest "outdoors voice," which at the time was still extremely light, I sang, "Jesus loves me, this I know; for the Bible tells me so . . . "

As I sang, I heard Daddy say, "Oh, hallelujah; oh! Hallelu . . . yer."

When I finished singing, I hopped back down the stairs into the waiting arms of Daddy. He was so proud of me.

From then on, I'd sing anytime and anywhere anyone asked me to. Daddy told us kids, "If someone asks you to sing one time, don't wait till they ask you a second time. Sing!" Consequently whenever I was asked to sing in church, I was always quick to respond.

I learned to read music before I could print my ABCs. When I was five years old, prior to starting first grade, I attended my first "singing school," a crash course in music training. Each summer, at least one of the churches in our area (and usually several churches) conducted singing schools. Classes were held daily on church property for a couple of weeks at a stint. Course requirements included the new Stamps-Baxter songbook, an A. J. Showalter *Rudiments of Music*, and a lined music notebook. From the Stamps-Baxter songbook, we learned some of the great old hymns of the church as well as the most recent gospel compositions. Showalter's *Rudiments* served as our textbook and provided an excellent overview of music theory for beginners, including scales, notes, rests, meter, and timing. The lined notebook was used for our own practice.

All of the Freeman children attended singing school. Some of us enjoyed it more than others, but we all learned how to project our voices and how to sing harmony. The music we learned and sang at singing school was gospel music, never show tunes or any other kind of music. Although we weren't conscious of it, while we were learning to sing, we were also being exposed to the gospel. We were not simply learning how to perform; we were learning how to communicate an important message. It was great fun, but it wasn't something we took lightly. Singing school was serious stuff.

One of the teachers who influenced me most at singing school was Jay (J. L.) Freeman, Daddy's cousin. Another was Ben Stevenson, a kind, gentle man who really knew how to inspire young people to sing for God. Both Jay and Ben had tremendous skills in music, but even more important, they had a heart for the music they were teaching. To them, the music was not simply words and notes; it was life.

Because I was kin to Jay, he didn't think twice about using me as an example in front of the class. After a few days of singing school, during which we studied, sang, and practiced, Jay graded our music work papers just as if we were in school. Then it was time for a real-life demonstration. Often Jay selected his daughter, Katherine, along with two of our relatives, H. M. Freeman and his brother, Junior, and me to be in a quartet. The students in the class—sometimes as many as fifty children—were allowed to call out any of the songs in their books, and the quartet had to sing them, whether we knew the songs or not. Jay wanted us to be able to sing by note, not merely by memory.

While I was in my early teens, my sisters Faye and Bobbie and I started singing as a trio during singing schools. Faye was six years younger than I was, and Bobbie was only six years old! Before long, we received invitations to sing in some of the local churches as well as at the county fair and other civic functions. Many of the nearby communities held talent contests during their fairs, so Mama entered my sisters and me as the Freeman Trio. We won every contest we entered!

Meanwhile our brother, Cat, was making a name for himself in music too. Daddy and Mama sent Cat to more music schools than any of us. Cat attended Vaughn's School of Music in Lawrenceburg, Tennessee, and studied "serious" music. He also went to the Stamps School of Music in Dallas, one of the most prestigious "proving grounds" for fledgling gospel artists. Daddy worked his fingers to the bone to earn enough money to send Cat to music schools. When Cat came home from one of his many music-education experiences, Daddy had him teach my sisters and me everything he had learned. Cat loved that. He had Daddy's authority to tell his sisters what to do. None of us Freeman kids could actually play the piano, but Cat could pick out a few notes, so he gathered us around the piano and made us sing parts over and over again, teaching us how to sing harmony. Then he'd make us switch parts and do it some more. In the years to come, knowing how to sing all the parts in a song would be a valuable asset. Sometimes Cat could get a bit overbearing in his big-brotherly attempts to turn us into "Cat's School of Music" students, but he really did help us to learn how to sing better.

A decisive event in my understanding of music occurred when I attended a singing school at a Methodist church in Geraldine, Alabama. The school was associated with Vaughn's School of Music, and the head instructor was a man named Dewey Yeager. Mr. Yeager saw potential in me as a singer, so he took a personal interest in helping me develop my voice. While the other students were doing notations, Mr. Yeager took me into one of the side Sunday school rooms and had me sing while he accompanied me on the piano.

One evening he and I were practicing my lessons alone in the Sunday school room. "Vestal, please sing 'The Old Rugged Cross' for me," Mr. Yeager instructed.

I began singing the well-known hymn. We had sung the song so many times in our church as I was growing up that I could almost sing it without looking at the music

I hadn't sung much more than the first line when Mr. Yeager abruptly stopped playing the piano. "No, no, no!" he said. "You aren't singing it. You're just singing *a* song; now sing me *the* song."

Mr. Yeager played the introduction again, and I started over. I didn't get any farther than the last time before Mr. Yeager stopped me again. He turned to me and spoke kindly but firmly, "Vestal, do you really want to sing?"

"Why sure, Mr. Yeager. I want to sing for the rest of my life."

"Well, if you really want to be a singer, and you really want your singing to be of any value, you must learn to sing with feeling. Right now, you are not singing with feeling."

Mr. Yeager's words stung me, but like many teenagers all I wanted to do was finish and get out of class, and my attitude was probably obvious. He could easily have given up on me at that point, but he didn't. Mr. Yeager continued, "Now, let's try it again. And this time, don't just sing the words and notes, but *see* in your mind what you are singing about. Close your eyes and see Jesus on that old rugged cross. Sing about what you see on that cross."

We began again. And again. And again. Over and over, Mr. Yeager had me sing that song. I never made it to the chorus before he'd stop me. "You still don't see it, do you?"

"Yes sir," I answered. I thought I was seeing Jesus on the cross, but Mr. Yeager was not convinced.

"Who are you singing about?" he asked me.

"I'm singing about Jesus on the old rugged cross."

"Can't you see it? Can't you see Him, hanging there with nails in His hands and through His feet? Can you see Him with a crown of thorns on His head? See the blood trickling down His face. Try seeing it, Vestal," Mr. Yeager implored.

Although I didn't appreciate it at the time, Mr. Yeager was giving me the most important singing lesson of all. He was teaching me it is not enough merely to sing the words and notes correctly or to perform some sort of vocal gymnastics. It is not enough simply to produce beautiful music. Mr. Yeager was teaching me that if I wanted to sing about Jesus, it was necessary for me to spend time with Him, to know Him, to have a sense of His heart, to be able to rejoice over the things that please Him, and to be brokenhearted over the things that break the heart of God.

Mr. Yeager was not minimizing the importance of proper voice inflections, hitting the notes on pitch, or any other part of my music skill. He was simply saying, "Vestal, your ability, without the anointing—God's supernatural touch—can never help a soul. People may hear you sing and go away impressed at your technique or your talent, but that will not help them make it through the tough times in their lives. Nor will it get them into heaven. If you are going to sing about Jesus, you have to *know* Jesus and let your audience see Him in you. Let them go away talking about Jesus, not just you."

To this day, I credit Dewey Yeager for helping me understand not just how to sing, but more important, why I sing. I am convinced that

I began to fall in love with Jesus that night in that Sunday school room as Mr. Yeager helped me see for the first time, really, the cross on which Christ died and the Christ who died on the cross.

Prior to that night I had not truly committed my life to Christ. Of course I had grown up hearing about Jesus, talking about Jesus, even singing about Jesus. I knew a lot of information about Him, but I didn't really know Him, and I certainly did not have a close relationship with Him.

I became conscious of sin in my life and my need of a Savior about seven years of age, but I resisted making the most important commitment a person can make. Why? Because a major stumbling block weighed heavily on my mind. I knew that the moment I committed my life to Jesus Christ I would be called to preach. Throughout my childhood and into my early teenage years, I could not shake Daddy words, "Vestal, someday you are going to carry the gospel." Although I went to church regularly with my family and friends, attended fever-pitched camp meetings and revivals, and prayed every night before I went to bed, I continued to ignore invitations to meet Christ. I preferred to continue in my sinfulness rather than become a lady preacher.

During my early teenage years, I became even more uncomfortable about my lack of a real relationship with God and my awareness of my own sinfulness. Of course, at that time my worst overt sin was sneaking off to a movie in Fort Payne with my sister Millie and our friends while Mama and Daddy thought we were attending revival services at our friends' church. Going to movies, according to our church, was strictly prohibited. Lying about where we had been made matters even worse! After each rendezvous with my friends at the movies, I'd live with horrible guilt and condemnation . . . until the next opportunity to go to the movies came along.

It took some work to keep Mama and Daddy from finding out about our movie excursions. The biggest problem was that I could never lie to Mama. If I even tried to tell Mama a lie, she could see right through me. She'd look me in the eyes and say, "Vestal, you're not telling me the truth, are you?"

Inevitably I'd begin crying and say, "No, Mama, I'm not." Immediately I would start confessing everything I had done.

But Millie . . . ah, dear sister Millie! My sister could look Mama directly in the eyes and spin the biggest tale, all the while vowing and declaring that it was the absolute truth. Millie and I quickly learned that if we had done something the night before that we didn't want Mama and Daddy to know, the way to avoid detection was to let Millie talk to Mama before I did. First, Millie and I would conspire on our story, getting all the details down so I could corroborate what she said. But Millie would be the first to face Mama.

Mama would grill Millie about where we had been the night before, what we had done, and who we had seen, and Millie would answer every question to Mama's satisfaction. She may not have answered a single question totally truthfully, but at least Mama's suspicions and concerns would be allayed. When I would come into the room, Mama didn't quiz me about the previous night, because she was perfectly content that she had already discovered all she needed to know from Millie. Only on rare occasions did Mama catch Millie in a lie.

Usually our lies were not blatant; they were more like half-truths (which is still a lie, in case you are wondering). For instance, the morning following one of our movie adventures, Mama asked, "Where did you go last night?"

"Why, Mama, we went to church," Millie answered semi-truthfully. We had indeed gone to church . . . for about fifteen minutes. The Straight Creek Church was holding revival services, so we stopped in long enough to see who was there and to be seen by the saints. At first chance, we slipped out of the service and headed off to a movie.

"Who did you see?" Mama asked.

Millie rattled off a list of friends or church folks who had attended the service.

"What about Sister Jones? Was she there?"

"No, Mama. I didn't see her," Millie answered truthfully. The previous evening Millie had paid careful attention to who was there and who was not. Sister Jones had not attended the service. "Maybe she's come down with something and isn't feeling well," Millie continued with feigned concern. "You might want to check on her."

"Yes, maybe I'll do that," Mama replied, as Millie and I went on our way.

One of my favorite teachers in school was my high school English literature teacher, Miss Grubbs. She was the sweetest teacher I ever had. I loved Miss Grubbs. Ironically, I was in the minority. Most of my classmates thought she was mean and cantankerous. Miss Grubbs was an old-maid schoolteacher—and she liked to be referred to as such. With her gruff, gravel-pit voice, she sounded as if she were going to bite off a student's head when she spoke.

Not me. I never feared her. If Miss Grubbs snapped at me, I turned right around and answered her in the same tone of voice.

Although Miss Grubbs did not want me to know it, she thought my replies were amusing. I did know it though, because every once in a while when I retorted, I'd notice a glimmer of a smile creep across her face. I was never disrespectful; this was the Deep South, after all, where students were expected to say, "yes sir, no sir, yes ma'am, no ma'am." But I knew how to make my statements sting.

Despite Miss Grubbs's gruff exterior, she inspired in me a great love for books. In fact, one of my favorite pastimes as a teenager was reading. I especially loved reading Grace Livingston Hill novels because they were filled with romance, intrigue, drama, and fascinating characters. When I read a Grace Livingston Hill book, I was no longer a teenage girl working in the cotton fields of Alabama. I was living vicariously through the characters in her books, transported through time to a variety of wonderful places and experiences. Grace Livingston Hill wrote more than eighty books, and I read all of them but two. (The only reason I didn't read those two was that I couldn't find them!)

I loved going to the library too. I felt like I was in heaven with so many wonderful books from which to choose. And I read many of them. I was always checking out an armful of books.

When I finished reading a book, I'd immediately write a book report on it. When a teacher assigned book reports in class, I had a ready supply. Miss Grubbs thought my book reports were awesome and told me so.

Sometimes we had to give oral book reports. While most of my classmates nervously anticipated standing in front of the class and talking, I looked forward to those times. Once Miss Grubbs invited Mr. Boston Massey, our school principal, to listen while I gave a book report. Just as I stood to give my report, I saw Mr. Massey slip in the back door of the classroom.

Miss Grubbs thought I might be intimidated by his presence. She needn't have worried. When I saw the principal, it enhanced my desire to do a great report. I mean, I burnt it up! I did one of the best book reports I had ever done, and later both Miss Grubbs and Mr. Massey told me that it was excellent. I am indebted to Miss Grubbs for helping me to become more comfortable with speaking in public, which would come in handy in the years ahead.

Six years later when my sister Faye took English literature, Miss Grubbs was still the instructor. Faye, however, did not enjoy reading as much as I had. Nor did Faye relish the opportunity to write a book report. One day Faye discovered a gold mine—a box in the closet full of book reports. The next time Faye needed a book report for class, she simply took one of my old reports, copied it in her own handwriting, and turned it in.

The day that Miss Grubbs returned the reports, as was her custom, she called each student by name to come up to her desk. There the student received a word of encouragement, some note of instruction, or sometimes a scolding.

"Faye Freeman," Miss Grubbs called. Faye hurried to Miss Grubbs's desk, anticipating words of praise for a fine book report. But when she looked at her paper, to Faye's surprise and chagrin she saw that Miss Grubbs had given her a B.

Barely looking up from the stack of papers on her desk, Miss Grubbs said, "I gave your sister an A for that report."

I was never a bad person . . . at least not by most people's standards. I never killed anyone; I didn't even dislike too many people. I didn't get drunk, take drugs, sleep around, or cause trouble. I was a "good" girl according to the definition of most folks living in Fyffe, Alabama, in the middle of the twentieth century.

Oh sure, I could get pretty angry at times. And sometimes I'd cuss a little or say bad words, things I never wanted Mama or Daddy to hear. My vocabulary wasn't filthy, but I knew Mama would not have approved and Daddy would have cried had they ever heard such language coming out of my mouth. Beyond that, I was the master of the snide remark; I could slice through someone with my words, and I often did.

Perhaps the problem that plagued me the most, though, was my stubbornness. I could be extremely strong-willed. And during my teenage years, I began to recognize that if I were to become a Christian I would have to surrender my will for God's will . . . and I wasn't sure I was willing to do that.

With me Christianity was an all-or-nothing issue. I had watched people "get saved," some of them for the fourth time in a month, but I didn't detect any changes in their lifestyles, vocabularies, or attitudes. I was repulsed by what I saw as fake Christianity. I believed in God; I believed in Jesus; and I felt that if a person gets hold of the real thing—a genuine relationship with Christ—it's gonna show up in his or her lifestyle. I was not content to settle for anything less.

One night my good friend Nellie Hartline and I attended a revival service at Highway Church of God. That in itself was not unusual. But for me, that night was going to be very different.

Nellie and I sat in our usual row on the left-hand side of the church near the back. Mama and Daddy would not allow me to sit in the back row, because that's where the rowdy kids usually sat, so I got as close as I could to the action. Nellie had already become a Christian, as had most of my closest friends. I was one of the few holdouts. Earlier in the week, though, I told Nellie, "I think I am going to do it."

"Do what, Vestal?"

"I think I am going to give my life to Jesus Christ."

"Vestal, that's wonderful!" Nellie gushed. "When are you going to do it?"

"I don't know. But I think it's time. Soon," I assured her. Nellie hugged me, and I knew she was praying for me. Still this had to be my decision. I knew what it would mean if I surrendered my will to Christ.

That night as the service progressed, I felt an unusual tugging at my heartstrings. God was speaking to me, and in my own way I was speaking to Him. Toward the close of the service, the preacher gave an invitation. He instructed those who wanted to trust Jesus Christ as Savior to come down to the front of the church to kneel and pray. It was not a particularly compelling altar call, but people responded. Men, women, and children gathered at the front of the church and began calling out to God, as the congregation sang a traditional altar-call hymn.

Meanwhile, a rather curious conversation was taking place near the back of the church. In my brash way I was telling God, "I want to go down to that altar. I want to get saved. I want to be filled with Your Spirit. But I don't want to play any games. Everything You have for me, I want. And when I tell You tonight that I'm gonna give You my life, I'm gonna mean it. And I'm gonna walk after You, and I want to be as much like You as You have ever allowed a human being to be."

As the congregation continued to sing that night at Highway Church of God, I continued talking to God. "I'm fixin' to go down there," I whispered to the Lord, "and before the public, I'm fixin' to give You my heart and life for everyone to see." In actuality, I gave God my life as I stood in the row, long before I took the first step toward the front of the sanctuary, but I insisted on clarifying the matter with God and for myself before I responded publicly. "I want everyone to see that I am not ashamed to make a public commitment of my life to You."

Suddenly I felt my body moving toward the front of the sanctuary.

From behind me I heard Nellie let out a "Whooop!" As I moved forward, it seemed as though I flew from the back of the church.

I hit the altar area, fell to my knees, and began to pray. Within three minutes I knew that God had done something supernatural in my life. I was changed. I felt clean. I was free. I felt His presence flow into me, through me, and out of me in a way I had never before experienced. I got so lost in the Lord's presence I became oblivious to everything and everyone around me.

People later told me that Mama and Daddy, who were in the service that night along with Faye and Bobbie, had a real hallelujah time. I'm sure that is true, but I would not be able to confirm it personally. I was in my own little world with God.

When Daddy saw me coming down to the altar area, he immediately started praising God. While I was on my knees, Daddy was on his feet, shouting and dancing, skipping all across the front of the sanctuary, from one side of the church to the other. Nellie, too, was dancing and praising the Lord, along with our friend Niva Bell Maddox. Mama was rejoicing as well. Mama was not as expressive as Daddy—she was not a shouter or a dancer—but she had a deep relationship with the Lord. When she saw me on my knees, Mama simply stood with her face tilted heavenward as the tears flowed.

I stayed on my knees for about forty-five minutes. When I stood, I knew that in a real way I was a different person. My commitment to God had been sealed. I felt as though everything had become brand-new, that indeed I had become, as Jesus described it, "born again." A new sense of joy permeated my being.

People were hugging me and telling me how much God was going to do in and through my life. Everyone seemed so happy for me. Nellie expressed what many people in the church were thinking. Nellie said, "If you think Vestal sang good before, wait till you hear her now!"

That night after the excitement had calmed down, Daddy and I sat by ourselves in two rocking chairs on the front porch of our house. A warm, gentle breeze caressed us. Daddy and I began discussing what had happened to me at church and what we thought it meant. Both of us knew what my conversion implied, but Daddy didn't want to rush me. On the other hand, I was still flying high, and I couldn't wait to tell him what he had waited so long to hear.

"Daddy, I don't know how long it will take," I began slowly, "but I have made my commitment to the Lord. I'm gonna start studying the Word of God; I'm gonna start learning scriptures more; I'm gonna walk closely after Him, and I don't know when, but I know that at the right time, He'll let me know and I'll preach His Word."

Words were not necessary to convey the love Daddy and I shared that night under the stars. We embraced, and tears of joy streamed down both our faces.

Over the next few days Nellie and I spent a lot of time talking about the call God had placed on my life to sing and preach His Word. Besides being one of my best friends, Nellie was a Sunday school teacher and a pianist in our church. She loved the Lord and knew a lot more about the Scriptures than I did, and I respected her opinion. I told her, "I don't know what to do, Nellie. Do you think I ought to tell the members of the church about my call?"

God gave Nellie great wisdom in that moment. Nellie replied thoughtfully, "No, Vestal. Don't be in too much of a hurry. Wait until you know it's time, and then you can tell the church." I took Nellie's advice and kept quiet about my calling, but I set about studying the Scriptures with a new passion, getting ready for whatever God wanted me to do.

Even though I had been in church all my life, the roots of my spiritual life were still fairly shallow. Like any new Christian, I needed time to grow stronger spiritually. I needed to allow God the opportunity to transform me. In the weeks following my conversion experience, one of the first ways I noticed God changing me was that I was kinder to everyone around me. Prior to meeting Jesus, if I didn't like someone, I wasn't bashful about saying so, no matter who I hurt. If I had an opinion about something, everyone knew it, whether they wanted to or not. After I committed my life to Christ, I was still outspoken and opinionated, but

Jesus took the sharp edge off my attitude. I no longer took joy in sarcastically skewering a person.

Instead I wanted my words to encourage and bless people, to lift them up rather than to weigh them down. For some people such a change may not seem all that significant, but for me it was earthshaking. It was also a clear confirmation in my spirit that Jesus was changing me into His image. I realized that He was remaking my life, just as the scripture says, "Therefore if any man be in Christ, he is a new creature: old things are passed away; behold, all things are become new" (2 Corinthians 5:17).

God did not put me on hold while He was deepening my relationship with Him—just the opposite. The Lord knew I had a lot of energy and enthusiasm that could be used to tell others about Jesus. Nothing is more contagious than the exciting witness of a new believer. And I was more than excited to tell everyone I met about the Lord.

During that time, Nellie, Niva, and I started a singing group called the Highway Church of God Trio. We sang for a number of revival services in our area. One week, we went to Guntersville, Alabama, every night to sing for Pastor A. N. Lee's revival services. Pastor Lee was a precious man of God, and one night after a service I told him about my daddy's prayer and my subsequent call to preach.

Brother Lee hugged me and said, "Yes, I know it, honey. I, too, believe you are called to carry the gospel."

Brother Lee's words were a confirmation to me about my calling. Nevertheless, it was a full six months before I told the members of our home congregation that I had been called by God to preach His Word. During a normal Thursday night prayer-meeting service, we experienced a mighty move of God's Spirit. Many members of the congregation were crying; some were praying, and a number of people were standing and giving testimony concerning what God had done in their lives. As I sat in the sanctuary that night, I sensed the Lord speaking to me, "Now is the time."

Obediently, but nonetheless nervously, I stood. When it was my turn to speak, I first reminded the congregation of the night I had committed my life to Christ. Many of the dear saints who were in the Thursday night prayer meeting had also attended the night I had met the Lord. They nodded in agreement as I spoke about my experience. I paused for a moment, took a deep breath before continuing, then said, "And I know that God has called me to preach . . . "

I didn't have to say anything more. In fact, it wouldn't have mattered if I had. Nobody would have heard me. Folks all around the congregation were praising the Lord. Some were shouting; others were crying tears of joy; all were rejoicing with me.

Chapter 5

Howard and Vestal

When interviewers ask me about the most important milestones in my music career, my mind does not immediately turn to Grammy Awards or singing before governors or presidents. My first response is usually, "I married the right man."

Some members of the media are stymied by my response. They can't imagine, in this day and age, that a woman as outspoken as I am could possibly view her success as being intricately bound with a man. But I believe that God has our steps ordered and had I not followed His plan for my life, I might have enjoyed some measure of musical success, but I would not have discovered the immense depth of satisfaction and fulfillment that I have known. Interestingly, the man I married belonged to a group of fellows that my big brother, Cat, desperately tried to keep me away from.

Cat was, by all accounts, one of the best tenors in gospel music. He moved away from home when I was still in grade school, but about the time I turned sixteen, Cat teamed up with Reverend C. T. Douglas, a traveling evangelist and a radio minister who was broadcasting over WSGN in Birmingham, Alabama. Reverend Douglas had another singer working with him, a portly fellow with broad shoulders, curly hair, and a wide smile. His name was Howard Goodman.

Before he took the position playing piano and singing for Reverend

Douglas's services, Howard had been singing and preaching throughout Alabama, Tennessee, Kentucky, and the Carolinas with his sisters, Ruth, Eloise, Stella, and Gussie Mae, and his younger brothers, Sam, Rusty, and Bobby. The family's enthusiastic gospel singing and Howard's fiery preaching often created a stir in churches and on street corners where the group conducted services. Their music was usually well received, but Howard's preaching made many people uncomfortable. He regularly spoke against moonshine, gambling, and immorality—three popular vices among many of his listeners. On more than one occasion, some drunken mountaineer with a jug of homemade whiskey resting in the crook of his arm threatened to silence not just Howard's preaching, but Howard himself. "You just keep it up, fat boy," one drunk hollered, "and you won't be long fer this world."

Howard never backed off his message. He continued preaching hard about sin.

The group called themselves the Happy Goodman Family, a tag they adopted in their youth when their mama once declared, "You Goodman kids are always laughing and having fun. We may not have much of this world's goods, but we sure are happy. We're not just the Goodman family. We are the *happy* Goodman family."

Happy or not, the Goodmans could not earn enough money to support themselves through the meager offerings they received at their meetings, often less than twenty dollars. Besides, Gussie and Stella had both married, and Rusty and Bobby were struggling through a rebellious streak. Howard decided it was time to enter a new phase of ministry. The Happy Goodman Family broke up, and Howard went to work with Brother Douglas; Brother Douglas did the preaching and Howard did the singing.

Shortly after Cat joined Brother Douglas and Howard, they scheduled a tent revival meeting on Sand Mountain, near Albertville, Alabama, about eighteen miles from Fyffe. Of course my family and I planned on attending. I was so excited to see Cat. It seemed as though he had been gone forever.

The week of the revival meeting I was ironing clothes, trying to help Mama. When I finished, I was in a hurry to get everything put away. Thinking I could cool the iron more quickly, I placed the hot iron in a pan of cold water. Whooosh! Steam erupted all around my hand, scalding my skin. I dropped the iron into the pan, yanked my hand away, and howled in pain. Big blisters formed on my hand almost instantly. I could barely move my fingers.

Mama heard me crying, and she came running, as did Faye and Bobbie. They got some ice, put it in a cloth, and gently held it against my hand. I was shaking so badly they could hardly keep the ice on me.

Despite the pain in my hand, I was determined to attend the tent revival in Albertville. I refused to miss a chance to see my big brother and to hear him sing again.

The night of the revival on Sand Mountain, Mama, Daddy, Millie, Faye, Bobbie, and I were among the first to arrive and the last to leave. We hugged on Cat, and then he introduced us to Brother Douglas and the burly piano player. Howard Goodman shook hands with Mama and Daddy and spoke respectfully, "I'm so glad to make your acquaintance." As Cat introduced Howard to me, Howard's eyes locked on mine. Suddenly a stunned expression came over his face, as though a surprisingly euphoric thought had interrupted our introduction. Howard quickly snapped out of his momentary daze, and it was then that he noticed my hand.

"My Lord, girl. What did you do to your hand?" he asked with genuine concern in his voice.

I told Howard that I had had an accident involving an iron and that my hand was severely burned. "Why we need to pray for you right now," he replied.

Brother Douglas and Howard prayed for my hand to be healed. My hand was not instantly, miraculously healed, although the burns did clear up rapidly in the days ahead. I must confess, however, that at the time it was not my hand that was experiencing startling sensations; it was my heart. Something about that Goodman fellow caused my heart to flutter. He was a big bear of a man with a strong voice, yet Howard seemed to possess an extremely gentle and sensitive spirit. I couldn't help thinking that I would feel mighty safe and secure in those big arms of his.

Although I didn't know it at the time, I later learned that Howard's heart had been affected that night too. On the way back to Birmingham, he told Brother Douglas, "I met my wife tonight."

"Who? Vestal Freeman?" he asked.

"Yes sir. I think she's just about the prettiest thing I've ever seen," Howard answered.

"Aw, Brother Howard," he drawled, "you don't mean it. You're joking, aren't you? That girl is just sixteen years old, and you're twenty-five."

"No, I do mean it."

"Well, Howard, you're sure gonna have one hard time courting her," Brother Douglas said with a grin, "'cause Cat won't let her date gospel singers."

"What?" Howard almost shouted. "What do you mean she can't date gospel singers? How come?"

"Cat's been around a lot of singers," the pastor replied as he slowly nodded his head. "He knows what some of them are like. He's not about to turn that pretty little sister of his loose with some hot-lipped gadabout. I don't know how he feels about you, but I do know he's told me several times that he'd kill the first gospel singer who tried to date Vestal."

"Oh, my soul!" Howard moaned. "I find my wife, and right away somebody's trying to kill me!"

Brother Douglas was right. Cat had discouraged me from dating gospel singers. Of course, to my big brother, no fellow was good enough for me. But Cat wasn't simply being overprotective. He knew that God had placed a call on my life, and he did not want to see me squander it by getting involved with someone who might draw me away from the Lord.

For the next four years, I didn't see Howard Goodman very often. Occasionally he stopped by our family home with Cat, and of course I'd go to see them when they were holding services anywhere nearby. But Howard and I never went out on a date. He was always going off on another crusade with Cat and Brother Douglas. As I continued through my high school years, I dated a number of young men, but I could never get Howard out of my mind. Something about him intrigued me.

I was fascinated by the fact that such a giant of a man could be moved to tears so easily when talking or singing about the Lord. Most young men I knew believed in God, but few of them ever got teary-eyed over Him. They talked about a "god" who was out there someplace; Howard talked about a God who was within him, guiding him, and maintaining a friendship with him. When Howard prayed, he didn't sound as though he was reciting the Gettysburg Address. Howard prayed fervently, passionately, personally. I liked that in a man.

I loved to watch Howard play the piano during the revival services. Howard didn't simply play the piano, he attacked it. With his large, strong hands, he literally hammered the keys into producing sounds. And what wonderful music it was! I could hardly believe it when one night after a service, Howard told me that he had never taken a music lesson in his life! In fact, Howard told me that his piano playing was actually a miracle.

As a boy of twelve, Howard developed an interest in the piano. His parents, Sam and Gussie Goodman, both loved music and attended singing schools as they were growing up. Howard's mama also learned how to play a pump organ as a child, so perhaps Howard inherited his fascination with the keyboard from her.

Howard's family was much too poor to own a piano, but while living near Vinemont, Alabama, Howard gave his life to the Lord and began going to church regularly. The church had a piano.

Every Sunday morning Howard was one of the first worshipers to arrive at the sanctuary. All by himself he'd sit on the piano bench, and with one finger hitting one key at a time, he attempted to plunk out tunes on the piano. One of the first melodies he learned was the old hymn "Nothing But the Blood of Jesus." After a while, he learned how to add a harmony part with a second finger.

Howard's piano practice was not appreciated by one woman in the congregation. Unfortunately she happened to be the church pianist. "That Goodman boy is nothing but a pest," she complained to the pastor. "Ever since he joined the church he's been fooling around with this piano. Last Sunday we couldn't get him in his Sunday school class because he wanted to sit up here and pick at the keyboard."

The pianist threatened, "Preacher, if you don't do something about it, I'm going to!"

Before long, the church pianist took matters into her own hands. Early one Sunday morning Howard was sitting at the piano excitedly picking out a new tune with his index fingers. Suddenly without warning the piano lid slammed down on his fingers!

Pain shot through the twelve-year-old's fingers. Howard yanked his hands out from under the heavy wooden lid and looked up to see the angry face of the church pianist, darts shooting from her eyes. "I told the preacher that if he didn't make you stop messing around with my piano that I was going to. Now you get up from this bench right this minute and get out of here. Don't you ever touch that keyboard again."

"I'm sorry, ma'am," Howard answered, as he flexed his fingers to see if they still functioned. "But how am I ever gonna learn to play unless I . . ."

That was more than the church pianist wanted to hear. She reached over and grabbed Howard by the ear and literally picked him up from the piano bench. "Don't you dare talk back to me, you little white trash!" she screamed at Howard. "Learn indeed! The likes of you don't ever learn nothing. What makes you think you could ever learn to play the piano anyhow? And even if you did, what would you do with it—

play in some honky-tonk? You'll never amount to anything anyway so get out of here and don't come back."

Not surprisingly, the church pianist did not become one of Howard's music mentors. Nevertheless, he wouldn't give up. Something deep within him kept telling him that he was destined to play the piano. He continued showing up early on Sundays, and continued to pick out tunes with his two fingers. And the church pianist continued to slam the lid on his hands every chance she could.

A kind neighbor woman who attended the same church owned a piano that her husband had loved to play before he died. The woman allowed Howard to stop by and play her piano. It wasn't like having one of his own, but it sure beat getting his fingers broken. Howard's daddy knew that his boy loved the piano, so one day he said to his wife, "'Taint right for the boy to have to play somebody else's piano. There's an old piano for sale for fifty dollars down at the feed store. I'm gonna get it for him so he'll have a piano of his own."

Fifty dollars was a colossal sum in 1932, especially for Howard's family as they worked long hours for little money, trying to make a living off a twenty-acre farm. But Sam Goodman wanted a piano for his son, and he was going to get one.

Howard rode in the buckboard wagon along with his daddy to pick up the instrument. On the way to the feed store, Howard asked, "What kind of piano is it, Daddy?"

Sam Goodman grinned and replied, "It's a 'Beat Up' brand."

"Oh, that's good," Howard answered naively.

At the feed store, several strong men helped Sam Goodman load the heavy upright piano into the back of the wagon. Howard was ecstatic; he finally had a piano of his own.

On the way home, however, the mule pulling the wagon got spooked, bucked violently, and tried to run. As the beast jerked on the reins, the piano lurched backward . . . and slid right through the back end of the wagon and crashed in a mud puddle in the middle of the road. As Howard heard the awful, resounding "dischords" emanating from the keyboard, his heart sank. He saw that the piano lid had been ripped off and was lying on the other side of the road. The keyboard was covered with mud. Howard sat down beside his new piano and cried.

Some men came from nearby houses and helped Sam hoist the piano back onto the bed of the wagon. "Don't worry," Howard's daddy assured him, "'Beat Up' pianos are the toughest kind." The men standing around all nodded in agreement. They followed Howard and his daddy home and helped safely unload the muddy piano.

Howard and his mama went to work wiping the caked mud from the keyboard. Sam replaced the lid, and when they finally got it cleaned up, Howard's daddy pulled out the piano stool and motioned for Howard to sit down. The entire family, as well as the men who had helped unload the piano, stood around and listened as Howard timidly plunked out his first two-fingered rendition of "Nothing But the Blood" on his own piano. Soon the whole crowd was singing along with Howard: "What can wash away my sins? Nothing but the blood of Jesus!"

Although Howard now had his own piano on which to practice, he could only play with two fingers. He longed for the day when he could run his fingers—all ten of them—up and down the keyboard, making great music as he had seen other pianists do. Yet every time he sat down to play, he could get only two of his fingers to produce music. He shared his frustrations and his dreams with his mama, and she suggested that just as God gives all Christians certain gifts of His Spirit, maybe the Lord would give Howard a special gift of playing the piano.

Howard had a deep desire to serve the Lord, and he felt that in some way it would be with his piano, so he began seeking a deeper walk with God. One Sunday morning at his Uncle Herschel's church, Howard was filled with the Holy Spirit as he gave a testimony during the service. Howard began to praise the Lord and had the powerful sensation of God's presence pouring over him.

After the service, when Howard got home, he couldn't wait to tell his mama about what had happened. Gussie Goodman began to shout praises to God. Then she said, "Willie Howard, the Lord said, 'Ask and you shall receive.' You asked and you've received. Now get in there and sit down at that piano and claim the gift the Good Lord has given you."

Hesitantly, Howard sat down at the piano. He looked at the keyboard and then stared at his fingers uncertainly. Was it really possible? Could God actually . . . would God actually give him a gift of playing the piano?

Howard began to play tentatively, using only his index fingers. As he played, he prayed. Suddenly he could feel his other eight fingers reaching out to the keyboard. Slowly they began to move on the keys. As Howard continued to praise the Lord, he could feel his fingers pressing on the keys . . . and there was sound . . . and it was actually music! All ten of his fingers were dancing up and down the piano keys, playing music such as Howard had never before heard. God had miraculously given Howard Goodman an ability to play the piano.

Now as I sat in revival services listening to Howard and Cat singing and watching Howard using the gift God had given him for His glory, I couldn't help wondering what other miracles the Lord had in store for this gentle giant of a man.

CHAPTER 6

AN UNUSUAL COURTSHIP

From the time I was sixteen until I was nearly twenty years old, Howard and I communicated mostly by mail. I looked forward to receiving his letters, but they always threw me into a quandary. Howard wrote such warm, wonderful letters, and I could feel myself falling in love with him, but I hardly ever saw the man! He was always out preaching or singing somewhere.

He did ask me to marry him when I was only sixteen. During a series of revival services at Albertville, Cat, Howard, and his sister Ruth were staying at our home. Each evening we rode to church together in Daddy's car. A week went by, and Howard and I saw each other every day. We talked a lot and enjoyed one another's company. It was obvious that his interest in me was more than a big-brother-little-sister relationship, and I knew I was attracted to him, even though he was nine years older than I was.

One night on the way to church, Howard and I were sitting in the backseat of the car, and Mama and Daddy were in the front. Suddenly Howard looked at me, put his arm around my shoulder, and gently kissed me on the cheek. "Will you marry me?" he asked sweetly. "Please say you'll marry me."

"Yeah, I will," I answered without a moment's hesitation. I truly believed that Howard and I were meant to be married. He didn't have to talk me into it.

Howard squeezed me tightly, and we went on to church. And that was it!

After that, we both knew that we belonged together, but Howard was always so busy! He never followed up on his proposal, nor did he ever give me any indication that he was ready to make a commitment concerning our future together. When we talked about marriage, it was always in a general way, never about *our* potential as a married couple. After a while, my frustration with Howard's procrastination caused me to cringe every time I saw one of his letters in our mailbox.

In Howard's absence, I eventually began dating a nice young man from our community. At first he and I dated merely as a matter of convenience—just friends going out and having fun. After we were together for a while though, people in our small town simply assumed we'd get hitched. Maybe that's why I wasn't surprised when he asked me to marry him. What surprised me was that I accepted!

Our engagement was "conditional." We agreed to get married when he had enough money to rent us an apartment. My fiancé decided to go to Detroit, where he had kin and could get a good job. He promised that as soon as he could save enough money, he'd come back for me, and we'd be married.

That sounded fine to me. It wasn't much of a commitment, but it was more than I had from Howard. I kept busy while my fiancé was gone; I worked on the farm and in the cotton fields with Daddy, and I continued singing with my sisters.

Meanwhile Cat took a job singing with the Statesmen, one of the top gospel singing groups in America. Howard continued traveling from town to town, preaching and singing, first with Brother Douglas and then on his own. He even pastored a church in Lanett, Alabama, for about a year. He later moved to Wingo, Kentucky, where he and his family reunited in evangelistic work.

In the fall of 1949, Howard and his troupe conducted a service on a Sunday night in Gadsden, less than an hour away from Fyffe. I thought about attending but decided against it. If Howard was truly interested in me, he knew where I lived.

Howard was planning to go on to Huntsville for a Tuesday night service, but before he left our area, he stopped to see an old, mutual friend of ours, Brother Bonds. As Howard related the story to me later, it wasn't long before my name came up in their conversation.

A dear, wise old man, Brother Bonds was extremely blunt with Howard. "I'm gonna tell you something, Howard," he said. "If you want Vestal Freeman, you better go after her."

"What do you mean, Brother Bonds?" Howard asked naively. "I've been writing to her for years, and she has never said that anything was wrong."

Brother Bonds looked at Howard as if he had just fallen off a turnip truck. "Now let me tell you a thing or two about women. Howard, you've been writing Vestal Freeman once every six months. That's not enough if you have hopes of getting married. She falls in love with some local boy and decides to get married, and then along comes one of your sweet love letters, and it tears her all to pieces. You just can't treat a woman like that. A woman needs to be loved—all the time—not just twice a year on paper."

Brother Bonds shifted in the old cane-back chair and continued sternly, "Vestal's in love with you, and you've been treating her like a dog. She's been going with a local boy and has finally consented to marry him. Yet when she heard over the radio that you were singing in Gadsden and Huntsville, she borrowed her daddy's car and came flying over here Sunday afternoon, thinking you'd stop by. She told me that if you went back to Kentucky this time without seeing her that you needn't ever write to her again. Here it is Tuesday, and I imagine she's about given up on you. You may be too late already."

"Too late? What do you mean too late?" asked Howard.

"She's already had her blood tests and is gonna marry that other fellow. If you want her, you sure better go after her."

Howard thanked him, said good-bye, and made a hasty exit. He drove directly to our farm. My family and I had moved to a new location about a half-mile from our church. I was outside hanging the washing on the clothesline when I saw Howard speeding down our road. I was dressed in faded blue jeans and a work shirt, with the shirttail hanging out—not exactly the desired wardrobe for a person about to be surprised by a long-lost friend.

Howard was waving jovially as he pulled in, but there was no way I was gonna let him see me looking like that. I ran for the house, hollering at Howard as I went. "Howard Goodman! That's just like you. I wait around here for a year and never see you, and then you come pulling up without any warning!"

Howard was saying something that sounded like, "Wait! Vestal, wait. I want to talk to you," but I couldn't be sure. I was already in the house, racing up the stairs. I ran into my bedroom and changed my clothes; I ran into the bathroom, washed my hands and face, and combed my hair. Then as if I had been expecting Howard all day long, I waltzed downstairs and out onto our front porch where Howard was waiting to greet me.

"Vestal, I really need to talk to you," Howard implored.

"All right, fine. Let's talk," I replied.

We embraced briefly and then walked over to Howard's old car and sat down in the front seat, out of the brisk autumn air. "I'm on my way to Huntsville for a concert tonight," Howard said breathlessly. "I can't stay long now, but I'll be back over on Thursday."

I couldn't believe my ears. Howard shows up out of the blue, and the first thing he says is that he can't stick around. I wasn't playing that game anymore. I looked him straight in the eyes and said flatly, "I guess you know I'm engaged to another fellow, don't you?"

Howard shifted uneasily as he answered, "Yes. Brother Bonds told me all about it."

"He did, did he? Did he tell you that my fiancé is in Detroit earning enough money to rent us an apartment and as soon as he gets back we're gonna get married? I don't know when he's coming for me—

could be tonight, maybe it won't be till Christmas. I don't know." I paused long enough to let my words sink in.

Howard looked at me tenderly. "Vestal, I heard you were about to get married, and that's why I came after you. You're not marrying anyone in this world but me."

I appreciated Howard's sentiment, but it was a little late. I stared blankly out the car window at a couple of white chickens scratching around in the yard. Howard shifted nervously in the seat but didn't say anything, so I said, "I love you, Howard. I'll wait until Thursday. But if you let me down this time, it will be the last."

Thursday was one of the longest days of my life. I wasn't sure what time Howard would return, but I felt fairly sure he'd be back. I anxiously peered up the road every time I saw or heard a car coming, hoping it would be him. It wasn't.

Toward sunset, I began to lose hope. Huntsville was not that far from Fyffe! *Where is Howard?* I worried. *Maybe he won't come.* A million thoughts—not all of them good—ran through my mind. After supper my family members were planning to attend the usual Thursday night prayer meeting at our church. As I got ready for church, I kept looking out the windows, wondering, *Where's Howard? Why hasn't he come back?*

"Vestal, are you coming?" Mama's voice broke in on my thoughts. "It's time to go. We don't want to be late."

"Yes, Mama. I'll be right there," I said as I cast a final glance out the window.

Howard was nowhere to be seen.

I reluctantly joined the rest of the family, and we went off to prayer meeting, but I didn't really feel much like praying.

The service had no sooner begun than the back door opened, and in walked none other than Howard Goodman. He hurried straight down the aisle to where I was sitting with my friends; he stopped there and stood next to our row. He had such a concerned expression on his face I couldn't help but smile. I moved over, and Howard slipped into the row and took a seat right next to me.

A rustle of whispers could be heard behind us, accompanied by a hushed chorus of "ooohhhs" and "aaahhhs" from some little old ladies in the seats across from us.

Howard got directly to the point. "Can you go with me to Nashville for a gospel singing?" he asked in what he considered a whisper. "I'll bring you right back on Saturday." With Howard's booming voice, even his whispers carried like they had been amplified by a loudspeaker. At that, two elderly ladies sitting behind us, leaning forward to catch every word of what he was saying, nearly lost their false teeth! They gulped, gurgled, and gasped, and one of them let out a loud "aaahhhh!" People all over the church turned to see what was going on.

In my peripheral vision, I could see that the women behind us were horrified, so for the fun of it, I said just loudly enough that I was certain they could hear, "Nashville? I don't know. When are you going?"

Clearly aghast that I might even consider accepting such an outrageous offer, a man and woman sitting in front of us turned completely around and stared at me icily.

Howard tried again to whisper—unsuccessfully. "We're going tonight. We gotta get to Nashville early in the morning." Howard might as well have made the announcement from the pulpit, because it seemed almost every eye and ear in the building was focused on us. Even the pastor had stopped speaking and was staring. Howard tried to lower his voice still further. "My sisters Ruth and Stella are in Nashville, and you can stay with them. Just ask your mother if you can go."

I knew better than to ask Mama such a thing. In my mind I could hear her response already: "That just ain't gonna happen!"

"She won't hear of it," I whispered out of the side of my mouth, trying to look nonchalantly toward the pastor. I turned and looked fully at Howard and whispered more loudly, "I am engaged, you know. Those are his folks sitting right over there." I looked across the room toward my fiancé's mother, who was glaring at us. Howard's eyes followed mine. When my fiancé's mama looked at Howard . . . well, as the saying goes, if looks could kill . . .

I figured, *Everybody's gonna be talking about me anyway. I might as well give them something to talk about.* I quickly wrote a note to Mama, telling her I was going to Nashville to attend a gospel singin' with Howard Goodman. I explained that Cat was there, singing with the Statesmen, and I could either stay with him or with Howard's sisters and that I'd be back on Saturday. I handed the note to one of my friends and said, "After I'm gone, please see that my mama gets this."

I nudged Howard and said, "Come on, let's get out of here and go somewhere we can talk."

I got up from my seat while the service was still going on and stepped into the aisle with Howard following closely behind me. Another round of shocked "ooohhs" could be heard from the congregation as we hurried toward the door at the rear of the church.

Just as we reached the double doors that led to the porch, the doors swung open, and I got the surprise of my life. A dark-haired young man stepped inside, and I stopped dead in my tracks. For a moment—a moment that seemed like an eternity—he and I stared at each other. He glanced at Howard and then back at me; I could feel the blood draining from my face. I must have looked like I had seen a ghost.

Without saying a word, I grabbed Howard by the arm, jostled past the young man, and squeezed through the doorway, pulling Howard behind me. Across the churchyard we ran toward Howard's car. "Vestal, what's going on? What's wrong?" Howard called.

"Come on! Let's get out of here. Quick! Start the car." Howard and I crashed into the front seat of his car, and he plunged the key into the ignition, slammed the vehicle in gear, and stomped on the gas pedal. We roared out of the church parking area like Bonnie and Clyde after robbing a bank.

As Howard and I careened up the road, I looked out the rear window. The young man was now out in the church parking area, waving wildly for us to come back. I turned around and slumped down in the front seat. "Whew!" I let out a deep breath.

Howard looked across the seat at me. "Who in the world is that?" he asked.

"That is my fiancé," I replied.

"Ohhhhh!" Howard said, slowly nodding his head.

For a moment we were silent as the car sped up the road toward the main highway. Just as we neared our house, I knew that I didn't want to take off for Nashville without telling Daddy. But Daddy was working late at the barber shop that night. He might not be home until after ten o'clock, and if we waited around till then, Mama would be home from church. Not only that, but my fiancé—now my former fiancé—might show up at any minute.

"You better pull in at my house so I can call Daddy."

Howard whipped the car off the road, and we ran into the house. I hurriedly cranked the old-fashioned phone on the wall while Howard stood close by to hear what Daddy said.

Daddy answered the phone, and before he hardly had a chance to say hello, I blurted breathlessly, "Daddy, I'm going to Nashville with Howard Goodman to attend a gospel singin'. When I get to Nashville, I'll stay with Cat or else with Howard's sisters, then Howard will bring me back home on Saturday."

Daddy caught the full implications of my statement immediately. "You mean you're not gonna get married?" he asked.

"No, Daddy. That ain't going to work," I replied matter-of-factly. "I want to go with Howard."

"Your fiancé's gonna have a fit. He came by the shop and asked where you were, and I told him you were at church."

"I know, Daddy," I answered nervously. "I saw him there."

"It's not gonna look good, you know . . ."

"Don't worry, Daddy. I'll take the consequences."

Daddy could tell by the resolute tone of my voice that I had already made up my mind between my two suitors. "Well, you better hurry and get your things together and go on," he said softly into the phone, "because if your mama comes home from church before you leave, she ain't gonna want you to go."

"Daddy, do you think it's okay?"

"Now, baby, you know I trust you. You do whatever you feel is right. Just be a lady."

I said a hasty good-bye to Daddy, hung up the phone, and headed for my room to get my clothes, shouting back to Howard as I went. "It will take me two minutes to get my things. You get the car started. I'll be right there." Within minutes, Howard and I were back on the road. We met Howard's sisters along the way, then drove on. We spent the night with Howard's family and were in Nashville early Friday morning.

That night we went to the Ryman Auditorium, which at the time was the home of the famous Grand Old Opry, the "mother church of country music." The Ryman was originally built as a church, and it still retained the look and feel of a large sanctuary: wooden church pews, low overhanging balcony, and all. Not surprisingly, country, bluegrass, and gospel music were closely related at the Ryman. On the first Friday of each month, Wally Fowler, an enthusiastic and successful promoter of gospel music, hosted a big, all-night concert—a singin' as it was known in music circles.

Howard and Wally had been friends for years. Wally was aware of the Happy Goodman Family and occasionally had booked Howard and his family to sing. While I freshened up just before the show started, Wally greeted Howard warmly. Their conversation (I learned years later) went something like this:

"Wally, I got my future wife with me tonight," Howard said with a twinkle in his eye. "We're gonna get married."

Wally was flabbergasted. "Aw, Howard, you're teasin' me. You ain't gonna get married. You've hardly ever been out with a girl. Who'd have you anyway?"

"You just wait here, and I'll show you."

A few minutes later Howard was introducing me to Wally Fowler. Wally looked me over as though he were evaluating a new automobile. "So, you're Cat Freeman's sister. Well, I'll say this much for Howard. He may have waited a long time, but he sure picked a winner!"

I had no idea what he was talking about. I looked at Howard and asked, "What's he mean, you've waited a long time? Waited for what?"

Wally burst out laughing as Howard's face turned red. "Why,

Howard just announced that you was his future wife!" Wally said jovially.

I didn't even bother answering Wally Fowler. I turned my attention to Howard and nearly yelled, "Howard Goodman! You haven't said a word to me about marriage. Now you've gone and announced it to all of Nashville?"

Howard grinned sheepishly. Before he had a chance to say anything, Wally Fowler—ever the promoter—put one arm around Howard and the other around me as he said, "Tell you what. Let's do it next month. You can be married right here on the stage of the Grand Old Opry. Wouldn't that be great? It will be the first Friday in December, and everyone will have the Christmas spirit. We'll broadcast the ceremony over WSM radio, and my sponsors will donate entire rooms of furniture. You will not only be famous, but you'll be rich too when we finish."

"Great!" Howard gushed. "Thanks, Wally. It sounds wonderful." He turned to me and asked, "What about it, honey?"

I was too shocked to say much of anything, but I nodded my head in approval. Wally, Howard, and I hugged once again, and it was showtime.

I hardly remember a thing about the concert that night. I can't remember who performed or what went on. I was in a daze, a giddy, wonderful daze. I do know it was several hours past midnight when Howard and his sisters and I left Nashville. We drove for a few more hours and arrived in Haleyville, Alabama, at 7:00 A.M. Howard got a room in the old hotel for his sisters, Ruth and Stella, and then he came to talk to me. I could tell he was a bit nervous, and we both were dog-tired.

Howard shuffled awkwardly from one leg to the other and finally asked me, "Do you suppose you could stay here with the girls in their room, and I could take you home this afternoon or tomorrow?" I looked at Howard's face and knew he wasn't trying to pull anything. He was simply too tired to drive any farther, and I couldn't blame him. I couldn't wait to get to sleep either. Still, to stay overnight when Daddy and Mama were expecting me home would be touchy.

"I don't know," I replied. "I'll have to call Daddy."

"Okay, I'll go with you," Howard offered. We went down to the hotel lobby and placed the call. Daddy had just arrived at his barber shop, getting ready for a busy Saturday, as the telephone rang. Howard talked to him first and explained that he couldn't possibly get me home today because he and his sisters had a singing engagement in Fulton, Mississippi, that night, then another engagement near Jasper, Alabama, on Sunday afternoon. He asked if it would be okay to bring me home on Monday. Howard was careful to emphasize that his sisters were along, that I would be staying with them, and that I was perfectly safe, my honor intact.

"Well, all right then," Daddy said. "You all be careful."

When I got on the line with Daddy, I asked him, "Daddy, what do you think about this? Will it be okay?"

"Aw yeah," Daddy answered, somewhat to my surprise. "I know you're bound to be dead tired. You go on and get some rest. Just be a lady. I'll explain this to Mama; don't you worry about it."

Howard took me back to Ruth and Stella's room, and I wasted no time before tumbling into bed. I fell asleep exhausted but exhilarated.

On Saturday night the Goodmans put on a concert at a high school auditorium in Fulton. I enjoyed watching Howard onstage; he was a great communicator, and I enjoyed hearing him and his family members sing about the Lord. Since I knew many of the camp-meeting-style songs they were singing, I hummed along with them on many numbers.

The next afternoon they were to sing at a church out in the hill country between Jasper and Haleyville for an "all day singin' and dinner on the ground." We arrived just in time for dinner, a family-style potluck picnic spread out on a makeshift table made of planks balanced on wooden sawhorses. Newspapers covered the planks, making a disposable tablecloth, and mounds of food covered the newspapers. It was a southern banquet, comprised of local favorites such as baked yams, sausage and grits, boiled turnips, field peas and fatback, and of course, plenty of baked ham, meat loaf, fried chicken, and meatballs. There was banana pudding for dessert along with the biggest assortment of pies and cakes I had ever seen. It all looked delicious too!

Howard and I took our turns going through the food line and then sat down on the ground to eat, close enough to be cordial, but far enough away from everyone that we could talk to each other without interruption. When we finished eating, Howard and I walked over to his car sitting in the parking lot. A brisk wind was blowing and the air was chilly, so we slipped inside the car. We talked about all sorts of things while we watched the country folks bustling all around us. Then our conversation turned more serious.

Howard reached over and put his hand on top of mine as he said, "If I take you back home . . . you know there are gossips everywhere. It won't matter that my sisters have been with us the whole time; you know what it's gonna be like around Sand Mountain. People will say that you've been gone with Howard Goodman since Thursday night, and now it's Sunday afternoon. They're not gonna say you've been off with my sisters and me; they're gonna say that you've been off with Howard Goodman. To save all that talk, let's just go ahead and tie the knot. You and I know we are going to get married. So why don't we forget about Wally Fowler's offer and get married right away?

"We can go on to Jasper and spend the night with my relatives, then on Monday morning we can go back over to Fulton, because you can get married in Mississippi without a blood test or a waiting period. Let's just go over there and get married. That way when we go home, folks can say whatever they want to because you'll be my wife."

"But Howard," I pretended to protest, "I *am* engaged."

"I ain't worried none about that," Howard answered sternly. Then almost as an afterthought, he asked softly, "Are you?"

"No, I guess not."

"Good, then will you marry me tomorrow?"

"Okay," I replied. It was that simple. I wasn't interested in having a big, fancy wedding (although Mama had much different ideas!); I knew Howard and I were meant for each other. That's all that mattered to me. I leaned over and kissed Howard smack on the lips—a rather forward gesture in those days. We were so enthralled with each other, we almost forgot that Howard and his family had a concert to do! We might have missed it altogether had it not been for Howard's sister Stella rapping on the car window and shouting, "You two can hold hands and stare at each other later. The folks are waiting for us inside."

We got out of the car and started toward the church. As we did, Howard took my hand in his and told Stella, "Vestal and I have decided to get married tomorrow."

Stella let out a loud whoop and hugged me so tightly I couldn't breathe. When she and Howard took the stage, Stella stepped up to the microphone. "I have an announcement I'd like to make," she said. "I want to introduce our future sister-in-law, Vestal Freeman."

A loud round of applause shook the rafters as the folks at that country church gave us their approval. Getting Mama and Daddy's blessing was another matter.

Howard and I were married in Fulton, Mississippi, on Monday, November 7, 1949. We didn't have time for a honeymoon, but on the first night we spent together, we gave each other one of the most precious gifts any couple can give one another—our virginity.

Back at Sand Mountain, Mama was waiting for us. "I'm scared to face Mama," I confessed to Howard as we got closer to home. "She's always dreamed of a big church wedding for me. I don't know what she'll say about this."

"Well, I've prayed about it," Howard replied, "and I know the Lord will take care of things."

"He sure better," I answered, my nervousness in stark contrast to Howard's confidence. "Mama sure has a powerful temper when she gets mad."

As we turned off Highway 75 at the sign that read "Highway

Church of God," I was clearly agitated. Howard looked across the seat at me and said quietly, "Don't worry. It will be all right."

A minute later we approached my family's frame farmhouse. Mama was in the front yard. She had an old broom in her hand and was sweeping the leaves away from our front porch. As Howard and I drove up, Mama stopped sweeping and put her hands on her hips. Howard got out of the car, while I was still sitting on the front seat, too afraid to move.

"Well, if this ain't a pretty sight," Mama said, her comment tinged with sarcasm. "There ain't no use telling me what you've done," she said. "I know already."

"Do you think you know?" Howard asked with a disarming smile.

"Yes, I sure do."

"Well, in case you were wonderin', we went and got married yesterday," Howard said with a big grin.

"I knowed it!" Mama shrieked, tossing her broom to the ground and grinning. "Come here, child," she called to me. "Come here and let your mama hug you!"

I bounded out of the car and ran to Mama's open arms. By the way she held me, I could tell that everything was okay as far as she was concerned.

When Daddy came home, we told him the news, and he was elated. He cried tears of joy over our marriage.

My former fiancé wasn't so happy to hear about my marriage. He repeatedly drove by our farmhouse, screeching his tires and blowing the horn, shouting words I had never before heard him use. Eventually he calmed down, and not long after Howard and I set up housekeeping, he married another young woman from Sand Mountain and moved back to Detroit.

I was thrilled to be Howard Goodman's wife and looked forward to working together with him. I was especially excited when Howard asked me to join his family singing group.

Chapter 7

Singing the Message

After a brief stay at Mama and Daddy's, Howard and I moved back to Wingo, Kentucky, a small town near Mayfield, where he had been living prior to our marriage. We moved into a big house, but we didn't have an abundance of space because the house was fairly well loaded down already. Howard's brothers and sisters were living there, too, so Howard and I basically moved into the back room of the big old house.

I didn't mind the crowd though. In fact, Howard's family welcomed me so wholeheartedly, I felt right at home immediately. They welcomed me into the family and into their singing group. We traveled from church to church, singing the gospel. I was constantly aware of Daddy's answered prayer, that one day I would carry the gospel to the world.

Admittedly, our world was rather small in those days. We traveled mostly in Kentucky, Tennessee, and Alabama, singing at revivals, camp meetings, and gospel singings. We also had a radio show on WNGO in Mayfield. The station didn't have a powerful signal, but people in neighboring towns heard the Happy Goodman Family over the airwaves, and we started receiving more and more invitations to sing. We did not charge for our services; instead we received a "freewill offering," whatever folks wanted to give. Usually the offerings were sparse, but sometimes the donations got as high as $150. Although a dollar had a lot more buying power back then, we were definitely not singing for the money!

We spent our weekends singing on street corners. Howard's younger brother Rusty played a beautiful ebony, six-stringed, Gibson steel guitar that Howard had bought for him. Sam Goodman, Howard's brother named after their daddy, could also pick out a few chords on an old, beat-up acoustic guitar. Together, Sam and Rusty accompanied us on some songs, and others we simply sang with no instrumental background.

We lived in Wingo for two years before moving across the Kentucky-Indiana state line to Evansville, where we were able to make a small down payment on a large, ten-room, frame house in a lovely section of town. Howard's family members moved with us, including their spouses and children. Soon my sister Millie moved in too. Gussie's daughter, LaBreeska, was living with us as well. We were one big, happy family, but with more mouths to feed, our meager financial resources were shrinking fast. We continued singing as much as we could and had a radio show on several small area stations, but it became apparent that something had to change—soon!

Change came quickly when it came, starting with Howard's brother Sam being drafted for military service. When Sam left for the air force, we knew he would be gone at least four years.

About that same time I became pregnant with our first child. Howard and I were thrilled to be expecting a baby, but my pregnancy cut into my ability to travel and sing.

Added to that, Rusty, always the restless rebel in the Goodman family, became disgruntled with all the transitions we were having to make. Rusty may have been the most musically talented of all the Goodmans. He had lofty dreams of becoming a famous music artist, perhaps even someday singing and playing on stage at the Grand Old Opry. Night after night he listened to Eddie Arnold on WSM radio, the Nashville station that broadcasted the live Opry show. Soon Rusty had learned almost all of Eddie's songs, accompanying himself on his steel guitar.

The "pop" singer Rusty most admired and whose vocal style he emulated was Perry Como. All the Goodmans—myself included—

enjoyed Perry Como's rich, lush vocalizing, but Rusty practiced until he could literally match Perry note for note.

Although he was clearly talented, Rusty's impatience often got the better of him. Once in his frustration over our lack of success in the music business, he told Howard, "Hovie Lister [piano player for the Statesmen] told me I had the best voice in the business, and I can go with any male quartet I want. If I wasn't about to be drafted, I'd leave right now." Rusty stomped out of the room, yelling back over his shoulder to Howard, "If Elvis can make it big, so can I!"

And he probably could have . . . except he was drafted into the army the following month.

With both Sam and Rusty gone, the ranks of the Happy Goodman Family were reduced to Howard's sisters, Howard, and me, and I was close to my delivery date. Three weeks after Rusty left for military service, I got up early one morning and stumbled into the bathroom. My head was throbbing and I could barely see. I knew it was daylight, but everything kept getting darker and darker. Suddenly the light disappeared completely.

Howard rushed me to the hospital where the doctors discovered that my blood pressure had skyrocketed. I had developed toxemia, a blood condition that threatened the life of both our unborn baby and me.

Howard called Millie at work and told her that the doctors had informed him I had only a fifty-fifty chance of surviving, and it would be a miracle if the baby survived. Millie called everyone she could think of and told them to get to praying. In the meantime, my body was so wracked by convulsions that by the time Millie arrived at the hospital, seven nurses struggled to hold me down.

Howard and Millie prayed continually, as did our other family members. For a while, it looked as though the doctors' worst fears might come true, but wondrously, Ricky Howard was born. My blood pressure slowly dropped and then finally returned to normal. I was out of trouble, but this would not be the last time I entered the valley of the shadow of death because of my blood pressure.

Before discharging me from the hospital, the doctors warned Howard and me not to attempt to have any more children. We thanked them for their advice, which we promptly disregarded. Two years later, while we were living in Swainsboro, Georgia, I gave birth to our daughter, Vicki Lynn.

Sam rejoined us after his stint in the military, and in 1955 the Happy Goodman Family received what we thought was going to be our big break in the music business. A television station, WLOS-TV, in Asheville, North Carolina, contacted us and asked if we might consider doing a daily, live program on the fledgling Channel 13. Consider it? We could hardly wait!

Our program on Channel 13 reached a wide area of the Blue Ridge Mountains of North Carolina and could be seen as far away as Greenwood, South Carolina. We were certain the exposure we received on TV would help us to expand our music horizons, which in turn would provide new ministry opportunities. We were unaware that the new medium of television, with its awesome power to create a reputation, could just as easily destroy one.

Through our TV show we met a concert promoter who had a country-music program with a large audience on the same station. The promoter invited us to help him put together a big concert including country, gospel, and bluegrass music for a July 4 celebration on his farm. He agreed to give the Goodmans 25 percent of the gate for our efforts. We helped promote the concert, cleaned up the farm, built a stage, and marked off a parking lot.

On the day of the show, more than twenty thousand people found their way to the promoter's farm. He charged each one fifty cents to get in; he also sold concessions throughout the program. At the end of the day, the promoter handed Howard a check for six hundred dollars.

Howard looked at the check and said, "You promised us 25 percent of the gate. Twenty thousand people at fifty cents a head amounts to ten thousand dollars you took in, which means you should be giving us twenty-five hundred dollars."

"I'm sorry about that, Howard," he said, "but I had some incidental expenses to take care of."

Howard spoke sternly to the promoter, "Well, where we come from, a man's word is his bond. If you went in the hole, we'd be glad to help you out. But I don't believe you did. I think you made money, big money. And I don't think it's right to take advantage of us this way."

At that, the promoter became belligerent. "Well, that's your tough luck, fella," he sneered. "You should have signed a contract. Over here we do things differently. If you ignorant backwoods folks can't keep up, you ought to shove off."

He didn't have to tell us twice. We got away from that guy as fast as we could . . . but unfortunately not soon enough. The next day, the promoter made fun of the Goodmans on his television show. Worse than that, he implied that *we* were shady in our business dealings. "There's some stupid gospel singers around here," he said on the air. "I won't call their names. But if you ain't careful, they'll try to fleece you good."

Anyone who had watched the station could assume he was talking about us. Consequently we were fired from our first TV show. A local merchant bought time and put us back on the air, but it was useless trying to overcome the bad publicity we had received. We decided to leave Asheville and move back to our big house in Evansville.

We started working our way back to Indiana, singing along the way at any churches that would have us. It was difficult to get concert dates or revivals. Few people wanted anything to do with the Happy Goodman Family when they heard what had happened in Asheville.

In those days we traveled in a large 1952 limousine—the whole bunch of us—Gussie, Stella, Eloise, LaBreeska, Howard's mama and daddy, his brothers Sam and Bobby, and a few nieces and nephews as well. Not exactly a skinny family (Is that what they call *understatement?*), we were packed into that car like cattle. On the way back to Evansville, Sam was driving when, from out of nowhere, a teenager driving a revved-up roadster, smashed into the side of our car. The impact of the crash drove us off the road and into a ditch.

This was one time when the Goodman girth gave us an edge. We were so tightly wedged in the car that no one was hurt. The limousine, however, was a total wreck. We tied the doors shut with rags and limped home to Evansville.

As far as we could see, the Goodmans' singing career was over. With Rusty still in the army and Ruth already married and living out of state, the remainder of the Goodman family members went separate ways. Sam went to work in a furniture shop. Eventually he switched careers and became a fairly successful insurance salesman. The Goodman sisters opened a small upholstery shop, and Howard's youngest brother, Bobby, went to work playing for a rock 'n roll band. For Howard and me, there was only one place to go—back into evangelistic work. It looked as though my singing career was going to be on hold for a while.

CHAPTER 8

A NEW VOICE

*I*n April 1957, Howard and I were invited to help evangelist David Epperson conduct a series of revival services in Madisonville, Kentucky, a town of approximately twenty thousand people located about fifty miles south of Evansville, Indiana, and one hundred miles northeast of Nashville, Tennessee. Brother Epperson was to do the preaching, and Howard and I were to handle the music. Rather than drive back and forth from Evansville every day with our two young children, we rented a small house and moved to Madisonville.

As we drove into the coal-mining community, it was impossible to miss the huge sign on a railroad trestle above the highway. The sign read: THE BEST TOWN ON EARTH. That sign, we were soon to discover, was a lie. In many ways, Madisonville was a charming, wonderful place to live, but the town's sedate appearance was misleading. Just beneath the surface, Madisonville was a seething cauldron of corruption. The town lay right along a main north-south drug traffic route, and because of its location and the lack of a big-city police force, drug runners found it a convenient place to do business. A strong "good old boys" network fostered political influence peddling that would have rivaled that of any major city and made cracking down on crime little more than a slogan tossed around during elections. Besides all that, or maybe because of it, Madisonville was rife with what can only be called demonic spiritual activity. In the years to come, Howard and I would discover just how pervasive those evil spirits were in Madisonville.

Despite its drawbacks I was instantly smitten with Madisonville. I loved the rolling hills of rural Kentucky. I loved the cool breezes that seemed to constantly drift through the pine trees that decorated the hillsides. Most of all, I loved the people of Madisonville, the majority of whom were hardworking, sincere, honest folk—people like those I had grown up around in Alabama.

The revival that took us to Madisonville continued for several weeks and resulted in many members of the community being deeply moved and drawn closer to the Lord. At the close of the revival, Lawrence Scaggs, a prominent local Christian, telephoned Howard and invited him and Brother Epperson to visit in his home the following evening. Howard accepted, and the next evening Mr. and Mrs. Scaggs welcomed Brother Epperson and Howard warmly.

Mr. Scaggs surprised the ministers when he revealed the reason for their gathering. "My wife and I have just received $9,000 in royalties from a coal mine," said Mr. Scaggs. "We want to divide the tithe of this money between your two ministries, $450 to Brother Epperson and $450 to the Goodmans."

When Howard came home and told me about the Scaggses' gift, I was ecstatic. "Howard, just think. We could buy this little house we are living in with a down payment of $500. Do you reckon the Lord is telling us to settle in Madisonville and start some kind of ministry here?"

Howard wasn't certain, but like me, he sensed that God was actively directing our steps, so he agreed to pray with me concerning the matter. What appeared to be an answer came the following day.

David Epperson stopped by our house with an idea that he couldn't wait to tell us. "Brother Howard, I've been praying about this $900 we've been given. I feel the Lord wants us to take that money, buy a truck and a big tent, and start traveling together in evangelistic work."

Howard was intrigued. "Do you know where we could get a truck and a tent for $900?" he asked.

"Yes sir. As a matter of fact I do," replied David. "The Lord has led me to a man who has an old truck and a big three-pole tent that we can buy at a bargain. I think God wants us to strike out on faith and hit the road for Him."

Howard looked at me for a confirmation that this was what we ought to do. I couldn't give it to him. I looked down at the floor. I knew Howard loved preaching and singing and that he had a passion to win the world to Jesus, but I had really hoped we could stay in Madisonville. Furthermore, although I was just learning how to discern the Lord's direction in specific details, I felt strongly that I had "the mind of the Lord" on this matter. When Howard finally asked me what I thought, I told him the truth.

"Howard, you're my husband, and I'll go wherever you go—even if I feel you're making a terrible mistake. But just 'going' and 'doing' is not always God's plan. Sometimes the Lord asks His people to stop and get to work where they are, rather than always looking for something really 'big' to do for Him. In this case, I think you are dead wrong." Howard has always valued my opinions and spiritual insights, but in the earlier years of our marriage, he sometimes ignored my input and made what he thought was the best decision in his own heart and mind. This was one of those instances. Howard disregarded my appraisal of the situation and handed over our portion of the nine hundred dollars to David Epperson. In the months to follow, Howard would desperately wish he had paid more attention to my reservations about David's "divine leading."

In the summer of 1957, we sold most of our earthly possessions and hit the road as an evangelistic team, traveling in an old truck and holding our services in a large three-poled tent. Our niece, LaBreeska, went along with us to sing the third part in our harmony.

Our first meeting was in Winnsboro, Louisiana. Large crowds attended our services, but times were tough in that part of the country, and few folks had much discretionary income to support traveling evangelists. Soon we pulled up stakes (literally!) and moved to Monroe, Louisiana, where we set up our tent right across the street from the Apostolic Pentecostal Church, pastored by W. T. Hemphill. We held old-fashioned tent revival services every night for two straight weeks, with lots of lively gospel singing and plenty of hellfire-and-brimstone preaching. Numerous people in Monroe experienced a fresh touch from God as a result.

Just as we were about to begin our third week in Monroe, Hurricane Audrey hit the Louisiana Gulf Coast. The town of Cameron was nearly blown off the map by high winds and torrential rains. Worse yet, Audrey's might did not dissipate after a full day's worth of devastation. The hurricane continued raging northward, straight up the state of Louisiana, ravaging everything in its path. The city of Monroe—and our revival tent—sat directly in Audrey's way.

The day after Audrey's wrath had been poured out on Cameron, we awakened to radio reports warning us that the hurricane had actually gained power overnight and was headed our direction. We prayed for God's protection; nevertheless, we felt we had no choice but to quickly cover and fasten as much of our equipment inside the tent as possible.

David and his wife, Sue, joined Howard and me, along with three men from Brother Hemphill's church, as we rushed around frantically in the strong winds that had already begun to kick up. Sue and I folded chairs and laid them flat on the ground, while the men struggled to get the church organ in a pickup truck so they could take it back to the shelter of the church across the street. Just as they got the organ in the truck, David screamed, "I hear it coming! I hear it coming! Everybody run!"

If God's wrath is anything like the fury of Hurricane Audrey (and we know from Scripture that it is much worse), I don't ever want to experience it. Sue and I ran for our lives toward David's car as Audrey hit us with awful power, the high winds ripping through the trees, roaring like the sound of a hundred Niagara Falls. Suddenly our big tent filled with air like a giant hot-air balloon, and the guy ropes that supported it and held it down snapped like threads. The winds whipped under the tent and swept upward, blowing the tent literally off the ground. The canvas split wide open in a dozen places, tearing from one side to the other. The three heavy poles that supported the weight of the canvas and cables came crashing to the ground with a loud thud. What remained of the canvas collapsed, looking like an enormous parachute had just fallen from the sky.

Sue and I leaned into the driving rain that followed the wind, stabbing us like a thousand tiny needles. The wind and rain didn't let up for a moment but continued to pummel us as we groped our way through the chaos. Struggling as though someone were pulling us backward with ropes, we trudged inch by inch to the car and, with both of us pulling on the door, finally were able to get it open. Sopping wet, we fell inside the vehicle. The wind instantly caught the car door as though it were a sail on a boat. Try as we might, Sue and I could not get the door closed. We simply clung to the car's seats as the wind and rain continued pouring in on us.

About that time we saw David and Howard. They had leaped off the truck and were frantically searching for us, fearing that we were trapped inside the tent and had been crushed by the heavy poles. It was a glad reunion when Sue, David, Howard, and I made it safely to Brother Hemphill's house, where LaBreeska was waiting for us. We were grateful to be alive, but it was no time for celebrating. Our tent and our sound equipment were totally destroyed. We had sold everything and had given everything to follow what David and Howard had felt was the Lord's leading, and now it was all in shambles.

The dark, torrential downpour continued throughout the remainder of the day and into the next. Not until the following afternoon did the hurricane finally subside. The dark clouds that still filled the sky were nothing, however, compared to those that filled my heart. I was deeply discouraged and depressed. As the rain stopped falling, my tears began falling. I cried and cried and couldn't stop, no matter what anyone said or did.

"I just don't see how we can take much more," I told Howard. "It seems that even God is against us."

Howard tried his best to comfort me, but I continued to weep. "It's just not fair, Howard," I wailed. "All your life you've been trying to live for the Lord. Every place you've gone you've been unashamed of the gospel. People have made fun of you, even tried to hurt you, but you've always stood firm. Now nature is against us. It's just not fair. Why doesn't God do something? Why doesn't He say something? Why has He turned His back on us like this?"

Howard bravely tried to put the best spin on events. "Honey, maybe God's just letting all this happen to show us a miracle," he said as he gently pulled me into his arms.

I wasn't so sure. "Well, we're supposed to hold a service tonight. It'll take a miracle for Him to resurrect that old tent," I sobbed. I twisted away from Howard and ran outside with no destination in mind. I was so depressed I didn't care where I went or what happened to me. I just wanted to be away from everybody. As I ran, I spied our car and headed toward it. I crawled inside and sat there, hunched over the steering wheel, half-bawling, half-praying. Howard stared at me from the door of the Hemphill home, no doubt feeling frustrated and helpless over his inability to draw me out of the deep pit into which I had sunk.

I don't know how long I was out there alone in that car, but it was more than a few minutes. My travail was only interrupted when I heard someone tapping on the car window. I looked up and was surprised to see Brother Hemphill standing in the drizzle, peeking in the car window. I rolled the window down, and he called to me, "How goes it, sister?"

How goes it? Has this man been asleep for two days? How goes it? It goes terrible! I thought.

I burst out crying once again. "Oh, Brother Hemphill," I said through my tears. "God has turned His back on us. We invested every dime we had in that old tent because Brother Epperson said it was God's will. Now it's gone. God destroyed it. Why?"

The old gentleman reached inside the window and patted my shoulder softly as he said, "Daughter, it's the Lord. Let Him do what seems good to Him." The pastor and I talked for several more minutes about how God does all things well and how He causes everything to work together for good for those who love Him and are called according to His purposes. Brother Hemphill assured me that we were on the brink of a miracle. The kindly saint seemed so at peace with whatever the Lord was doing through all this and so confident that God had good things in store for Howard and me that after a while I couldn't help shouting, "Hallelujah!"

Brother Hemphill and I walked casually back to the house. Once inside, he announced with a radiant smile, "Tonight we'll go inside the church and finish the revival there. I'll get some spots on the radio so the folks will know we're still in business."

That night the little church was packed with people. Nothing like a devastating storm to get people thinking about eternity! Many people came to church with reports of how God had spared them during the storm. Others came grieving over their losses. It was a time to rally together as the family of God, encouraging each other.

Howard and I were concerned about one problem, however. The inexpensive sound system we had been using outside for the tent meetings had been destroyed by the hurricane. Brother Hemphill's church did not have a sound system in the building. We knew that Howard could preach without a microphone and still be heard, but my singing voice needed all the amplification it could get. Although anyone who has heard me sing within the past twenty-eight years might find it hard to believe, in those days my voice was a soft, sweet-sounding soprano. When I sang publicly, Howard had to constantly nudge me closer to the mike.

That night, Howard looked worried as he asked, "Honey, what are you going to do without a microphone?"

I was so fired up by Brother Hemphill's pep talk that my faith was soaring. "We'll just forget about it and sing," I replied, "even if they don't hear us past the first pew." I sat down on the front row and began thumbing through the hymnal, searching for the songs I felt that the Lord wanted me to sing that night. I stopped short when my eyes fell on a song called "I Need No Mansions Here Below." I had never sung the song; in fact I couldn't even recall hearing it. Nevertheless, I knew God wanted me to sing that song that night.

When I showed the music to Howard, he looked puzzled. "Have you ever sung it?" he asked. "I don't think I know it."

"I don't know it either, so you better get up there and play it ahead of time," I replied, nodding toward the piano. "Because the Lord told me to sing it."

After handling the preliminaries, Brother Hemphill turned the service over to Howard and me. Howard began playing the song I had picked out, and I stood up on the platform in front of the audience. I took a deep breath. It would be the first time in my adult life that I would sing publicly without a microphone. I reared back, closed my eyes, opened my mouth . . . and nearly fell over from shock! I could hardly believe the incredible freedom with which I was singing. More than that, my voice was no longer soft as a feather and sweet-sounding. People who heard me sing that night later described my voice as sounding like a trumpet or a clarion bell. Without a microphone I was singing stronger, more clearly, and with an entirely new tonal quality. I didn't know what was happening, but I felt sure God was performing a miracle. Tears streamed down my face as I sang. People in the audience sensed the miraculous nature of what was occurring, and many sat with their mouths gaping as I continued to sing in my new voice.

A mighty revival broke out among the congregation that night. It continued unabated for the next two weeks. Each night I sang with a fresh sense of God's presence in my life. And amazingly, my new voice did not go away after a day or two. It grew stronger as I continued singing about God's glory.

On Tuesday night of the second week of services, Brother Hemphill asked me to preach. I was reluctant at first, but in light of the recent miracles God had been doing in my life, I could hardly refuse. Besides, Daddy's words kept echoing in my mind, *Someday you are going to carry the gospel.* I knew the time had come. That night, after Howard and I sang and led the congregation in worshiping the Lord, I stood up behind the pulpit and preached a simple gospel message. The sermon itself was not profound, but I sensed that the Lord was helping me, so I felt incredible freedom to say what I thought He wanted me to say. The result was another outpouring of God's Spirit with numerous men, women, and children acknowledging Jesus as Lord.

Daddy would have been blessed right out of his shoes.

CHAPTER 9

A NEW ADVENTURE

*S*hortly after the dramatic transformation in my voice, Howard and I felt we should set ourselves apart from the ministry of Brother Epperson. Although finances were a factor, our decision to part company was more for spiritual reasons. Howard and I felt that God had directed us to sing and preach the gospel, and we did not want to be tied to Brother Epperson's coattails. Wanting to make certain there could be no question concerning our motives, Howard and I gave him everything that was left from our original $450 investment. It wasn't much, but it was all we had to give. We returned to Evansville with only the clothing on our backs and what was packed in our suitcases.

We were starting over once again.

It's easy to talk about living by faith; it is quite another thing to actually do it. It is especially disconcerting to have to pick up and start your career or ministry from scratch again. The older we get, the more possessive most of us become; we want to hang on to what we have. Yet Howard and I felt strongly that the Lord was directing our steps, and we continued to trust Him by faith. If God couldn't or wouldn't take care of us, then we were in the wrong line of work.

Early in November, Howard received a telephone call from the pastor of a small congregation in Madisonville, Kentucky. The pastor had heard Howard preach at a revival in that town. "You know, Brother

Goodman," the pastor said, "I'm getting old, and I'll be looking for someone to take my place before long. You're the best preacher I've ever heard. If you'll come and preach a revival that will last until Christmas, I might even want you to stay on and pastor this little church."

Howard and I agreed to return to Madisonville for what we thought was going to be a month-long stay. As we drove beneath the sign THE BEST TOWN ON EARTH, I couldn't help thinking that we were supposed to have been here all along. I didn't have to say "I told you so" to Howard. He sensed it too. I snuggled a little closer to him in our car. We felt as though we were going home.

Home or not, we were not prepared for the surprising events that followed. On the first night of services, the pastor encouraged Howard to "tell it straight" in his preaching. "You just preach like the Lord leads," he said. "Preach it hard 'cause these are hard folks, and they need to have their toes stepped on."

Howard took the pastor at his word and delivered some powerful sermons, seething with God's judgment and preaching against sin. (We hadn't yet learned to balance our message with God's grace and love as we did in later years.) For the first few nights, the little church on Madison Avenue was packed. The building held only about one hundred people when it was standing room only, but we felt good about the number of people attending the services. In the middle of the first week, however, attendance plummeted, and Howard candidly called attention to it.

After listing several distractions that might have kept people away from church that night, Howard "went to meddlin'." He started picking on television viewers. Prior to the mid-fifties, televisions were owned by a privileged few, but by now they were becoming more accessible to the common folk. Most folks—even sincere Christians—were enamored with the new source of entertainment, although many preachers railed against the "sinful idiot box."

One of the most popular shows on television was *I Love Lucy*, starring Lucille Ball and Desi Arnez. Naturally when Howard thought of a popular show that might tempt people to miss church, *I Love Lucy* came quickly to mind. "And some people love Lucy more than they love the Lord," he preached. "They've stayed home tonight to watch *I Love Lucy* rather than come to church."

Little did Howard know that one of the leading, closet "Lucy-holics" in the church was the pastor's wife! She, too, had stayed home from church that night to watch Lucy, although her viewing was more clandestine. Pastors in her denomination were preaching that television was "of the devil," so like many of her ilk, she and her husband had to hide their television in the bedroom so their parishioners wouldn't know they owned one. Ahead of her time in many ways, the pastor's wife wasn't much for legalism. She liked to dress in pretty outfits . . . and she liked to watch Lucy.

At the following service the pastor stood up and brusquely announced, "The revival meeting will close tonight." He offered no further explanation.

Howard and I were baffled. *Close tonight? Why, we were planning on being here for at least a month!* We had even rented a small apartment, thinking we might be there much longer, as the pastor had insinuated. Hadn't he told Howard to step on some people's toes? Apparently he hadn't meant his wife's toes.

Howard and I returned to our little-bitty apartment and prayed most of the night. What was God doing to us? We both felt that the Lord had directed us back to Madisonville, but why? To have a revival shut down just as we were getting started? It didn't make any sense. We didn't get an answer from God that night. I was ready to pack up and shake the dust off my feet as we left. Nevertheless, Howard and I were both convinced that we had not been brought to this town by accident.

The next morning Howard got up early and walked the streets of downtown Madisonville, praying and wondering why we were there. A side street, just off the town square, led past an old theater building, the

Cameo Theater. The building was vacant and boarded up tightly. Howard walked back and forth in front of the building several times. Each time he felt the Lord was telling him, "This is where I want you to begin My work."

He asked around concerning the building and received a wide variety of responses. One man said, "There aren't any seats in that building."

Someone else told him the old theater was being rented as a warehouse to store refrigerators and other appliances.

A lady told Howard, "That old place is infested with rats and cockroaches. You don't want that building. Stay away from it."

Another man told Howard, "The man who owns that old building lives in Nashville. He hates preachers. Several have tried to rent that theater for a church, and he's just laughed at them."

Meanwhile I was back in our apartment, praying and begging God to get us out of this place. I honestly did not want to stay any longer, but when Howard returned, he was excited about what he felt God was saying to him about the old theater. I wasn't so sure, but we got down on our knees and began to pray.

Howard prayed, "Lord, I've heard all kinds of stories about that old building. I've heard that the seats have been ripped out and that the man who owns it won't rent to preachers. Now Lord, I'm not asking You to do anything about the dirt, rats, and roaches. Me and Vestal can take care of that—"

I almost stopped Howard right there. I hate rats and cockroaches! If we're prayin' for a miracle, let's go all the way.

Howard continued praying, "If it's Your will, Lord, for us to get that old building to start a church, then we're asking that You will touch the owner's heart so he will rent it to us and that You will arrange for the seats to be in the theater." Howard was about to conclude praying; he was content with that, but I wasn't.

I interrupted Howard and prayed, "Now, Lord, I don't mind cleaning up dirt and trash. I've done that all my life. But Lord, You know I can't stand cockroaches . . . and rats scare me to death. So if You want us to have that old building, then don't let it have any bugs or rats either! Amen."

That afternoon Howard called the theater owner in Nashville. "Oh yeah, I know about you folks," the owner said. "I heard you at the all-night singing at the Ryman Auditorium. I'll be glad to rent the theater to you. The rent is $150 a month, with six months due in advance."

Howard gulped hard. Nine hundred dollars! In advance! We could barely afford our little apartment. Where in the world were we going to get $900? "Does it have any seats?" Howard wanted to know.

"Yeah, the seats are still in it. I'm not sure what condition they're in though."

Howard told the owner he'd call him back. He turned to me and said, "Well, praise the Lord! He'll rent it to us. Not only that, but he says the seats are still in it. The only catch is he wants $900 in advance."

Ironically, I had been praying that the Lord would not allow us to get the building. Finally I came to the point where I said, "Okay, Lord. If You want us to have the building, let it have seats in it, and let them be good seats. Let there be no bugs or rats in the building. And give us the first month's rent. Then I'll believe that You want us to be here."

I knew my prayer was a tall order, but I was desperate. When a Christian gets desperate enough, he or she will not be bashful about making brash pleas to God. I genuinely desired to know what God wanted us to do, and God knew my heart, that I wasn't being fickle or presumptuous. Wherever the Lord wanted us to be is where I wanted to be, but I needed to know it was God's idea, not our own. We had already learned a hard lesson with the tent we had purchased, thinking it was God's plan. This time I wanted better confirmation.

The theater owner told Howard where we could pick up a key to the building, and together Howard and I went to examine the property. When we walked inside the musty theater—it had been boarded up for six years we learned later—we were amazed. The theater was in excellent condition, filthy dirty, with cobwebs hanging eerily, but nothing that soap and water and some "elbow grease" couldn't take care of.

I had asked God to let there be seats in the theater, and there were.

Good seats—plush, padded theater seats that looked almost brand-new, with genuine leather upholstery and spring cushions at that! Oh, sure, they were covered with dirt, but they were there—all 357 of them.

I looked around the theater carefully, searching for signs of rats, bugs, or other vermin. What I saw excited me. "Howard, I don't see a trace of rats or bugs, do you?"

Howard concurred. There were no cockroaches or rats, not even a little mouse, anywhere to be seen.

We had the seats; we didn't have bugs; one other aspect of my prayer remained to be answered.

The next day Howard called the theater owner back. "We've decided to rent the theater," said Howard boldly. "We'll sign a lease for six months, but we can't pay the full amount right now."

Amazingly, the owner agreed. "All right," he said. "I'll take half now and you can pay the rest as you go along."

"I'll mail you a check for $450 this afternoon," Howard nearly shouted into the phone. He hung up and looked at me, his face beaming. I was excited, too, but we did have one small problem; well, actually we had over four hundred problems. Howard and I had only $20 to our name! That left us quite a bit short of covering a $450 check. There was only one thing to do.

We dropped to our knees and prayed. Howard prayed specifically, "Lord, it's almost one o'clock now, and the banks close at four. We're willing to give every penny of what we have, but that still leaves us $430 short. Would You mind selling a few of those cows out there on Your hills and arranging for us to get the balance so I can mail this man a check? After all, Lord, it's for Your work."

I don't usually recommend trying to put God on the spot, but when you are attempting to do something for His honor, and it is so far beyond your own resources that only He can do it, God frequently answers in extraordinary ways. Several families in Madisonville were upset at the way we had been treated in the "Lucy affair" and had offered to help start a church if we were willing to stay on. That very afternoon Lila and Lonnie Scaggs, the couple who had so generously donated money to Brother Epperson and us earlier that year, approached Howard about starting a church. "Brother Goodman, I'd like to give the first $200," said Lonnie. He also gave Howard the name of another family who felt similarly.

Following the Scaggses' lead, Howard and I walked to the home of Clarence Harris. When Mrs. Harris opened the door, we nearly fell over as she said, "Why, Brother Goodman! I'm so glad you came by. The Lord has just told me to give you $100 for your new church." Howard and I looked at each other in amazement. We thanked Mrs. Harris profusely and walked on down the street.

Madisonville was a small town. To have two people within an hour approach us unexpectedly, nearly thrusting money into our hands to begin a church, was already miraculous. Walking back toward the theater, we "happened" to see Bill Eppley walking toward us. "Brother Howard, I hear you're thinking about starting a church in the old Cameo Theater."

"We're talking about it," Howard replied. "We're just waiting for the Lord to answer our prayers."

"Well I'd like to be part of the answer. Here's $50 to put toward your first month's rent," Bill said, as he reached into his pocket and pulled out some cash. It was the same everywhere we went. People couldn't wait to give—$5, $10, sometimes more, often much less. But by four o'clock that afternoon, Howard was able to go to the bank, get a cashier's check for $450, and just as he promised, and as God had provided, Howard put the check in the mail that same afternoon. It was the first of many lessons in which we were to learn that God can supply our needs when our goal is to give Him glory.

That night as we lay in bed, exhausted yet exuberant over the events of the day, a verse of Scripture kept running through my mind. "And we know that all things work together for good to them that love God, to them who are the called according to his purpose" (Romans 8:28). I quoted the verse aloud to Howard. "You know, Howard, I've been lying here thinking."

"About what, honey?" Howard asked, sleep nearly overtaking him.

"You know that $450 the owner wanted to rent the theater?"

"Mmm-hmm."

"Well, that's the exact amount Brother Scaggs gave us back in April, but we went and spent it on that old tent."

Howard perked up a bit and replied, "I guess God had to let that hurricane come along to blow us back where He wanted us all along."

I smiled at Howard in the darkness. It's a great man who is willing to admit when he was wrong. I squeezed his hand tightly. "But ain't God grand? If we hadn't gone off like that, maybe my voice wouldn't have changed. Maybe I'd still be singing with that soft little voice." I could feel the tears trickling down my face.

My, how I wanted to sing for God! And I couldn't wait to sing in Life Temple, the name we had decided to call our new church. But before God allows you to stand up on the platform to sing in front of the masses, sometimes He has you down on your knees in obscurity, doing the dirty work that few people know about.

CHAPTER 10

PASTOR VESTAL

People who have known me only through my music career are sometimes surprised to learn that I have been actively involved in leading a local church. My years in the pastorate provided an excellent opportunity to learn compassion and concern for individuals, rather than simply looking out at full auditoriums and seeing masses of faceless people. Nowadays when young people ask me what they can do to enhance their music careers, I tell them, "Get involved in a local church. Not only will you learn music, but you will learn volumes about life."

Much of what I learned through starting a church I learned on my knees, not praying—although I did plenty of that too—but scrubbing. The old Cameo Theater was filthy when Howard and I first walked through its doors into the dingy lobby. As Howard looked at all the dirt, he brushed his brow, and said, "Whew, we've only got two weeks if we want to get this place ready before Christmas."

"Don't worry, Howard," I told him. "We'll make it. Some of the women who have supported us are coming in to help me scrub and clean. You just get out and start contacting folks. Let them know that Life Temple is a reality."

It took us a full two weeks, working all day every day, to clean out the theater. We scrubbed everything that didn't move. We filled bucket after bucket with ammonia and water, scrubbing inch by inch on our hands and knees. We scrubbed every aisle, every seat, and every piece of carpet runner in that place. By the end of the first week, my knees had blisters the size of half-dollars on them from crawling across the concrete. We scraped enough chewing gum from under the theater seats to fill a large garbage can.

As we were getting ready to move into the Cameo, Howard's brother Sam came down from Evansville to help us get the place open. At first, Sam drove back and forth between Evansville and Madisonville, but after a while we all began to feel that Sam belonged on our team full-time. When Sam met Barbara Gibson, a pretty young woman from Madisonville, he felt the "call of the Lord" more strongly. He moved to Madisonville and dug right in with us, cleaning and scrubbing.

One day Sam was up in the old theater's projection booth, sweeping it out in hopes of making it into a Sunday school class. "What are y'all doing here?" he heard a young man ask. Sam looked up from his work and saw a little guy staring at him quizzically.

"We're fixin' to open this old theater for a church," Sam replied jovially.

"Do you want me to help ya?" the lad asked.

"You're sure welcome to do that!" Sam answered as he shook the boy's hand. "I'm Sam Goodman and my brother Howard and his wife, Vestal, are going to be the pastors around here. Thanks for lending a hand. We sure can use the help."

"I'm Bill Cox," the young man replied. "Glad to help out. Where do I start?"

Working together on their hands and knees, Bill and Sam transformed that dirty projection booth into a clean, inviting Sunday school room. More important, Bill became the first member of Sam's Sunday school class and joined our fledgling church. He grew up to be an outstanding citizen, eventually going on to become the U.S. federal highway administrator during Jimmy Carter's presidency. Bill continues to be a hard-working leader to this day, serving most recently as the mayor of Madisonville.

We officially opened Life Temple on New Year's Eve 1957 with a big singing and preaching service. All 357 seats were filled, and we had a powerful, enthusiastic meeting. Sam joined Howard and me to help with the music, and it felt good to be singing together as a family once again. That night, fifty-three people found Jesus Christ at Life Temple. At least thirty others were filled with the Holy Spirit and experienced God in a deeper way than they had known Him before. Our ministry in Madisonville—both through music and preaching—was up and running.

Sam and Barbara were married shortly after we opened the church. Sam felt a strong concern for the common folks in town. He told Howard, "I think God wants us to build a church where people can worship without respect to outward appearances. I think He wants a church where the emphasis isn't placed on what a person wears, whether he or she uses the right grammar, or makes a lot of money. We're all poor folks ourselves, and I believe the Lord is leading us to build a poor folks' church."

Sam was right. The poor were attracted to Life Temple; so were the blacks. In contrast to some churches that sought to exclude anyone whose skin wasn't lily white, we welcomed people of every ethnic background and skin color into our congregation—no small scandal for a small Kentucky town in the pre–Martin Luther King Jr. days. Interestingly, the more we opened our hearts to the poor and downcast of our community, the more the wealthier folks wanted to be a part of us. There's something about a church that reaches out to the poor that is attractive to society and pleasing to God. Consequently our congregation soon had a good mixture of Madisonville, the rich and the poor, the young and the old.

We stayed in the old theater for a year and a half before we received word from Nashville that the owner was selling the building and we had to get out. Immediately we began searching for a place to worship. The only place we could find on short notice that was big enough to hold our congregation was another filthy, empty building. Instead of being downtown, right in the heart of the community, this building was on the other side of the tracks, both literally and figuratively. Worse yet, it had last been used as a pet shop, and the building reeked of foul pet odors. Once again, we gathered our cleaning crew, grabbed our buckets, brushes, and ammonia, and hit our knees.

I made a mistake, however, in not taking the time to ask God to rid the place of rats and roaches before signing the lease. Vermin were everywhere, scurrying across my hands as I scrubbed. I like to have died right there!

One night as I nursed the blisters on my knees, I told Howard, "If another of those horrid creatures runs across my hands while I'm scrubbing floors, I think I'll pack up and go back to Alabama. Besides, I ain't so sure there's not other varmints living in there. I think I'd die if a snake slithered out of one of those holes in the wall."

We opened for services in the former pet shop at the worst possible time, during the stifling heat of a Kentucky summer. Despite our best efforts to clean and disinfect the church, a rank odor continued to permeate the place. Worse yet, the smelly old building had little ventilation, so it didn't take long for things to heat up. Maybe it was the heat or maybe it was the noise that brought an unexpected visitor.

The first Sunday we held services in the pet shop things started quite well. We sang, prayed, and worshiped the Lord, and then Howard began to preach. Just as he got to an important point in the middle of his sermon, a huge highland terrapin came crawling down the aisle! This was no little turtle, like the ones in pet stores. This turtle was as big in diameter as the steering wheel of an eighteen-wheeler!

As the giant turtle inched its way down the aisle, Howard desperately attempted to hold the congregation's attention. But as more and more people saw the turtle, Howard realized his efforts were in vain. Soon the congregation was abuzz; some of the men were snickering, while some of the women were struggling to keep from screaming.

Finally Howard couldn't handle it any longer, and he burst out laughing. By now, everyone was on their feet, trying to see—or get away from—the turtle. The whole congregation broke up. Some people were laughing uproariously, and others were screaming in terror.

Howard quickly dismissed our first service in the pet shop. At the door one fellow teased, "The least you could have done was baptize him, preacher."

"Baptize him nothing. I've got him in a box behind the pulpit," Howard quipped right back. "We're going to take him home and eat him!"

During that time in our ministry, a bowl of turtle soup would have been more to eat than we were often used to. Our congregation dwindled over the long, hot summer, and with fewer faces, the offerings that supported the church, and us as the pastors, dropped as well. We were living on about thirty dollars a week.

Our church met in that pet shop for three months. Meanwhile the congregation of the Church of Christ built a new sanctuary and parsonage across town, and by September they were ready to vacate their property on Grapevine Road. The little white stucco church building had enough room to regrow our congregation. The sanctuary was small but pretty, and in the basement were several rooms that had been used for Sunday school. Beside the church was a parking lot and a four-room, cement-block parsonage. It had two bedrooms, a living room, and a kitchen. The house wasn't much to look at, but it sure was a lot better than the cramped garage apartment where Howard, Vicki, Ricky, and I were living.

It seemed impossible that we would be able to purchase the vacated facilities on our income, but Howard and I, as well as what remained of our congregation, began praying for another miracle. The leaders of the Church of Christ agreed to sell the property to us for a mere $19,000. That was great, except we were about $18,900 short. We continued praying.

Wanting to help us, the owners agreed to take a $4,500 down

payment and allow us to pay off the balance in payments of $150 a month. We kept praying.

On a warm September Sunday morning in the pet shop, Howard stood before about seventy-five people and laid out our situation. He knew that if we didn't make a move soon even those seventy-five faithful would be gone. Howard informed the congregation about the available property and then boldly declared, "If we can raise $2,000 this morning, I believe the Lord will open up a way for us to buy that church."

A man who owned a real-estate company was the first to stand up and donate. "I will give $500 toward the purchase of a new church," he promised.

Another man pledged to give $100; others could give only nickels and dimes, but before the service was over, we had raised $1,700. The real-estate man stood again and contributed $300 more to make our goal.

With $2,000 in his hand, Howard went back to the Church of Christ leaders and offered to give them the money and $500 a month for the next five months, after which we would pay them $150 a month. The leaders had to talk about that one.

In less than an hour, our telephone rang. "Brother Goodman, we'll accept your proposition."

As Howard hung up the phone, his eyes were moist with joy. I was excited, too, and impressed by Howard's great faith. With feigned concern in my voice I asked, "Howard Goodman, now where in the world are you going to get $500 per month? Our church isn't raising $50 per week, and we've got to have something to live on ourselves."

Howard smiled broadly as he pulled me into his arms. "I'll tell you how we're gonna do it," he said with a laugh. "We're going out on one of those thousand hills owned by the Lord and sell some cattle!"

The following week we moved into the parsonage on Grapevine Road, and our congregation worshiped in the little white church. Over the next five months, our congregation never missed a payment . . . and we took in enough extra money to buy groceries too. The congregation's enthusiasm began to return, and before long our little church began to fill with people every time the doors were open. But it wasn't until the fall of 1962 when our church—and the Happy Goodman Family—and my music career really exploded.

It started with a telephone call from Howard's brother Rusty. Howard answered the phone in our parsonage and called for me to get on the extension. "It's Rusty," Howard shouted to me, "and he's in trouble!"

Chapter 11

Rusty Returns

Howard's brother Rusty loved God as much as any man I have ever known, but he also had a rebellious streak in him that set him apart from the other Goodman boys. When Rusty left our family for the army, he vowed to someday make it big in the music business . . . without us. He had been discharged from the service prior to Howard's and my move to Madisonville, so he could have easily come along with us had he wanted to, but Rusty wanted no part of our ministry at that time. Instead he struck out to fulfill his dream of singing at the Grand Old Opry in Nashville.

He made it, too, although not as a headliner. While we were busy doing evangelistic work and starting a church, Rusty joined country singer Martha Carson as her rhythm guitarist and master of ceremonies. Martha was singing at the Opry at the time, but when she felt she had outgrown the show (country music was a far cry from what it is today), she and her band struck out for New York, hoping for a shot at the big time.

In the Big Apple, Rusty rubbed shoulders with Broadway's music crowd and soon got sucked into a party world he had hardly known existed. He did know that his New York lifestyle contradicted everything he believed, so despite a potential appearance on *The Ed Sullivan Show* and a three-week stint at Lake Tahoe, Rusty quit Martha's band and came home.

Once home, however, he quickly became bored. Coming from the bright lights of the big city nightclubs to our tiny town was too difficult a transition. Besides, Rusty's life was his music, and at that time the Goodman family was not making much music. When Eastmon Napier of the Plainsmen Quartet called Rusty from Dallas, Texas, and asked him to join their group as the baritone singer, Rusty readily accepted the offer.

The good news was that Rusty was now singing songs about the Lord rather than tears-in-my-beer country songs. The bad news was that he continued living like someone who didn't know the gospel, even though he was singing gospel music. Strange as it may seem, in those days many four-part harmony groups sang gospel music, not so much as a means of spreading Christ's message, but merely as a show. And some of them were incredible showmen who, onstage, could stir an audience to tears or transport them to heavenly places, while offstage they talked and acted more like the devil. Consequently Rusty found ready acceptance among his musical peers and a casual tolerance of his spiritual compromise, all of which made it easier for Rusty to continue carousing.

But Rusty couldn't fool God, and the Lord had not given up on Rusty either. The Lord kept speaking to him, calling his prodigal son home. Unfortunately the prodigal son had not yet come to the end of himself.

Rusty and the Plainsmen got a break when Jimmie Davis, former governor of Louisiana and a popular gospel singer himself, invited the group to sing background for him. Jimmie Davis ran for reelection that year, and the Plainsmen stumped with him from one corner of Louisiana to the next. With his combination of down-home wit and wisdom—and a little bit of God and country thrown in—Jimmie Davis was reelected, and the Plainsmen moved from Dallas to Baton Rouge to work for the governor.

About a year later Howard, Sam, and I were invited to sing and preach at the Kansas City Camp Meeting of the Pentecostal Church of God.

While we were there, Rusty called and said that the Plainsmen needed a "front" group for a concert in Wichita. He immediately had thought of us. "They'll pay you a hundred dollars for coming," Rusty said.

We weren't concerned about the money—although it didn't hurt—but Howard, Sam, and I were not going to pass up an opportunity to see Rusty again. I couldn't wait to get to Wichita, but I wasn't prepared for what I saw when we got there.

Rusty met us at his hotel that afternoon, and when I saw my brother-in-law, I almost wished that we hadn't made the trip. Rusty looked terrible, and I could smell whiskey on his breath. He talked about his music and how successful the Plainsmen had become, but he carefully avoided talking about anything personal, especially his spiritual condition. Later that night I approached him backstage. He was smoking a cigar and laughing loudly along with some of his singing buddies. When he saw me coming, he instantly got defensive. "Now, Vestal, don't come at me with your preaching," he said defiantly. "I've heard just about as much of that stuff as I can stand. I don't want to hear any more—from you or anyone else."

I was so taken aback by Rusty's attitude I didn't know what to say. He and I had always shared a close, open relationship. Because Rusty was so much younger than Howard, Rusty sort of regarded me as a substitute mother figure. We talked candidly, and he often discussed things with me that I knew he dared not mention to Howard or Sam. I had always felt that we could talk about anything. I couldn't relate to this "new" Rusty, so I didn't even answer his snide remark.

I reached over and hugged him and said, "I just want you to know that I love you, Rusty, and I'll be praying for you."

Rusty turned and walked away, and I cried all the way back to Kansas City that night.

The next afternoon Howard was preaching under the big, open-air pavilion at the camp meeting. It was hot, with hardly a breeze to cool things down. I was trying my best to stay riveted on Howard's sermon, but my mind kept returning to Rusty. My heart ached for him; he knew better, yet he insisted on running from God. While I listened to Howard, I prayed for Rusty.

Howard was preaching on Judges 11:30: "Jephthah vowed a vow unto the LORD." Howard's theme from that verse was, "If you make a vow to the Lord, keep it." He told of an incident from Rusty's infancy, a time when Rusty had developed a life-threatening sickness. At their wit's end, Howard and his mama took Rusty to the old camp-meeting tabernacle nearby to ask the preachers to pray for the baby. Howard carried his baby brother down to the altar rail and literally held him up before the Lord. Howard prayed fervently, "Lord, You gave him to us, and You have the right to take him back. But if You will heal him, I will serve You the rest of my life."

God did heal Rusty, and Howard kept his vow to the Lord.

As Howard was telling the story, adding that this vow often kept him going in the ministry, even when he felt like quitting, I began to sense God speaking to me in a most unusual way. He spoke clearly to my heart and mind, telling me, "I want you to write a letter to Rusty. Do it now. Do not delay. Seal it and at the close of the service, take it to the pulpit. The preachers will lay hands on it and pray. Mail it to Rusty. If you will obey me, one year from today, Rusty will be in this same camp meeting, saved and filled with My Spirit, and he will preach at this same camp meeting."

I grabbed some paper out of my purse and began writing. I didn't know what I was going to write, but suddenly the words began to pour out of my heart onto the paper. To this day, I have never discussed with anyone the specific words God had me say in that letter, but the essence of it was, "You have run from God as long as you could get away with it, but now it's time to return to the Lord."

I put the letter in an envelope and clutched it tightly for the remainder of the service. At the conclusion of the afternoon service, the state superintendent came to the pulpit and asked if there were any further announcements. I knew it was now or never. I got up from my seat and started walking down the aisle, waving the letter in my hand as I went.

"Yes sir," I said when I was within earshot. "The Lord told me to write this letter and ask the preachers to pray over it before I mail it." I went on to explain how my brother-in-law, a young man who many at the camp meeting knew from his singing, was away from the Lord. "But God said if I will do this, one year from now Rusty will be saved, filled with the Spirit, and will come with us to this same camp meeting, and he will preach."

The superintendent took the letter out of my hands and gently laid it on the altar rail, as though he were placing an exquisite, priceless treasure on the altar—which in a way he was. He asked all the preachers who were present to come forward, and together they prayed over the letter, asking God's Spirit to anoint it. The superintendent then gave the letter back to me, and at the first opportunity, I mailed it to Rusty.

We didn't hear much from Rusty over the next nine months, but God was working in his life. Earlier he had fallen in love with Billie, a pretty little blond woman from El Dorado, Arkansas. Rusty and Billie married, and a year later their beautiful little girl, Tanya, was born. God used Tanya's birth to remind Rusty of the miracle of spiritual rebirth.

The world's attention was focused on the showdown between President John F. Kennedy and the loud, portly leader of the Soviet Union, Nikita Khrushchev, as they prepared to square off over the issue of nuclear missiles based in Cuba. Many people, including Rusty Goodman, thought this confrontation might easily lead to World War III or worse. That's what prompted Rusty's telephone call to Howard in October 1962.

"Howard, I've gone just about as far as I can," Rusty said, as Howard and I listened on separate extensions.

At first Howard thought Rusty was in financial trouble and needed money in an emergency. We didn't have a dime to spare, but Howard offered all we had. "Rusty, all I've got in the world is a ten-dollar bill. It's not much, but I can send it to you if you need money."

"No, no, it's not that," Rusty said as he began to sob. "Billie and me have got to get back to the Lord. The radio says that this Cuban missile crisis could explode at any moment, and it really bothers me. Howard, we're not ready to die. We want help, and we need it now."

"What do you want us to do?" Howard asked.

Rusty told Howard that he wanted to go hear Joel Hemphill preach. Joel was the son of W. T. Hemphill, the pastor of the church in Monroe, Louisiana, where our revival tent had been destroyed by the hurricane. Joel had married Howard's niece, LaBreeska, and they were now holding evangelistic singing and preaching meetings back in Winnsboro.

Rusty said, "We're gonna drive up there tonight and go to church with them, but we really want you all to come down and pray for us."

I could hear the pain in Howard's voice as he said, "Rusty, I don't know how in the world we can come down there. This ten dollars is all I've got, and it ain't near enough even to buy gas."

"Rusty, we'll be there," I heard myself saying. "We'll leave here within the hour. We're on our way."

"Honey, we can't go," Howard said to me through the phone.

"But you don't have any money," Rusty began to take up Howard's protest.

"We'll get it," I replied. "If God provided a whale to get Jonah to Nineveh, He can provide gas for us to get to Louisiana." In my heart I knew God would provide. We encouraged Rusty to respond to what the Lord was telling him and promised we would get there as rapidly as we could.

Howard and I hung up, and I walked back into the room where he was still sitting. "Let's get packed, hon. God's moving in a hurry."

We packed some clothes in a suitcase and prepared to leave, wondering the entire time where we were going to get money enough to buy gasoline. As Howard was loading the car, the telephone rang, and I answered it. The caller was a woman from our church. "Vestal, this is Lucille Wells. I was praying just awhile ago, and the Lord spoke to me. He said you needed fifty dollars. I don't know what it's for, but I've got it here at the house. Do you want me to mail it or bring it over to you, or would you rather come get it?"

"Honey, you wait right there. We're on our way out of town and will stop and pick it up as we leave. I'll explain more when we get there." Lucille had never before done such a thing, but this would not be the last time she obeyed God by taking a step of faith.

Howard and I stopped at Lucille's home, gratefully picked up the fifty dollars, and headed south toward Louisiana. In the meantime, Rusty and Billie were driving to Winnsboro. When Rusty and Billie arrived at the church where Joel and LaBreeska were conducting the revival, Joel rushed out and met them. He threw his arms around Rusty and Billie and said, "I prayed that you'd come."

That night at the close of the service, Joel extended an invitation for those in the audience who were not right with God to come forward for prayer. Rusty and Billie were among the first to respond.

Howard and I drove straight through the night, arriving in Baton Rouge the next day. We rejoiced with them, laughing and crying and praising the Lord for His faithful love, a love that never gives up on people, even prodigals who run from Him. We spent the next two days studying the Bible and praying with Rusty and Billie. Rusty arranged for Howard to preach that Sunday at a church in Baton Rouge. At the close of the service, Howard baptized Rusty and Billie. It was a glorious new start for the young couple.

Rusty continued singing with the Plainsmen for several more months, but he grew increasingly dissatisfied with what he was doing. Ironically, it was just after the Plainsmen had completed a successful tour with a new, up-and-coming country artist by the name of Johnny Horton that Rusty came home and told Billie, "Honey, I've just quit the quartet."

Billie understood Rusty's decision, but she was still new to the whole idea of living by faith. "What are we going to do for a living, Rusty?" she asked pensively.

"Well I don't know yet," Rusty replied. "But God will provide. Maybe we can sing with Howard, Sam, and Vestal."

Meanwhile back in Madisonville, on Friday morning of that same week, I was making breakfast when Howard came into the kitchen. "Hurry, hon, let's eat and get cleaned up," I said. "We're going to Owensboro to buy an organ for the church today."

Howard was flabbergasted. It was bad enough that we were struggling to survive financially as it was, let alone hearing such an outlandish idea on an empty stomach. "We don't need an organ," Howard answered kindly.

"Yes, we do," I said emphatically. "The Lord told me to go buy an organ . . . today."

"But, Vestal, we don't have any money."

"I know it, but I also know the Lord wants us to go buy an organ."

Howard acquiesced and agreed to go to Owensboro. All the way there, he kept saying things such as, "But we don't even have anyone who can play an organ. We don't need it."

"God will send us someone," I assured Howard.

We went to Shuttlers' Music Company in Owensboro, and with barely enough money to buy gas to get back home, we walked in and told the salesman we wanted to buy an organ. "We have no money," I told the salesman, "so we'll have to make payments on it, but we need a good Hammond organ for our church." It's a wonder the salesman didn't show us the door. Instead he showed us a fabulous, slightly used, Hammond B-3 organ with a "Leslie" speaker that another church had just traded in.

Howard and I signed the papers, agreeing to make the payments ourselves, out of our own money.

"Now, we need it delivered in the morning," I said.

"Oh, I'm sorry, ma'am," the salesman said. "We can't possibly get it to you until next week sometime."

"No, we have to have it tomorrow." I had a sense of urgency that the organ needed to be in the church before Sunday. The salesman and I talked further, and I finally convinced him that if he could get the organ to us before noon the next day, we'd take it.

That evening we received a telephone call from Rusty. "I want to come home," he said. He and Billie packed all their earthly possessions into a small, U-Haul type trailer, hitched it to their car, and headed toward Madisonville.

"Rusty, what *are* you going to do after we get to Madisonville?" Billie asked as they pulled away from Baton Rouge.

"I don't know," he answered. "Maybe I can play the organ at the church."

Billie sat up straight in the seat and looked at Rusty in amazement. "Rusty, you can't play the organ. You've never played one in your entire life. You can't even play the piano. All you play is the guitar." Billie sighed and slumped back down. "Besides, they don't have an organ at that church."

About seven o'clock the following morning, just as Howard and I were sitting down for breakfast, I looked out the window and saw Rusty, Billie, and their daughter, Tanya, pulling their car into our church parking lot, towing their belongings behind them. What a hallelujah time we had! We shouted and rejoiced and praised God that Rusty and his family were home. We had no idea where we were going to house them, but we were glad they were home.

Just about the time we were going into the house, a truck from Shuttlers' Music Company pulled into the parking lot. "Where do you want your new organ?" the driver called out the window of his vehicle.

"Organ?" Rusty said as he raised his eyebrows. "What's this?"

"Well, we just went out and bought one," Howard told him.

"But you don't have anyone in the church who can play, do you?" Rusty asked. "Are you going to play it?"

"Me? Oh no, not me," Howard said with a laugh. "I sound like a circus coming to town when I try to play the organ. But we figured the Lord would send somebody along to play it," Howard said, looking at me with a twinkle in his eye.

Rusty stood in the parking lot and began to cry. He and Billie told us about the conversation they had had as they pulled away from their only source of income at that time. Although we didn't understand it completely, that organ was a confirmation to Rusty and Billie that they had made the right decision. Before long, we were all somewhere between laughing and crying, but our tears were tears of joy.

When we finally calmed down, we gathered for breakfast, excitedly talking and catching up on recent events in our lives. "Tomorrow, Vestal and Sam and I are scheduled to go to the Kansas City area camp meeting," Howard was telling Rusty.

"Oh, Rusty, you'll have to come along with us and help us sing at the camp meeting," I said hopefully, not really certain how he might respond. I didn't have time to find out.

Suddenly Aileen Richey, a young woman who was living with Howard and me, burst into the conversation. Aileen had been at the camp meeting in Kansas City the previous year, and she had heard me tell how God had instructed me to write Rusty and present the letter for the pastors to pray over it. Now she jumped up and reminded us of that letter.

"Vestal," she said excitedly, "Rusty is supposed to preach at this year's camp meeting. Remember?"

I looked at Rusty. He was nodding his head. "I know," said Rusty. "I remember too."

The next morning we left for Kansas City, and Rusty went along with us. Howard, Sam, Rusty, and I sang together on Monday and Tuesday nights. On Wednesday afternoon, during the youth service, Rusty preached his first sermon. It was more of a testimony than a sermon, and as the young people listened, the Spirit of the Lord moved in and began to touch their hearts. Many of those teenagers had looked up to Rusty because he was becoming a well-known gospel singer. When Rusty confessed his sin in front of them and acknowledged how unworthy he was to be standing on that platform, the kids identified with him. Dozens and dozens of kids responded to a simple invitation to meet the Lord in a fresh way.

When we got back home, Rusty's practical side took over. "What am I going to do here, Vestal?" he asked. "Howard, you don't need me in the church. I don't even play the piano."

I said, "No, but you're going to play the organ."

"I don't really know how to play the organ," Rusty objected.

"That's all right," I replied. "You go on over to the church and check it out."

Rusty went over to the church and began to press some of the keys on our "new" Hammond B-3. He was crying and praying and saying, "Lord, what am I doing here? I don't even have money to rent a house."

Rusty was right. A darling little house not even a block away from us was for rent, and the owner wanted only fifty dollars a month, but Rusty couldn't afford it. Until they could find a place, Rusty, Billie, and Tanya slept in the basement of the church.

The following Sunday Rusty was playing the organ in our morning worship service. His playing was a little rough at first, but it didn't take him long to master the keyboard and pedals, producing some fairly good music.

On Sunday afternoon Rusty joined Sam, Howard, and me as we sang for a small Methodist congregation near Madisonville. The church gave us an offering, and we split it evenly among us, six dollars apiece. Rusty wanted to give his portion to the rest of us, but we made him take it. He had no other money to live on, and he had a wife and child to support.

The next afternoon Rusty went into the church and sat down at the organ. After a while he got off the organ bench, got down on his knees, and began to pray. "Lord, you're gonna have to show me what to do," he said, "because we're out of money and just about out of food. We don't have anything left. You promised that you would provide for us and supply all our needs, so I'm trusting you to do that."

A few minutes later Rusty returned to the organ and began to play and sing. As he did, God inspired him to write a song. The words and music practically flowed through Rusty. He played the song once and then scribbled the lyrics and some chords on a piece of scrap paper.

Rusty came out of the church and called for Howard and me. "Come here, quick; I want you to hear something." Howard and I hurried across the parking lot from our house, and Rusty told us what had happened. He reached into his pants pocket and pulled out a sheet of paper on which he had written these words:

> *Many times I bowed beneath a heavy load*
> *And on bended knees to God a prayer I'd pray;*
> *As I knelt there on the floor,*
> *He'd remind me just once more*
> *That the answer was already on the way.*
>
> *Oh yes, the answer's on the way this I know.*
> *Jesus said it, I believe it, and it's so.*
> *Our Heavenly Father knows the need before we pray;*
> *And we can rest assured the answer's on the way.*

Rusty sang the song to us, and Howard and I joined in as we learned it.

The next day the postman brought a letter to our house for Rusty. The letter was from Gov. Jimmie Davis. Rusty opened the envelope, and great big tears began pouring down his face.

He looked at Howard and me and said, "Now I know what the song was about." In the envelope was a letter from the governor. The governor wrote, "Rusty, I know that you weren't in good financial shape when you left, and I admire you. I miss you, but I admire you for going home to work with your family in the church. And here is a little gift you might need." Along with his letter, Governor Davis enclosed a check for fifteen hundred dollars that he said he owed Rusty for past services.

Rusty looked at the postmark. The envelope had been mailed the day before yesterday.

The answer really *was* on the way.

We sang Rusty's song in our church service the following Sunday. By the time we got to the second verse, our congregation was nearly shouting!

If there is a special need in your life, my friend
And you are seeking for an answer every day,
If by faith, you will start believing,
Mighty soon you will be receiving,
The answer is already on the way.

We could hardly have imagined at the time that we would soon be singing "The Answer's on the Way" all over America.

CHAPTER 12

THE FIRST GOODMAN ALBUM

With Sam and Rusty rejoining Howard and me, it was only natural we should start singing together as a family again, mostly for our own church services at first. But as the word got out that the Happy Goodman Family was available for singin's, we began to receive invitations from other congregations. We weren't out beating the bushes looking for places to sing. Just the opposite. As the founders of Life Temple, Howard and I were content to stay busy at the church. We had already experienced plenty of life on the road as a traveling ministry. We were delighted to stay in one town for a while, to sleep in our own bed, to eat our own food, and to have something like a normal life.

Rusty and Sam, however, were hoping we could do more singing outside the walls of our church and beyond our community. Just such an opportunity came along when the WLTV television station went on the air in Bowling Green, Kentucky, about seventy miles southeast of Madisonville and about sixty-five miles north of Nashville. Sam hosted an early talk show on WLTV, and his guests included musicians, Christian singers, politicians, and preachers. When Rusty heard about the new station, he immediately realized the potential a television program featuring the Happy Goodman Family might have.

"Howard, we ought to go over there and audition," Rusty suggested excitedly. "Sam said they were crying for talent."

Howard held lingering suspicions about television and the fickleness of anyone associated with it. "I don't know about this TV thing, Rusty," he said, shaking his head. "You weren't with us when we had that terrible experience with a television personality in Asheville. If that's the way it has to be to work on TV, I don't want any part of it."

The next day Howard and Rusty were watching television at our house when the announcer said, "If you have talent, and you would like to appear on TV, contact the program director at WLTV, Channel 13, Bowling Green."

Rusty and Howard stared at each other in awe. "Howard, we're going over there tomorrow," Rusty said. "I believe that was a message from God."

The following day we drove to WLTV. Howard, Sam, and I stayed in the car while Rusty went inside to talk to someone about an audition. Soon the program director was herding us into a small studio, where we sang one of our favorite songs, "Born to Serve the Lord." A few minutes later the program director was back in the studio asking, "When can you start a regular program?"

One week later the Happy Goodman Family began a weekly, thirty-minute program on WLTV. The program aired live on Monday nights, which meant we had to drive the 140-mile round trip to Bowling Green every Monday evening. Soon, however, that wasn't the only traveling we were doing. Invitations for concerts began to pour in from Kentucky and Tennessee. The Happy Goodman Family was on the road once again.

Rusty was ecstatic. He was doing what he loved to do—sing the gospel. Ever the innovator, Rusty was constantly urging us onward to the next level in our musical presentation. Not surprisingly, Rusty was concerned about the professionalism of our performance, and shortly after our program began airing, Rusty brought up the subject with Howard.

"Howard, if we're gonna start doing concerts," he said nervously, "we've got to have a better sound system. This little old amplifier and loudspeaker we're using just can't handle what we're tryin' to put through it. Things are changing in gospel music, and we need to change our methods too. When I was with the Plainsmen, I realized that if gospel singing groups don't update their equipment and start using modern methods, we'll never make it professionally."

Howard didn't care a lick about sound systems or making it professionally, but he was passionately concerned about reaching people with a message about Jesus. He expressed his concerns to Rusty. "I ain't against progress, Rusty," Howard said, "but I'm just afraid as soon as we start changing our methods, we'll water down our message."

Rusty understood Howard's anxiety. He was convinced, however, that we were in the communication business, and we could get the message across more clearly to more people if we used the best equipment we could get our hands on. "If we can't sing and testify to the glory of Jesus," Rusty said, "then I don't want any part of it. But I think the Lord wants us to use the best methods available to communicate His message. And that means getting a better sound system."

Rusty's logic made sense to Howard, and the next day Rusty and Sam began their search for a better system. What they found was three microphones (we had all been singing around one mike), a fifty-watt amplifier, and two speakers. Total price: $250, less than the price of one microphone today.

The decision to go first class when it came to our sound equipment set a precedent for us and also established a reputation among our music colleagues, a reputation that followed us throughout our career. It was common knowledge among musicians: "If you're on the same concert as the Goodmans, use their sound equipment, because they have the best."

With our newfound popularity came a deluge of invitations to sing all across the country. That created a problem, especially for Howard and me, since we were already committed to being in our church every

Sunday morning. We made our living by singing and didn't take a salary from the church, so it was not money that motivated us to be home for church; it was a spiritual commitment. Howard and I had promised the Lord when we started singing full-time that if at all possible we would be home in our own pulpit every Sunday morning and evening and every Wednesday night for prayer meeting. The local church was still our priority. Consequently we decided that we needed a bus so we could not only travel to concerts more comfortably and conveniently, but so we could also sleep on the way home Saturday nights.

Rusty said he knew where we could get a good price on a used bus, so he and Howard went to Dallas to check it out. When Howard saw the 1947 Trailways clunker that Rusty had found, his countenance dropped, and his mind filled with misgivings. "Rusty, I can just see us broke down with this old junker."

Howard's words proved to be prophetic. That old bus was always breaking down. On more than a few nights, I woke up to find the floorboards torn up and somebody working diligently beneath the bus, trying to get us back on the road.

With a new television program, a new sound system, a bus in which to travel, and a growing church, one might think that Rusty would relax, slack off a bit. He didn't. He knew there was a whole world that had never heard of the Happy Goodman Family. He also knew that one of the best ways to familiarize folks with our music was through a recording.

One morning as Rusty, Howard, and I were drinking coffee at our kitchen table, Rusty said abruptly, "Howard, we've got to make a record."

Howard nearly choked on his coffee, but he finally cleared his throat enough to say, "Whoa! Now wait just a minute, Rusty. I went along with you on the sound system and the bus, but we can't make a record."

"Why not?" Rusty wanted to know. "Sure we can," he said before Howard had a chance to object. "Lots of people enjoy our style of music. Our style of music will sell," he said, pacing back and forth across our kitchen.

"Who would record us?" I asked.

"I don't know yet, but I'd like to find out," Rusty replied.

Howard sighed a huge sigh and said, "Talk to Sam. If he agrees, then see what you can do."

That was all Rusty needed to hear. The next day he drove to Nashville, looking for a record company that might want to record the Happy Goodman Family.

None did.

Not Heartwarming. Not Songs of Faith. Not John T. Benson. Nobody wanted to take a risk on such an unknown entity as the Goodmans.

Mr. Benson was at least interested enough to make a follow-up trip to Madisonville to visit us. He seemed sincerely concerned for us and even made an offer. Mr. Benson told Howard, "If I invest the money to record the Goodmans, you will have to guarantee that you will sell a certain number of albums every month."

"Mr. Benson, we can't do that," Howard replied. "We don't have any idea how our records will sell."

John T. Benson scratched his chin, thought awhile, then said, "Well, then, I will have to have a financial lien against your bus."

Howard didn't even think twice about that one. "Mr. Benson, do you see that little old typewriter sitting over there on the desk? I wouldn't even give you a lien against that. Because if I did, it would be like saying I don't believe we're going to sell enough records. And that simply isn't true. I believe that when we record, people will want to buy Goodman albums."

The meeting ended amicably, but Mr. Benson walked out without a lien on our bus, and we walked out without a recording contract.

In desperation Rusty went to see Russell Sims, a man who owned a small recording business. Rusty was at his persuasive best as he talked with Russell. "You don't know this group, but we want to make a record," Rusty told him. "We feel like we can make you some money out of it, because one day the Happy Goodmans are really going places."

Russell was unimpressed. "Rusty, I'd like to help you, but I'm just as broke as you are. In fact, I've been thinking about going out of business. I'll tell you what though. If you can come up with six hundred dollars to pay the union musicians, I'd be willing to pay the six hundred dollars it will cost for studio time. If you can get the cash, we might be able to work something out. Otherwise forget it."

When Rusty brought home his report, we were all disappointed. We hadn't really thought much about making an album up to this point, but Rusty's enthusiasm had been contagious. Now a record seemed to be the next logical step in our music career. But even with Russell's generous offer to pay for the studio time, we didn't have six hundred dollars to pay for musicians.

Mulling over the situation as we sat around the living room, Sam had an idea. "Vestal, do you reckon we could borrow the six hundred dollars from Daisy Troop?"

Daisy was a close friend of our family, and more important, she was a member of our congregation. She, too, had been encouraging us to make a record. Daisy owned a school of cosmetology, a beauty school, in Madisonville, so although she wasn't wealthy, she at least had assets which allowed her to borrow more money than most of us. I didn't want to impose on our friendship, but I figured it wouldn't hurt to ask.

Daisy was delighted to loan us the money to make our first record, and two days later we signed a contract to cut our first album with Sims Records. We promised to pay Daisy back just as soon as we sold our first batch of albums.

For the benefit of all the budding recording stars reading these pages, I need to warn you that nowadays many so-called producers make lucrative livings by luring unsuspecting talent into recording studios with empty promises of hit records, glamour, and success . . . all for a fee, of course. Actually, most modern record deals work in exactly the opposite manner. You should never have to pay to sign a recording contract. Unless it is a "custom" recording—one that is not contracted by a label—or a demonstration project (a demo to be played as a sample of your music and not to be sold), the artist does not pay to record. If a record company wants to record an artist, the record company pays the production costs of the album. The artist then repays the company gradually out of royalties that are earned as the product sells. After the company recoups the up-front money it has invested in producing the album, the artist is paid a royalty for sales in excess of the costs.

That's the way the recording business works today. But in 1962 we were glad to find someone (anyone!) who was willing to record us. Fortunately for us, Russell was a legitimate businessman rather than a ripoff artist.

The studio where we recorded our first album was an old Quonset-hut type of building in the heart of what is now Nashville's famed Music Row, the area between Sixteenth and Eighteenth Avenues. When we went into the studio, we didn't have three thousand studio musicians in Nashville from which to select, as there are today. Back then, only twenty studio musicians worked regularly. But they worked around the clock, recording a session with Patsy Cline in the morning and going into the studio with Eddie Arnold in the afternoon.

Amazingly, Rusty and Russell secured the services of some of the finest studio musicians in Nashville at the time, including "Pig" Robbins, Walter Haynes, Junior Huskey, and others. The leader of our session musicians was a young man named Harold Bradley, who was just beginning to make his mark on the Nashville music scene. Today Harold is the president of the Nashville musicians' union. Harold's brother, Owen, also greatly influenced "the Nashville sound," playing on and producing albums for numerous country stars. Eventually Owen developed Music Mill studios on Music Row, where he recorded a relatively unknown bunch of boys from Fort Payne, Alabama. The group, known simply as Alabama, went on to superstardom in country music. Harold and Owen's sister, Connie Bradley, also became enmeshed in the Nashville music business, heading up the Nashville division of the American Society of Composers, Authors, and Publishers (ASCAP).

The fact that we used such a variety of musicians was a first in itself. Prior to our first album, most gospel music was recorded with piano accompaniment and not much more. The Blackwood Brothers had

Wally Varner and the Statesman had Hovie Lister playing the piano. The Goodmans went into the studio and used the same musicians that were playing on George Jones's and many other country stars' records. Almost unwittingly, the Goodmans built a strong bridge between country and gospel music.

Much of our "progressiveness," of course, was due to Rusty's insatiable desire to produce excellent music that would bring honor to God. As the Happy Goodman Family, we didn't realize just how innovative we were, deciding early on to use guitars in our music, making use of television to promote our group, and incorporating top-of-the-line equipment. Later on, when our son, Ricky, learned how to play the drums, we were also one of the first gospel groups to add drums to our live concerts, as well as on our records.

Once we completed the recording process, Russell Sims explained to us that it would take about a month to produce the master and plates from which the vinyl records would be pressed. We also had to get an album jacket ready. Woodmont Baptist Church in Nashville allowed us to take a picture of the beautiful stained-glass window adorning their sanctuary, and that became the album cover of our first long-playing record, which we titled *I'm Too Near Home*.

While we waited for the albums to be done, we kept busy in the church throughout the week and sang at concerts on weekends. One Friday night we were to do a concert in the tiny town of Pall Mall, Tennessee. We were still looking for the church when it was almost time for the concert to begin. We drove all over that part of the country and succeeded only in getting more lost. Finally around eight o'clock we gave up. Fortunately we later learned that only five people had found their way to the church. It was downright embarrassing.

Rusty, however, was not so much discouraged as determined. He got Howard and Sam together and said, "Tell you what let's do.

Tonight's the night of the all-night singin' at the Ryman Auditorium in Nashville. Let's drive down there and ask if Wally Fowler will let us on the program."

Sam and Howard shrugged their shoulders. "Sounds good. Let's go," said Sam.

We arrived at the Ryman around ten o'clock that night. The auditorium was already packed with more than three thousand enthusiastic music lovers who were on hand for the eleven o'clock show.

Wally Fowler greeted us like long-lost cousins. Although he had not heard the Happy Goodman Family sing since Howard's sisters had left the group, he had been hearing about us and was more than willing to take a chance by putting us on the program . . . as a warmup act before the main show. He explained to Howard, "I want you to sing a couple of numbers. You know we go on the air live at eleven o'clock for an hour over WSM radio. My program is already full, but I can put you on at 10:45, and you can sing for fifteen minutes before we have the regulars come on for the broadcast."

Beggars can't be choosers, as the saying goes, so at exactly 10:45 the Happy Goodman Family took the stage at the Ryman. We started out strong, singing the rousing, "Born to Serve the Lord." It was a fabulous feeling to stand on that grand old stage and sing about Jesus. When we finished the song, three thousand music fans roared their approval. Rusty had just written a new song that we had sung only a few times on our television program. In the sterile quietness of a television studio, it had been difficult to tell how the song was being received by the audience. But when we did the song as our second number at the Ryman, it received such a thunderous ovation, we knew immediately that it was going to be a signature song for the Happy Goodman Family.

Rusty had been inspired to write the song by observing Shorty, an old fellow who attended our church occasionally. Shorty had a habit of interrupting the service, just before Howard was about to start preaching. He'd stand and wave his hand high above his head so Howard could see him. "I want to testify, Brother Goodman. I want to testify."

Howard always respected Brother Shorty's wishes and allowed the little man to speak. Shorty wouldn't talk long, but he always witnessed to how much he loved the Lord. When Shorty was done "testifyin'," he'd step into the aisle, twirl around two or three times, and then just before sitting down, he'd look up at the congregation and say, "I wouldn't take nuttin' for my joo-ney now."

Shorty didn't have much by this world's standards. He had a slight speech impediment, and some people made fun of him behind his back. But the man's faith in God melted Rusty's heart every time he heard him. Rusty was so touched by Shorty's phrase that he wrote "I Wouldn't Take Nothin' for My Journey Now," a song that has become a gospel classic. On the sheet music, we dedicated the song to Shorty.

It was now close to eleven o'clock, and the appreciative Ryman audience was clapping and shouting for more of "I Wouldn't Take Nothin' for My Journey Now." Howard cast a worried look toward Wally Fowler who was standing backstage in the wings. Wally grinned and waved us on. "Keep going," he mouthed the words. "Whatever you're doing, keep doing it!"

Good thing. The enthusiastic audience was not going to let us quit anyhow! They kept calling for one encore after another. It was 11:30 when we finally left the stage, and even then, the audience was clapping, whistling, and shouting for more! What an incredible feeling to experience that kind of reception to our music.

Wally met us as we came offstage. "That was fantastic!" he shouted above the din. "Here's $75," he said as he thrust some bills in my direction. "And we want you folks back next month."

"Wally, we didn't expect any pay," I said as I tried to give him back the money. "We're just grateful for the chance to be on your program."

"Well, if you come back next month, I'll give you $150," Wally gushed. "Those folks out there sure enjoyed the Goodmans tonight."

The first Friday of the following month we were back at the Ryman Auditorium. This time we were on the program with several other gospel groups that made up The Gospel Singing Caravan, including the Statesmen Quartet, the Prophets, the Blackwood Brothers, the Johnson

Sisters, the Blue Ridge Quartet, the LeFevres, and the Sego Brothers. The Gospel Singing Caravan was the hottest gospel ticket traveling the country in those days, and we were honored simply to be performing on the same stage as them.

Better yet, Russell Sims showed up that night with our new album, literally hot off the presses. The albums were so new, they weren't shrink-wrapped in cellophane; in fact, they didn't even have covers. In the parking lot behind the Ryman, our son, Ricky, and Russell hurriedly inserted the records into white slip covers and ran them back inside, where we sold them off the front of the stage during intermission. People crowded around Ricky as though he were giving away hundred dollar bills to get their copy of the Happy Goodman Family's album.

All of the groups on the program that night had albums. Some of them were running special deals on their records, three albums for ten dollars, two for five. We had only one album, which we sold for full price, but we could hardly keep up with the demand. We sold every record that Russell brought that night, enough to completely repay Daisy Troop's six hundred dollar loan with money to spare, which we promptly put toward purchasing more albums.

We later learned that John T. Benson was in the audience that evening. When he saw the crowd clamoring for our albums, Mr. Benson shook his head and said to a friend, "I've messed up. I've missed a good thing."

We recorded our second album at the prestigious RCA Studio B, the same studio in which Elvis Presley, Red Foley, George Jones, and a host of other famous artists had recorded hit records. The studio is still there on Eighteenth Avenue in the heart of Nashville's Music Row, with a full complement of instruments and studio equipment, looking much as it did the day the Goodmans first walked through those famous doors.

Today, however, RCA Studio B is a museum, open to the public, where music fans can see what it was like to create some of Music City's most famous music.

I didn't know enough to be awed by one of the music industry's most notable recording facilities, and I probably wouldn't have much cared anyhow. I've never been one to be impressed by money, monuments, or other "sacred cows." To me, it was just a recording studio, and I would have been just as excited if it had been in somebody's barn. Rusty and Sam, however, were well aware of the studio's history, and they were teeming with enthusiasm as the musicians arrived and we began to roll tape to record our first song on our album *It's a Wonderful Feeling*.

The session moved along quite well until we got to the song "What a Friend We Have in Jesus." I was singing a solo on the second verse, when out of the corner of my eye, I saw a man crawl on all fours through the studio door and then slide along the wall of the studio. Slowly he pushed his torso up just high enough that he could turn his back to the wall, then with his legs stretched out toward the center of the room, he propped himself up slightly and leaned his head back against the wall.

I didn't know what to make of the unusual character, but I knew enough to keep singing. In those days, all the singers and instrumentalists recorded in the studio at the same time. Unlike today's multitrack recording process, back then if anyone stopped or made a mistake, the entire ensemble had to play and sing everything again. Despite our intruder, the musicians continued playing, and the red light stayed on, indicating that we were recording, so I had no alternative but to keep right on singing. At every pause in the song, however, I turned my head away from the microphone to stare at the strange figure on the floor.

To describe him in today's terms, he looked like a homeless person, someone you might see sleeping on a cardboard box in many major cities. He was horribly emaciated—his skin barely hung on his bones—and his black shirt and black pants were disheveled. He looked as though he hadn't eaten or slept in days, and I noticed immediately that the man was in his stocking feet! His eyes seemed glazed, as if he was in an alcohol- or drug-induced stupor.

The man listened to us sing the entire song, and as we finished the take, he said wistfully in a low, gravelly voice, "God, I wish I could sing like that. That's the kind of singing I want to do. I want to sing about *that.*"

Without saying a word directly to us, the shadowy figure crawled out of the studio, again on all fours.

Sam and Rusty were instantly buzzing between themselves.

"What's going on?" I asked. "Who was that man?"

Sam replied excitedly, "Why, Vestal, that was Johnny Cash!"

"Who's Johnny Cash?" I asked naively.

Rusty and Sam quickly informed me that Johnny Cash was one of the music world's premier stars.

"Well, whoever he is, that man is miserable," I answered. "We need to pray for him. He needs Jesus."

Johnny Cash was going through the valley of the shadow of death. Years later he would reveal to the world that that was one of the lowest points of his life. Ironically, he had already achieved a level of success most music artists dream about. His songs "Ring of Fire," "How High the Water, Mama," and others had been chart-toppers. Yet in the midst of his skyrocketing superstardom, Johnny Cash had fallen victim to drug addiction and alcoholism.

Years later Johnny met and married a friend of ours, June Carter, of the country and bluegrass singers, the Carter Family. June Carter was a sincere Christian, a praying woman who literally prayed Johnny Cash into the kingdom of God. Johnny went on to have numerous hit records, among them "I Walk the Line" and "Folsum Prison Blues." Johnny Cash may not remember the day he crawled in on a Happy Goodman Family recording session. In his condition, he would have been lucky to have remembered his name! But I couldn't forget that forlorn figure dressed in black. I prayed for him every time his name came to mind. In many ways, Johnny's plaintive cry in the studio that day was a prayer that God heard and answered far beyond what Johnny or we could have imagined. Johnny has become a prominent spokesman for Christ, and he has gone on to sing about Jesus at Billy Graham crusades and other Christian events around the country.

On another occasion we were working in the studio with an outstanding group of studio "pickers." From our earliest recording efforts, Howard, Rusty, and Sam realized that the background music was an important part of the package in which we were wrapping the gospel message. The music was not merely the icing on the cake; it was what made the cake delicious and attractive. Consequently the Goodmans always held musicians in the highest regard, and we tried to book the best session players available for our recordings.

When we were working on a song for our album *What a Happy Time,* our background musicians were the cream of the crop. Most of them were the same musicians who had done so well for us on our first album. One guitar player, however, was a newcomer. His name was Jerry Reed. Chet Atkins had brought him to Nashville and had helped him to get some studio session work while he was getting ready to record an album of his own.

We started recording, and I was singing a solo on "The Old Rugged Cross" when suddenly the engineer's voice came over the talk-back microphone in the studio control room. "Hey, we need you to play, Jerry," the engineer said as he stopped the tape.

We all looked over at Jerry. He was sitting in a chair, leaning over his fire-truck red Gibson guitar with his head bowed and tears dripping down his face.

"What's wrong, Jerry? We need you to play," the engineer implored.

Jerry didn't answer. He simply raised his face, still wet with tears, looked over at me, and said, "You got to me, mama."

Don't ever let anyone tell you differently: Those old hymns still can reach into somebody's heart. "The Old Rugged Cross" sure reached

Jerry. A few weeks later Jerry Reed recorded his first solo album. One of the songs from that album was a career-breaker, "U.S. Mail," which propelled Jerry to stardom, but Jerry has always reminded me that it was in a Goodman session that a gospel song touched his heart.

We recorded three records with Russell Sims before he sold his company and we were forced to look for another record label. By that time we had become regulars on Wally Fowler's program at the Ryman. Beyond that, we were receiving invitations to sing in concerts in Atlanta and cities all over the South. Because of our increased visibility, finding another record company posed an entirely new set of problems.

CHAPTER 13

SIGNING WITH WORD

When the Goodman family began negotiating the next recording contract, several questions arose immediately. First, with whom should we sign? No longer did we have to convince record-company executives of our viability as a recording group. By now several record companies were actually courting us. Howard, Rusty, and Sam spent long hours meeting with record executives, fielding offers, and trying to carefully and prayerfully decide between them.

One such meeting took place in a hotel in Memphis, where we were staying prior to a concert. Jarrell McCracken and Marvin Norcross visited us to tell us about a new record company they had formed known as Word Records. At the same time representatives from Sing Records, a label owned by our friends the LeFevres, were also visiting us, hoping to convince us to sign with them. Neither the men from Word nor the men from Sing were aware of the others' presence in the hotel.

While Howard, Sam, and Rusty negotiated with the two record companies, I was in my hotel room right down the hall from them. I didn't know much about record deals, but I figured the Lord had a plan for the Happy Goodman Family, and it was important that we be in tune with His will for us, regardless of whether it was the best record deal or not. I prayed, "I need an answer, Lord. What are we supposed to do?"

I opened my Bible and began searching for God's answer. I knew better than to take the first verse I came to as a divine directive. I had often heard the fictional story concerning the fellow who opened his Bible looking for specific directions. The fellow let his finger drop onto a verse which read, "Judas went out and hung himself." Not content that he had found the right answer, he allowed his Bible to fall open again. He placed his finger on the page and read the verse that said, "Go ye and do likewise."

That sort of direction I could live without. But I was desperate to know what God wanted us to do, so I scanned the pages of my Bible. All the while I was praying, "Lord, please show me either the word 'sing' or 'word,' and I will believe that it is You." I opened my Bible three times to the Old Testament. The first time it fell open to the book of Jeremiah. I looked at the page and read, "Jeremiah said, 'I heard the Word of the Lord.'"

I said, "That's one."

I looked in the Scriptures again, and they opened at Isaiah, where the prophet declared, "I heard the Word of the Lord."

Again I shut my Bible and then allowed it to fall open one more time. Sure enough, it fell open to another passage containing something about the Word.

"Well, that is in the Old Testament," I said. "Now let's try the New Testament." I let my Bible fall open in the New Testament, and it plopped open at John 1:1: "In the beginning was the Word, and the Word was with God, and the Word was God."

Every time I allowed the pages of my Bible to fall open, "Word" was somewhere on the page. Try as I might, I could not find "sing" anywhere in the Scriptures, even though I knew it was used often in Psalms and other places in the Old Testament. I shut my Bible and started to cry, praising the Lord for His answer.

After a few minutes I realized that I better let the boys know I had received an answer from God. I jumped up, took off down the hallway, and knocked on the door where Jarrell and Marvin were meeting with Howard, Rusty, and Sam. I called the Goodman brothers aside and said, "Forget it, boys. Don't even bother negotiating. There's no need to discuss it anymore. Whatever the deal is, we are signing with Word." To make sure they understood I was not speaking simply on my own initiative, I added, "God said 'Sign with Word.'"

We signed with Word Records and became their flagship artists on the Canaan label, where we recorded for the next twenty-five years and sold literally millions of albums. Marvin Norcross and his wife, Chic, became two of our closest friends and most loyal encouragers. Marvin sat in on nearly every one of our recording sessions, encouraging us in every way possible. He attended every Goodman concert he could, often standing backstage with tears streaming down his face as we sang. Marvin was one of the true princes in gospel music and a tremendous influence on the Happy Goodmans' music.

Before we actually inked the pact with Word, however, God gave us another sign as a confirmation. This sign was more for me than for the other members of the group.

As we started singing more often, it became apparent that our bus was not going to serve us well. It was nothing but a piece of junk when we bought it, with no bathroom and no air conditioning, but Rusty and Sam had worked hard to build some bunks on the bus, and we had all pitched in to make the coach as comfortable as possible. Unfortunately the old bus had a way of breaking down at the worst possible times, such as when we were hurrying home on a Saturday night to get back for Sunday morning services at Life Temple.

The boys decided they wanted to buy a new bus. Howard, Rusty, and Sam found out that we could order a brand-new Silver Eagle Coach, the same sleek model used by Continental Trailways at the time, for a down payment of six thousand dollars. The total cost of the new vehicle, including shipping from the factory in Belgium, was around sixty thousand dollars. That was an astronomical amount of money, which, of course, we did not have. We believed that God could provide whatever we needed, and right now we needed a reliable means of transportation, so we began to pray and save toward that end.

Everyone in the Happy Goodman Family was excited about the

possibility of getting a new bus . . . everyone, that is, except me. I didn't want a new bus. At that point I didn't even want to travel and sing anymore. I was perfectly content to stay in Madisonville, Kentucky, and work in our church. I loved the church and didn't want to leave it. I was always extremely disappointed when we had to miss a service in our home church because we were on the road. But as our schedule began to include more and more West Coast locations, it became obvious that Howard and I would not be able to make it back in time, every time, even with the help of red-eye flights from California.

Three days before the down payment on the bus was due, we still didn't have the six thousand dollars. My heart was torn between two allegiances. I wanted my family to travel and sing, and yet I didn't want to give up the church to do so. In deep travail, I called Hannah Jackson, a member of our church who was one of my dearest friends and strongest prayer partners. I said, "Hannah, we've got to fast and pray for three days."

"Okay, sure," she replied as though I were asking to borrow a cup of sugar. "About what, Vestal?"

I said, "Hannah, I need you to agree with me in prayer. We are going to ask God, 'If this music ministry is really of You and You want us to travel and sing, we have to have the new bus, so we can get back every Sunday for church.' And Hannah, we need to ask the Lord to give us ten thousand dollars, more than enough for a down payment on this new coach, and we need it in three days. If God provides that amount, I will believe that He wants me to travel and sing."

And then I said something that shocked both Hannah and me. "If God doesn't answer by Monday, Howard and the boys will be able to raise the six thousand dollars somewhere and get the coach, but I'm going to tell them, 'You go ahead without me. I will help you all I can, but I am not going to travel and sing. You will have to get somebody to take my place.'"

It was a bold prayer request, especially since the Goodmans were receiving rave reviews everywhere we were singing. Besides that, I had recently been proclaimed the "Queen of Gospel Music" by the readers of the *Singing News*, a monthly newspaper that covered gospel music.

Now was definitely not the time to shake things up by threatening to quit. For that reason, I kept the more personal elements of my prayer request between Hannah, the Lord, and me. I didn't want to get the other members of the group all upset.

I said, "Hannah, I don't want to travel and sing, but I will if the Lord shows me that is what He wants me to do."

For the next three days, Hannah and I fasted, eating no food and drinking only limited liquids. On the third day, at three o'clock in the afternoon, Rusty came flying into my house, whooping and shouting. I was lying on the couch, half-sick since I had been fasting, and I was beginning to get nauseous. Rusty grabbed me and wanted me to get up, to jump up and down with him, to yell and scream.

I said, "Rusty, settle down and tell me what is going on."

He said, "Vestal, you ain't going to believe this! Marvin Norcross from Word Record Company called. They want us to sign a three-year contract, and they will give us an advance of ten thousand dollars! Think of it, Vestal. That's more than the amount of money we need by today to order the Silver Eagle bus we've been wanting."

I said, "Call and order the bus, Rusty."

Then I called Hannah and said, "Forget it, Hannah. Go ahead and eat; the fast is over. We got the money and we're buying the bus. And, oh yes, I guess I will be going along on the road."

Hannah understood exactly.

We ordered the custom-made bus, the first one that Trailways ever sold to any music group. Acquiring the new bus was a major milestone, not only for the Happy Goodman Family but for me personally. It was a confirmation to me that God wanted us to sing. There was no question about it. It was as plain as if He had written me a letter. Consequently from 1965 to 1980, nearly every Wednesday night after prayer meeting, Howard and I boarded a bus bearing the name THE HAPPY GOODMAN FAMILY and headed into the night for concerts on Thursday, Friday, and Saturday. Wherever we were on Saturday, whatever concert location we were in, we left in time to get back to the church for Sunday morning worship services.

Chapter 14

Rough Roads Bring Out the Best

We hit the road hard in the mid-1960s, traveling the length and breadth of America. We were not only riding in a new bus, we were riding a phenomenal wave of popularity. Everywhere we went, we sang to huge, enthusiastic crowds. We achieved the respect of our peers with our singing and our musicianship. The boys put together a great band, including Ernie Maxwell as lead guitarist, Bobby on bass, Rusty on rhythm guitar, Larry Strzelecki on pedal steel guitar, and Ricky on drums. Occasionally we had Aaron Wilburn playing acoustic guitar and Eddie Crooks helping Howard on piano. It was a dynamic group of musicians who never failed to bring down the house.

We were one of the highest paid gospel groups on the road, receiving a minimum of thirty-five hundred dollars per program—a whopping figure in those days—yet a sum most promoters were only too happy to pay since the Happy Goodman Family was one of the hottest "draws" in gospel music at the time. Back home, the church was growing faster than we could keep up with, nearly bursting at the seams from all the new people who had made Life Temple their church home. Everyone was doing well . . . except for Rusty.

Sometime in 1967 Rusty slipped into a deep pit of depression and couldn't seem to get out. Every time I saw him, he looked despondent, as though he was about to cry. He was so down I could hardly stand it. Howard and I prayed with him, but he continued to despair.

We went to Nashville to tape some *Jubilee* television shows, and Rusty remained aloof, spending most of his free time in his hotel room by himself. Ordinarily when Rusty wasn't depressed, he loved to be around folks, having fun, going to restaurants with us to eat dinner or to a coffee shop with us for breakfast before going to the studio each morning. But on this trip Rusty wasn't doing any of that.

Howard and I prayed for him nearly all night long the first night in Nashville. The next morning as we were sitting in the hotel coffee shop, I said, "Honey, we gotta do something to get Rusty out of this depression. I can't stand to see him like this. It's killing me." Just then Rusty walked through the door of the restaurant. When I saw him, I said, "Howard, look, something has happened to Rusty."

Rusty walked over to the table and sat down with us. He slid a scrap of paper across the table and said, "Here, Auntie, read this and see what you think of it."

I picked up the paper and started to read aloud. As I did, Rusty sat quietly, with his hands up to his face. Tears dripped down his face, through his fingers, onto the table. I read, "When I think of how He came so far from glory, came and dwelt among the lowly such as I. He suffered shame and such disgrace, went to Calvary and took my place. But I'll still ask myself the question: Who am I?"

I knew the hidden message that Rusty was expressing in this song. Rusty never thought he was good enough; he always felt unworthy of God's love and forgiveness. It was almost more than he could comprehend that a King—the King of kings and Lord of lords—would bleed and die for him. That's why he wrote the chorus:

> *Who am I that a king would bleed and die for?*
> *Who am I that He would pray, "Not My will but Thine" for?*
> *The answer I may never know;*
> *Why He ever loved me so;*

That to an old rugged cross He'd go
For who am I?

Rusty wrote many wonderful, beautiful songs, but "Who Am I?" will always be one of the most special to me. That morning in the coffee shop, Rusty sang the song for Howard and me. As he sang, great big tears streamed down his face. Before long, Howard and I were crying too. People began to stare at us, but we didn't care; Rusty was practically oblivious to the customers around us, singing even louder, his strong voice filling the room. The busy coffee shop grew quiet as Rusty continued to sing. Even the waitresses stood still; several of them bowed their heads until Rusty finished the song.

I wiped the tears from my cheeks and said, "Rusty, you ought to ask God for another valley. You'd never have gotten that song if you had stayed on the mountaintop. The richest soil is always down in the valley."

We recorded "Who Am I?" on our next album, and the song became an instant gospel hit. It was one of the most requested songs the Happy Goodman Family ever sang. Dozens of other artists and groups recorded the song, and everyone that sang it sensed a special touch from God when the song was performed.

As "Who Am I?" raced up the gospel charts, we raced around the country from one concert to the next, trying to keep up with our own success. We worked for many great concert promoters, such as J. G. Whitfield, W. B. Knowlin, Lloyd Orrell, and a few shady ones. Most of the promoters with whom we worked gave us absolute freedom to sing, talk, or preach about Jesus any way we wanted to do it. Those promoters who tried to restrict us from expressing what we felt God wanted to say through us ran smack into Howard Goodman's stubborn side.

W. B. Knowlin promoted the biggest gospel concerts in Texas. Knowlin had enjoyed success with his secular concerts featuring such groups as the Ink Spots and artists such as Boots Randolf, Chet Atkins, and Floyd Cramer. We always knew that when W. B. booked us, it was going to be a well-run, well-attended show. W. B. didn't sponsor many flops. On the other hand, he didn't like his concerts to be too ministry oriented. In fact, he preferred that his gospel concerts be as benign as possible. If we wanted to dance, shout, or stand on our heads, it was okay with him just as long as his box-office receipts remained strong. But he was constantly trying to get us to tone down our message. In fact, W. B. holds the dubious distinction of being the only promoter to demand that we zip our lips except when we were singing.

One night before a concert in Fort Worth where we were appearing with the Speer Family, the Oak Ridge Boys, the Florida Boys, and others, W. B. handed us a letter. Although he had distributed the letter to all the performers, we were targeted specifically. W. B. gave us the essence of the letter in person. He said, "You can't talk onstage tonight. Nothing but singin'. No testimonies. Just sing. No preachin'; these people paid their money to hear you sing, not preach." Knowlin turned his back and walked away.

"That's fine," Howard said without argument. "Boys, go tear our equipment down." The boys had already set up all our instruments and were nearly ready for the concert to begin. Nevertheless, at Howard's word, they dutifully started undoing what they had just taken an hour to assemble.

The auditorium was nearly full by now, so when people saw the Goodmans tearing down their instruments, word spread like wildfire that we were not going to be performing on the program that night. People lined up at the box office, demanding their money back—so many people that W. B. Knowlin came scurrying out to our bus to find Howard.

"What's going on here, Howard?" he roared.

"Well, W. B.," Howard replied calmly. "We're leavin'. If the Happy Goodmans can't tell these folks about Jesus, then there ain't no cause for us bein' here. We're gettin' our stuff off the stage right now, and we'll be out of your way real quicklike. Just give us a few minutes, and you can go on with your concert."

"You can't do that!" Mr. Knowlin yelled.

"Oh yes we can. And we are," answered Howard. "Unless, that is, you want us to do the program you booked us here to do, to let these people hear the Happy Goodman Family, not some sugarcoated version of us."

W. B. looked out the window at the people already heading for their cars. "Can you not do it my way?" he asked Howard.

"No, we can't. If we're on that platform and one of our group feels that the Lord wants us to say something, we have to be free to do it. You go ahead and have your concert, but you'll do it without us."

"Oh, all right," he growled. "I can't let these people have their money back. Go on up there and do what you want. But try to take it easy, will ya?"

"We'll have a time," Howard said with a big grin.

Despite not wanting us to minister to the audience, Mr. Knowlin continued to book us though the years. He never gave up subtly trying to tone us down. We always told him, "We have forty-five minutes on the platform. We're gonna do what we feel like we are supposed to be doin' there. We're gonna sing about Jesus. We're gonna talk about the song, we're gonna talk about the Lord, salvation, healing. We'll do whatever the Lord tells us to do."

"But why can't you just go out there and sing?" Knowlin would say, the exasperation clearly evident in his voice. We knew W. B. loved us, and we always had a good relationship with him, but we were not going to compromise what we felt was right. Obey W. B. Knowlin or obey the Lord; now tell me, how hard a choice is that?

CHAPTER 15

The Church on the Move

Throughout the mid-1960s and early 1970s, Goodman music ventures mushroomed. We opened a recording studio, formed a music publishing company, and co-hosted a syndicated television program, *The Gospel Singing Jubilee,* which aired on more than one hundred stations across America. Concert promoters called night and day, wanting us to perform on their venues. Despite the phenomenal acceptance of our music, I continued to feel that my main purpose in being in Madisonville was to minister at our church. The church was growing in numbers and in spiritual depth, but that growth did not come without a price.

In the mid-1960s we were having revival services at our church, but nobody was getting saved, nobody was getting delivered from addictions or other bondages, and few people seemed permanently affected. We had booked a popular evangelist for the meetings, and we were having good crowds. But the services were just meetings, that was all. Nothing supernatural was going on . . . or so I thought.

I started fasting and praying, asking God to do whatever was necessary to bring revival to our people. I prayed, "Lord, whatever You want to do in me, please do it. And whatever I need to do, just show me and I'll do it, but we need Your Spirit to move mightily in this church, because as it is right now, we're accomplishing nothing."

In my wildest, most active imagination, I could not possibly have concocted what happened next. In fact, even to tell this story I must rely on details provided by others who witnessed it. You'll soon understand why.

One night after church, about 10:30, I felt a strong urge to pray. We had had another long, spiritually unfruitful service, so Howard had retired for the night. Two women were at our house, awaiting a ride home, so I told them, "I am going over yonder across the parking lot to pray at the church." I went into the foyer and reached out my hand to turn on the light switch, when to my surprise I felt a hand over the switch. I couldn't see anyone, but I could feel the hand, just as sure as I was living, and it seemed as though it was keeping me from turning on the light.

Not sure what to think, I went on into the church through the swinging doors and attempted to turn on the lights inside the sanctuary. Again the hand prevented me. By now I was scared, so instinctively I said, "Oh Jesus."

At that, I heard a distinct, gravelly voice say, "Don't use that name!"

Again I cried out, "Oh Jesus, help me!"

Once again, I heard that awful voice, this time even louder. "Don't use that name."

I walked as far as the first row of seats, just in front of the pulpit area. Every bit of my physical energy suddenly drained away. I collapsed, slumping into the seats, feeling helpless and vulnerable. From that point on, it seemed as though I was starring in my own horror movie. I felt like I was having a vision, but this was certainly no vision from God.

An ugly figure came and sat down beside me and said, "I have come to take you to hell."

"You can't do that," I answered boldly. "I am a child of God."

As if to show me the foolishness of my faith, the figure picked me up, grabbing me beneath my arms. He held me for a few terrifying moments over a huge pit and then dropped me. I could feel myself falling . . . falling . . . deeper into the abyss. I knew I was in hell. The vision before me was horrible beyond description. Words do not exist that can portray the anguish, pain, and utter torment I felt all around me. "Oh God! Help me!" I cried out. "Oh God, what am I doing here?" No answer came, nor did I hear His voice; worst of all, I could not sense even a trace of God's presence in that place.

About that time the evangelist who was preaching for our revival services sensed something was wrong. He was staying with a family who lived about two miles down the road from the church. Without anyone informing him of what was going on, the evangelist said to his host, "I've got to get to the church. Sister Goodman is in trouble!"

"Hang on, I'm going with you," the host cried, as he followed the evangelist out the door, throwing his clothes on as he ran. They jumped into the car and raced toward the church.

Back at our house, Howard woke up just then and went into our kitchen, where the two ladies were still waiting for me to drive them home. It was now about 1:30 in the morning.

"Where is Vestal?" Howard asked the women. "The Lord woke me up and told me to go find her." Howard's brow wrinkled. "Where is she?"

"She has been over at the church praying since 10:30," one of the women replied.

Howard and the two women ran to the church. Just as he stepped up to the front of the building, the evangelist and his host roared into the parking lot.

"Howard, wait!" the evangelist called as he ran toward the church. "The Lord woke me up and told me that Sister Vestal is in trouble and that I should get up here."

"Me too!" Howard called back, bounding up the stairs leading to the church foyer.

Think about it: God's timing is so perfect. Just as I had plummeted to a point lower than I even knew possible, God sent word to both Howard and the evangelist, warning them that I was in trouble. And He supplied them with three prayer warriors to come along on their search-and-rescue mission. That's an important lesson: Anytime you plan to do battle with Satan's crowd, make sure you are covered with prayer.

When the men went into the church, they could not turn the light switch on; the hand was over it. Then they saw me—writhing in pain at the front of the church, totally oblivious to their presence. The men ran to me and attempted to pick me up, but as their hands reached out to touch me, they could not break through what can only be described as a force field all around me. The men could get within a few feet of me and no closer. The shield was all over me. Howard was a strong man, young and husky, and not even he could touch me.

The group started praying for me, and as soon as they mentioned the name of Jesus, the "voice" bellowed, "Don't use that name!"

The men continued praying in the name of Jesus. Suddenly the evangelist shouted, "Watch out! Here is Michael." The swinging doors from the foyer burst open with such force they nearly flew off their hinges. The men whirled around to see.

"There's nobody there!" someone shouted.

The evangelist was adamant. "Oh yes there is," he shouted. "It is Michael, the angel. Don't be afraid."

Michael entered the room and hurled a huge sword in my direction. The sword pierced the force field and went all the way through me.

Only then was I free to move. Groggy and disoriented, I slowly became aware that other people were in the church with me.

"Vestal, what happened?"

"Are you all right?"

"Talk to us! Are you okay?" Everyone was talking at once, their words swirling around my head.

"Quiet!" Howard roared, his voice startling all of us. He pulled me close to him. "Now, Vestal, tell us what happened."

As best I could, I recounted the horror I experienced as I saw for myself the terrors that await people who leave this world without a relationship with Jesus Christ. The utter darkness was frightening enough. The awful, perpetual pain that people in hell experience is far worse than mere words can convey. Perhaps the most horrendous aspect of hell was the sense of absolute loneliness that I felt. Contrary to images of hell portrayed in Hollywood movies and rock music, hell is not one big eternal party attended by the worst of sinners.

It is isolation. Absolute aloneness. The absence of hope that this condition will ever change. It is separation from God. That is hell.

After a lot of prayer that afternoon, the evangelist, Howard, and I agreed that I should report my experience to our people. We were obviously occupying territory on which some heavy spiritual battles were taking place, and our people needed to be aware of it.

Using the simplest of terms, and trying my best not to scare anyone in the congregation, I told them what had happened to me. As I described what little I could about hell, the Holy Spirit swept through the sanctuary, bringing a strong sense of conviction. People streamed to the front of the sanctuary, fell on their knees, and cried out to God for mercy. People were not simply admitting that they were sinners in need of God's amazing grace. They were repenting specifically, crying out, "Oh, God, I did this; I did *that!* Please forgive me." Nobody wanted to spend eternity in the place I told them about. At the same time, a Spirit of peace permeated the room, as people experienced true forgiveness and knew—some for the first time in their lives—that God loved them, that He did not want to destroy them in hell, but had sent Jesus to make a way that we can all be clean before the Lord. Several dozen people came to know Jesus Christ during that service.

Not only was it a turning point in their lives, that night was a milestone in our church. We began to see miracles happen, almost on a regular basis. But if we thought Satan would give up his grip on Madisonville without a fight, we had another thought coming!

One night at the close of our regular church service, a young woman named Virginia responded to our invitation to meet Christ. The main part of the service had concluded, and only fifteen or twenty people remained in the sanctuary. Most of them were praying quietly on their knees, while Howard sat at the piano on the platform maintaining an attitude of worship by playing softly. From my position near the pulpit,

I watched the young woman linger at the rear of the sanctuary, just standing there glaring at us, as most of the regular church folk began to leave.

Suddenly Virginia stepped forward and made a beeline for the altar. I could tell immediately that she was in dire need, so I left the platform and knelt to pray with her. Trying to lead her, I said, "Virginia, just say 'Jesus, come into my heart.'"

The young woman started to say "Jesus," but every time she tried to say His name, she started gagging and choking. She could not say the name.

I said, "Now, honey, say, 'Jesus, save me.'"

This time, when she started to say "Jesus," a litany of profanity spewed from her mouth—right there in church! I had rarely heard some of the words she used, let alone heard them at the altar where people were seeking God. I could hardly believe my ears. In fact, I grabbed her by her shoulders and shook her because the voice that was coming out of Virginia's mouth did not sound like her own!

Howard was so shocked to hear those horrid words in the church he stopped playing the piano and stared down at the young woman and me. Everybody else in the sanctuary was equally dumbfounded. I said, "Virginia, don't say that again." I was not angry with her; I recognized that she was not the one speaking. Ordinarily Virginia spoke in soft, demure tones, but the voice we were hearing was not that of a girl. To my utter shock, I realized it was a demonic entity speaking through Virginia!

With eyes that looked as though they could burn holes in concrete, Virginia looked up at Howard and bellowed, "Play that piano!"

Immediately I said, "Howard, don't you touch the keyboard. That is Lucifer speaking. That is Satan telling you to play, so don't do it," I warned him.

I turned to the members of the congregation, most of whom didn't know whether to laugh, cry, or run for the exits. "Don't anybody in here move or do anything or say anything," I cautioned them, "because these demons are coming out, and when they come out, you be praying. I don't want them entering you. Your temple better be clean!"

Both of our children—Vicki, who was seven, and Ricky, who was nine—were waiting for Howard and me in the sanctuary, as they usually did after the service. Their eyes were as big as saucers as they watched the spiritual drama unfold before them. But they didn't seem to be afraid. They knew, even at that young age, that the strongest demons were no match for Jesus.

Meanwhile Virginia was dropping in and out of demonically inspired personalities. For a while, she was her normal self, and she'd break down and cry. She looked into my face so pitifully and said, "Sister Goodman, I am sorry. I don't want to do that. I don't want to say those awful things."

I said, "Virginia, just say 'Jesus, come into my heart.'"

Each time she tried to say the name of Jesus, she began choking. Then the profanity began again.

After she had repeated this pattern for about thirty-five minutes, suddenly she leaped from the altar area onto the platform, landing like a cat. She stood over Howard and roared, "Play that piano!"

I said, "Howard, don't do it."

Virginia banged on the keyboard, causing the ugliest discord that piano could produce. Howard got up from the piano and stepped away. The woman was clearly dangerous. Meanwhile Virginia was walking around the piano again and again, cursing something awful.

We had received an offering during the early part of the service, and the money was still in the old-fashioned, aluminum offering plate, a container that looked like a large pie pan with a green felt bottom. The offering plate was sitting on the piano as Virginia circled it.

I reiterated to the church members, "Everybody, just keep your heads bowed and pray."

Just then, Virginia walked over to the offering plate, grabbed it by the edge, and hurled it like a Frisbee against the concrete wall about twenty feet away. She threw the offering plate with such awful force that it hit the wall and folded like an accordion.

Finally Howard and I and several others took hold of her, anointed her with oil as we prayed over her, and rebuked the devil in Jesus' name.

We commanded the demons—you can't speak nicely when you are casting out demons—to come out of Virginia and go find another place to live.

Virginia fell to the floor and almost instantly began to sob. We could tell it was the real Virginia this time. We wrapped our arms around her and prayed for her some more. She was soaking wet from perspiration and exhausted from the battle that had been raging within her, but she was free. She was delivered in a matter of moments, and she cried and apologized. Virginia became a great worker in the church, a sweet person with a true servant's heart. She is still serving the Lord to this day.

Throughout our ministry in Madisonville, we had confrontations with evil spirits. Messing with demons is no game, and it certainly wasn't something Howard and I went looking for, but when situations arose that required us to come against the enemy in Jesus' Name, we were never reluctant to do so. I truly believe that many sincere Christians are struggling in their walk with the Lord because some sort of demonic oppression has come on them, and they need to be set free. And when Jesus sets us free, we are free indeed!

When the Lord begins to use your life, you need to be aware that the devil is going to come against you. That's why it is important that you "war" against him. It is a war that will continue until Jesus returns. You dare not let down your guard. If you neglect your spiritual life, you are a sitting duck for the devil's attacks. You can't stay away from church; you can't slack off in your prayer life; you can't neglect your time in the Scriptures or other basic disciplines of your Christian life. You may be able to stand up and speak or sing for the Lord—and God will honor His Word—but inside you know that you are dry, empty, and in need of a fresh touch from God. And that's the good news: When we acknowledge our need of Him, God fills us afresh with His strength and power.

What are we to do when Satan tries to tempt us? We should do what Jesus did. When the devil tried to mess with Jesus, tried to tempt Him in the wilderness, Jesus used the Word of God against him. Three times Jesus told Satan, "It is written." This was the weapon Jesus used to put the devil in his place, and it is still the weapon we must use to conquer the devil's devious devices in our lives.

Scripture says we are overcomers by the word of our testimony and the blood of the Lamb. When Satan comes to tempt us, we dare not forget that. When the devil tries to plant negative thoughts in my mind, I don't even argue with him. I just start saying, "Praise the Lord! Jesus, I love You. I praise You, and I thank You for the promise of Your Word."

And Satan can't stand that. He cannot stay for long in the midst of praise. So if you want to whip the devil and cause him to leave your mind, start praising the Lord *aloud*. When you start praising the Lord aloud, Satan will leave.

I found that out the hard way.

CHAPTER 16

GIVE AND IT SHALL BE GIVEN

*I*t's better to give than to receive, but sometimes receiving a gift can be harder. That was an extremely important lesson for me to learn. I have always been quick to give—I learned from my daddy long ago that I could never outgive God—but to be on the receiving end of things was sometimes awkward for me.

As I mentioned earlier, for most of the years Howard and I served the church in Madisonville, we did not take a salary from the congregation. We earned our living by our music, and it was always a joy to share our blessings with the church. When we had money, the church had money. That's just the way we did it.

But in the early days, money was tight in our little town. Often we had to make do on next to nothing. I can vividly recall taking the only money in my purse and purchasing five yards of material for a dollar, so I could make two dresses, one for my daughter, Vicki, and one for me. Many of the dresses I wore onstage during the early years of my music career were ones I had sewn out of material from the Dollar General store.

Once a woman in our church brought a package to me at home. "I bought you a dress at JCPenney's," she announced cheerfully.

"You did what? Er, uh, I mean, ah, thank you very much," I replied, trying to hide my uneasiness. "That's real sweet of you and I appreciate it." I desperately needed a new dress to wear on the platform, but I didn't realize it had been that obvious. My mind quickly filled with horrible images of the kind of dress this woman might have bought for me—not to mention what size. When the woman left, I said, "Now, Lord, why couldn't You have had her give me the money, so I could buy my own dress?"

No answer came from heaven. "Okay, Lord. I repent; I'm sorry. I don't mean to sound ungrateful, but I pray that this dress will be great."

I opened the package and to my amazement, the dress was not only beautiful, it was the correct size. I wore that JCPenney's dress at church and in concerts all over America for years.

Occasionally God had to remind me that He could bless me with extraspecial things too. I almost fainted when Daisy Troop brought a beautiful diamond ring to Howard and said, "Give that to your wife. My pastor's wife should have a diamond on her hand."

Diamonds! I was trying to scrape up enough money to pay the phone bill; I certainly wasn't worried about jewelry. Not only that, but both Howard and I came from a church background that frowned on wearing rings of any kind. We were married for a number of years before Howard bought me a simple gold wedding band. And when I bought a ring for Howard and he actually wore it, even my mama thought he had backslidden!

But Daisy insisted, so I wore that diamond ring . . . and I enjoyed wearing it. That inspired Daisy to go a step further. One day Daisy came to me with a gorgeous watch with two small diamonds on each side of the face.

"Daisy, I can't wear this!"

"Yes, you can. Doesn't the Bible say it's better to give than to receive? Well, I want to give it to you. Now you don't want to rob me of a blessing, do you?"

"Well, no . . ."

"Then put on the watch."

I was soon to discover that God wanted to remind me of an important lesson through that watch, a lesson that had little to do with telling time and a lot to do with obedience.

Howard and I were singing for a camp meeting in Hillsdale, Michigan, at which Bro. A. W. Thomas, the district superintendent, introduced a

My life hasn't always been easy, but I can truthfully sing from my heart, "Lord, I wouldn't take nothin' for my journey now."

Auntie Mary and Uncle Ernest Freeman—the sweetest Auntie and Uncle in the world. Auntie never spanked me, not even when I made mudpies in her bathroom sink.

Gordie and Mae Freeman, my mom and dad, on their fiftieth wedding anniversary. Mama was the disciplinarian and Daddy was our counselor. He was a sensitive man and lots of fun.

Niva Maddox, Nellie Hartline, and me (1945). Two of my best friends who joined me in forming the Highway Church of God Trio.

The handsome man I fell in love with!

An early family portrait: Ricky, Howard, Vicki, and me.

Howard and I went back into evangelistic work after the birth of our first child.

Signing our first talent agency contract with Don Light Talent. *Left to right:* Bobby, Vestal, Howard, Rusty, Don Light, Duane Friend (our guitar player), and Sam.

An all-night singin' during our early days on the road as the Happy Goodman Family.

Much of our lives centered around "Life Temple," our church in Kentucky. We later built a new sanctuary that seated more than a thousand people.

The bus Hannah and I prayed about. The answer confirmed that I should be on the road with the group.

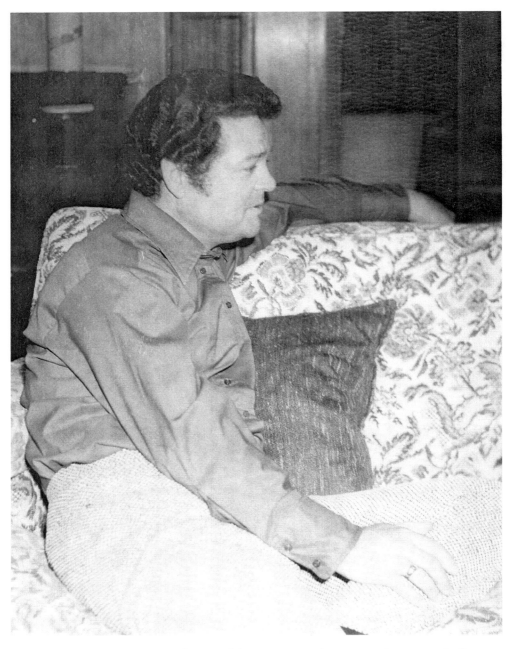

As the primary composer of many of the Happy Goodman songs, Rusty saw God's handiwork in all of life. Rusty's death shook my faith to its foundations.

One of the first tapings of our television program, Gospel Singing Jubilee.

Here we are accepting our first Grammy Award. We were thrilled!

Sam, Vestal, Howard, and Rusty.

Howard and me backstage at a television taping with Tennessee Ernie Ford.

In the White House Rose Garden with First Lady Rosalynn Carter. Mrs. Carter asked me to sing one of her favorite hymns, "Jesus is the Sweetest Name I Know." I later recorded the song and dedicated it to the First Lady.

On the White House lawn with President Jimmy Carter. The president told me, "Vestal, don't ever stop praying like that!"

At the Dove Awards. How about those "Elton John" glasses!

On stage with the Happy Goodmans. My hair really was almost a foot high!

Here we are at one of the Homecoming concerts doing what we love best—sharing our love for the Lord with a whole lot of friends.

Very few people can capture truth and emotion in words like Gloria Gaither does. Her songs touch my heart in a such a very special way. Gloria's tribute to Rusty was one of the highlights of the benefit concert for him.

Janet Paschal and I at a Homecoming taping. Janet still has one of my makeup- soiled handkerchiefs, and recently wrote me a great song.

Bill Gaither, who had the inspiration and vision to produce the Homecoming videos that have touched the hearts of millions of people around the world. I thank God for allowing me to be part of these videos.

Mark Lowry—the one guy who can joke about my hair and get away with it!

Rick, Jake Hess, and me taking a break during the taping of one of our TNN Hawaiian Homecoming videos.

Mark Lowry, with Angie and Guy Penrod, Andrew and Amy Hayes (Bill and Gloria's son-in-law and daughter), and me.

Larry Gatlin and me clowning around at a recent taping of a Homecoming video. Some of our "Homecoming friends" are in the background. Larry and his brothers have been successful in various styles of music, but their roots are in gospel.

David Byerly preparing Johnny Minick, Howard, and me for a video shoot.

Cam Floria, president of Christian Artist Seminars, presenting a Lifetime Achievement Award to Howard and me at Estes Park, Colorado (1997). *Left to right:* Our good friend Bill Gaither, Howard, Vestal, Cam, and Gloria Gaither.

What a wonderful night we had at the Gospel Music Hall of Fame induction (1998). *Left to right:* Amos and Sue Dodge, Vestal, Tara (Dodge) and Travis, Leslie, Dianne, and Rick.

The Happy Goodmans today—
Howard, Vestal, and Johnny Minick.

young missionary couple to the congregation. Brother Thomas explained that the couple needed about three thousand dollars to complete their itinerary and get them to the mission field in Indonesia. He laid the need before the camp meeting congregation and asked folks to give whatever God led them to give.

I was sitting on the platform praying, "Oh God, please cause the people to give. This young couple has a desire to serve you in missions, and the least we can do is give our money to help get them there."

The Lord spoke to my heart and mind and said, "Will you give?"

Me? I wasn't expecting that. After all, I had already been giving and giving and giving, at our home church, at numerous camp meetings where we had sung, and through several fund-raising programs. My funds were totally depleted.

I wasn't going to argue with God, but I felt it would be okay to remind Him, so I said, "Lord, I don't have anything to give."

"You could give that watch."

I looked down at the beautiful watch on my wrist, with the two diamonds on each side of its face smiling back at me. I thought, *Man, I ain't had it but thirty days! And what about my friend, Daisy? What would Daisy think if I gave away a beautiful watch she had paid hard-earned money for?* But I knew it was decision time.

I decided to give the watch to help send the young couple to the mission field. I didn't want to make a big deal about it though, so I slipped the watch off my arm and whispered to one of the young people sitting near me. "Take this watch to Brother Thomas and tell him somebody wants it to be in the offering."

The pastor took the watch from the boy and said, "Well, look at this. Somebody has sent a watch up here. It's even got little diamonds on it. We'll see what this is worth and see if we can sell it and get the money for it."

A man sitting in the audience stood up and said, "Whatever the watch is worth, I'll pay for it. Give it to the little girl going to Indonesia so every time she looks at it, she'll know there are people back home who love her."

Brother Thomas held out the watch and gave it to the young woman going to Indonesia.

Meanwhile I'm sittin' there thinkin', *Oh, God, there goes my watch.* I prayed, "Oh, Jesus, please don't let Daisy get mad at me because I gave this watch away."

God had bigger plans for that watch than my concerns. When the young woman received the watch from Brother Thomas, she took it tenderly in her hands, thanked everyone, and started crying; she was so grateful for the gift. Then something even more wonderful happened. The gift of the watch opened the door, and suddenly a spirit of generosity came over the people. Before the gift of the watch, we had barely raised three hundred dollars toward the three thousand dollars the young missionary couple needed. But after the watch was given and received, people began to give freely, and we raised over eight thousand dollars for the couple's trip.

I was pleased to be a part of God's plan for that couple, but when I got back home, I was not looking forward to seeing Daisy Troop. News travels fast in a small town, so before I even had a chance to explain, somebody told Daisy about my giving the watch away.

The next time I saw Daisy at church, she stared at my wrist and asked, "Where's your watch?"

I didn't flinch as I said, "I gave it in a missionary offering."

"Hmph! You'll know it when I buy you something else that pretty."

"I knew I was supposed to give it so I gave it. And if you ever have anything you don't want me to give away, don't give it to me, because if the Lord tells me to give something away, it's gone."

A few days later Daisy called me and said, "Let's have lunch." I didn't think anything about it. Her beauty school was downtown, and we often had lunch at a little diner around the corner from her school.

I met her at her school, and as we headed toward the diner, Daisy stopped in front of a jewelry store. She said, "Wait a minute. Come in here; I want to show you something." Daisy implied that she wanted me to help her pick out something for her daughter, Maryanne.

We went into the jewelry store, and Daisy said to the jeweler, "Lay some watches up here. We want to pick one for my daughter." The jeweler laid a strip of velvet on the counter and then gently placed five diamond watches on it. "Which one do you think Maryanne would like?" Daisy asked me.

I thought, *Maryanne, you're gonna owe me big-time!* I pointed to the prettiest watch of all, with a beautiful face surrounded by diamonds and a band decorated with diamonds. "That one," I said.

"Are you sure?" Daisy asked.

"Oh yeah. That's the prettiest one."

"Well, if you were buying one for yourself, which would you pick?"

"That one," I said, pointing to the same watch.

"You're sure? You like that one better than any of them?"

"I'm sure."

"Okay. We'll take this one."

Daisy paid for the watch and put it in her pocket. We walked out of the store and started down the street toward the diner, when she stopped, took that gorgeous watch out of her pocket, and handed it to me. "Try your best to keep this one," Daisy said with a smile.

I had given a watch with two tiny diamonds to the missionary girl—a watch that had been a free, unearned gift to me in the first place—and I received back a watch worth ten times as much or more. God was reminding me again, "Every good gift you have comes freely from your heavenly Father, so don't be afraid to sacrificially give anything you have. In the same way you give, you will receive. Give and it shall be given back to you."

Over the years God has blessed me abundantly with material things, but I have never been interested in simply amassing earthly possessions. I want to use what I have, whether it's a lot or a little, for His glory. Jesus said to lay up our treasures in heaven, where they can't be stolen or corrupted. The way we do that is to live "openhandedly," accepting what God gives us, and then giving it back to Him by using it in a manner that is consistent with His priorities expressed in His Word. I'm convinced God wants to give His children good things. The issue is: Can He trust us to use His gifts for His glory?

CHAPTER 17

COUNTRY FRIENDS

*I*n 1968 the Happy Goodman Family was nominated for a Grammy Award in the "Best Gospel Performance" category. It was a compliment to the entire gospel-music industry and a testimony to the increasing popularity of our music that the governing body of the National Academy of the Recording Arts and Sciences (NARAS) deemed it necessary to establish a new award category for gospel music. Prior to that year, gospel groups had received Grammys for their work with artists in other fields of music. The Blackwoods had won an award for their recordings with country artist Porter Wagoner, and established secular artists had won Grammys for their renditions of gospel songs, but no gospel group or artist had ever won a Grammy strictly on their own gospel recordings. The Happy Goodman Family was the first to do so.

That year NARAS held simultaneous award shows in New York, Los Angeles, and Nashville. The awards in Nashville were held at the old National Guard armory building, the largest facility for a dinner banquet in Music City at the time, and emceed by Dick Clark of *American Bandstand* fame. Entertainers on the show included Booker T and the MGs, Tammy Wynette, Joe Tex, and some of Nashville's finest pickers, led by Owen Bradley and the same fellows who had played on all our early albums. Also on the program that evening was Jerry Lee Lewis, whose song "Great Balls of Fire" was already well on its way to becoming a classic.

When it was announced that we had won a Grammy for our album *The Happy Gospel of The Happy Goodmans*, we went onstage and offered our thanks to the academy and to our producer and musicians and of course to the Lord. Then we went backstage to meet the press.

As we entered the press room, Jerry Lee Lewis and his manager, Audrey Williams (the former wife of Hank Williams Sr.), were carrying on loudly over in the corner. As they wobbled around the room, Jerry Lee was blowing cigar smoke like a smokestack and Audrey was cussing about everything. Her language nearly peeled the paint off the walls.

Jerry Lee turned around and saw Rusty and me. I greeted him warmly, although briefly. As he turned back to Audrey, she was still cursing a blue streak. Jerry turned to Audrey and said loudly, "Don't you use that kind of language anymore. Don't you know this is a lady?" he said as he nodded toward me. "There's a lady in the room, so don't be talking dirty anymore."

Audrey looked back at Jerry as though he had just dropped in from outer space . . . but she stopped her cussing.

I didn't want to cause any trouble between Jerry Lee and his manager, but I did appreciate the backhanded compliment he had given me. I had known Jerry for a number of years and had prayed for him many times. He had grown up around Christian people, and Jerry Lee knew a good deal about God and the Bible and what was right and wrong. He just refused to bring his life in line with the Scriptures. But that didn't mean I should give up praying for him.

One night the Goodmans were doing a concert in Knoxville, Tennessee, in an auditorium that seated several thousand people. The auditorium was attached, back to back, to an arena, where a country music show was booked. During a break in our program, Rusty and I decided to walk around to the country artists' backstage area, just to see if we could spot any of our friends.

Sure enough, as soon as we rounded a corner in the hallway, we ran right into Jerry Lee Lewis. He was surrounded by important music-business types. Jerry Lee stopped and hugged me and was extremely kind in his comments. He asked me how everyone in the group was doing, and we started talking informally. We were just getting caught up on everything when one of his music-business associates interrupted us. "You have to go, Jerry Lee. They're ready for you in the press room."

Jerry Lee waved the man off and said, "Well, wait just a minute. I'm coming."

The man was insistent. "Jerry Lee, you have to go *now*," the man growled. With that he let fly a string of expletives that caused my face to turn red. Jerry Lee whirled around angrily and roared at his handler, "Don't you dare talk like that in front of a lady. This here is a Christian lady," he said pointing at me. "Don't you ever use that kind of language in front of her."

Jerry Lee apologized to me and went on with his entourage. For all his faults, and he would be the first to admit that they are many, Jerry Lee knows what is right and wrong, and I continue to respect him and pray for him to this day.

The Goodmans have always shared a great deal of respect with country music artists, which is rather ironic since we never sang a single country song. But we have known many of the CMA legends and many of the genre's rising stars. Although we performed a different sort of music, the country artists knew that the Goodmans loved and respected them. I didn't always agree with their lifestyles, and at times, if artists asked my opinion, I'd let them know it. But whatever was wrong about their lives might easily have been part of my life had Jesus not come and fixed it.

One of my favorite female country artists has always been Barbara Mandrell. My! What a gifted woman she is—singer, instrumentalist, dancer, actor. I don't know how so much talent can be wrapped in such a petite package! She's a great sport too.

One night Barbara was hosting her own television special at the new Opry House in Nashville. I was working on another show and was backstage in the hallway when Barbara and her mother and daddy and sisters came out into the hall. They didn't see me coming, so I tiptoed up behind Barbara and said, "There's that little ol' Mandrell girl who can't sing!"

"Vestal Goodman!" Barbara squealed as she turned around and hugged me. We laughed together and talked awhile. "You know, Vestal," Barbara said seriously, "I have every album you've ever recorded." I was deeply touched and honored by Barbara's comment.

Another country artist for whom I have always had a special place in my heart is Larry Gatlin. I've known Larry and his brothers, Rudy and Steve, as well as their sister, LaDonna, since they were little-bitty kids. Larry says they grew up attending Goodman concerts, listening to the Happy Goodman Family records, and watching our television programs. (Thanks, Larry, for making me feel so old!)

In the late 1970s when we were taping our television program, Larry came on and sang several duets with Rusty. I loved every moment of it—what a treat it was to hear two of my favorite singers! We also did several Goodman Family songs on that show, with Larry singing along, so I got to sing with him too!

During the late 1970s and early 1980s, the Gatlin Brothers were a prime ticket in country music. Their records topped the charts ("All the Gold in California" was a hit on both the country and pop music charts). They were playing to sellout crowds, and they had even opened their own music theater in the Mall of America in Minnesota. Then Larry got the bad news. He had developed nodules on his vocal cords, a problem that could destroy not only his singing voice but his speaking voice as well.

Larry's doctors told him that the growths were large and dangerous. Even if he had surgery, they refused to say whether Larry would sing again. But when I went to Larry's home to see him and to the hospital to pray for him right before the operation, I felt led to give him a different prognosis. I said, "Don't worry about your throat; you're coming out of here fine. Whatever the doctors find in there, it's gonna be small and easy to take care of."

When the doctors operated, they discovered the problem was small and easy to take care of. Within months, Larry Gatlin was singing again, better than ever. He was one of the first artists to accept Bill Gaither's invitation to get together "to sing some of the old songs" in Nashville, the gathering that resulted in the original Gaither *Homecoming* video.

Dolly Parton is another country artist with whom I have shared strong ties. We go way back, when Dolly was still singing on television with Porter Wagoner. Early in our careers we'd see each other occasionally at music events. When we both signed booking contracts with Top Billing, a booking agency run by superagent Tandy Rice in Nashville, we saw each other much more frequently. We never sang on the same shows, but our agency often booked us in tandem, with one of us coming in as the other was leaving a concert venue.

Just as the Goodmans were big fans of the Grand Old Opry and Porter and Dolly's show, Dolly was a big fan of our TV show, which we recorded at WSIX-TV in Nashville. Our show regularly featured the Florida Boys, the Dixie Echoes, Steve Sanders (then a soloist, more recently of the Oak Ridge Boys), and the Happy Goodman Family. Occasionally we hosted guest artists.

One day Dolly said to me, "Vestal, when are you going to invite me to travel along with you some weekend on your bus?"

"Dolly! There ain't no way I'm gonna let you on our bus," I said with feigned indignation.

"But why?" Dolly protested.

"Honey, I have a hard enough time keeping all those boys on our bus saved without you tempting them!"

Dolly giggled that inimitable laugh of hers.

On another occasion Howard and I were having lunch near Rivergate Mall in Hendersonville, just north of Nashville, when Dolly and her sister Stella walked into the restaurant. Dolly was wearing a short, light brown wig and looked cute as a button. Every eye in the building followed the two beautiful women as they walked toward Howard and me. The hostess was attempting to guide them quickly to a booth in the rear of the restaurant, so Dolly simply tapped me on the shoulder as she walked past our table. As soon as the hostess had seated them, Dolly peeped her head around the corner. "Psst, Vestal," she whispered, as she motioned for me to come over.

I waited until she had ordered, and then I went over and sat down next to Dolly in the booth. We small-talked for a while, and then Dolly shocked the daylights out of me when she said, "Vestal, I'm going to Hollywood, California, and I'm gonna make movies."

"You can't be serious," I said.

"Yes I am," she answered with a laugh. "They're gonna put me in the movies, and they're gonna make me into a superstar," she giggled again. Then in a more serious tone, Dolly looked at me and asked, "What do you think about that?"

It seemed to me that Dolly was looking for more than just another affirmation of her talent. It sounded to me like she was hoping for some advice, so I took her hand in mine and said, "Dolly, if I ever met anybody who has all that it takes to do it, it's you. But darlin' . . . ," I paused for a moment and gripped both her hands in mine and looked her straight in the eyes. "Darlin', promise me that you won't sell your soul."

For a moment I thought Dolly was going to cry right there in the restaurant. "I won't," she said softly. "It won't happen."

Dolly went on to Hollywood and starred in the hit movie *Nine to Five*, along with Lily Tomlin, Jane Fonda, and Dabney Coleman. I didn't see her for some time after that, as she got busier and busier, crisscrossing the nation promoting her movies, music, and her theme park in the Great Smoky Mountains, near Gatlinburg, Tennessee.

The next time I saw her she was singing at the Tennessee Performing

Arts Center in Nashville on the Dove Awards, the Gospel Music Association's version of the Grammys. Dolly had recorded "He's Alive," Don Francisco's song about Jesus' resurrection, and backed by Nashville's Christ Church choir, Dolly had received a standing ovation at the Country Music Association Award show in October. Now, nearly seven months later, she was to do the same song on the GMA awards program.

Prior to the show I was sitting in the auditorium doing an interview with a young writer from *Gospel Voice* magazine. Suddenly I felt strongly that I needed to see Dolly before the program started. I excused myself and told him, "I'm going backstage."

"Fine," he replied, "I'll go with you." The writer followed me around to the side doors where we were stopped by a security guard. "Do you have a backstage pass?" the young man asked.

"Are you kidding?" I answered. "I don't need a backstage pass around here. If you don't know who I am, then go on home." I was joking with him, but I said it so seriously that I must have stunned him, because he let me pass on by, the writer in tow.

When we got past the guard, the writer said, "Man, they would have thrown me out of here if I had tried that. How did you do that?"

"Under ordinary circumstances, they might have thrown me out too," I told him, "but these aren't ordinary circumstances. I believe God wants me back here to see Dolly for some reason." The writer simply shook his head, whether in amusement or amazement I wasn't sure.

We walked past the artist lounge to the dressing-room area. I had been backstage at the center enough to know where the better dressing rooms were located, and that's where I figured Dolly would be, so that's where I headed. The hallway was crowded with people, some getting last-minute details ready for the show and others simply milling about. As I attempted to pass, another security guard blocked my path near the front of the hallway.

"Mrs. Goodman, you're supposed to come in this dressing room," he ordered.

"I'd rather go down here right now," I told him. "I'm going to hunt Dolly."

"No ma'am," he said more emphatically. "You're to come in here." He nodded toward the door.

"Well, okay. I guess I'll go in here," I said as the guard opened the door for me and then hastily closed it behind me.

Sitting inside the dressing room was Dolly Parton. She had posted the security guard in the hall to watch for me, she later told me. Dolly was getting her makeup on as we began to talk. I told her how proud I was of her and how pleased I was at her recent success. "Ya did good, Dolly."

"Well, I kept my word to you, Vestal."

"What do you mean?"

"I tried to tell you!" Dolly said, pretending to be exasperated. "Didn't you hear it?"

"What are you talking about, Dolly?"

She said, "Vestal, don't tell me you don't know. I wrote it in a song so you would know that I kept my word."

"Dolly, I still don't know what you are talking about."

"Have you heard my song, 'White Limousine'?"

"I can't truthfully say that I have," I replied.

"Well, the lyrics say, 'She was in the city of lights, where the devil was in control. But she never sold her soul.' I wanted you to know that I was okay."

I was glad to hear that Dolly had survived her Hollywood experience relatively unscathed, but I really felt that God wanted me to see Dolly that night for some other reason. "Are you okay now, Dolly?" I asked, knowing the answer before I posed the question.

Dolly's expression grew serious.

"Dolly, I don't know what's wrong with you," I said, "but the Lord wanted me to come in here and tell you that He is going to heal you."

"Oh, Vestal, don't make me cry. I've got to go onstage in just a few minutes."

"Tonight, He's going to heal you," I repeated. "I don't know what's wrong with you, but I feel deeply in my spirit that the Lord wants to heal you tonight."

"When we get a chance, I'll fill you in on the details, but let's just say I've been having some physical problems," Dolly said, "and I need a healing."

"Then tonight is your night."

Dolly knew she was supposed to see me that night. Neither of us had contacted the other prior to the show, but we both believed that God had arranged our meeting.

As Dolly made her entrance onstage that night, she had to pass between the members of the Christ Church choir. As she swept by Joy Gardner, coleader of the choir along with her husband, Landy, Joy heard a swishing sound. Joy turned to some of the women in the choir and said, "Whew! Dolly's gettin' a healing."

When Dolly came offstage, she attested to the truth of Joy's statement. After her performance, Dolly said, "I got healed on the stage awhile ago! When I started through that choir, I felt the Spirit of the Lord come all over me, and I knew I was healed."

I am not condoning every song Dolly has sung or every movie she has played in. I wish she wouldn't use some of the language the scriptwriters give her to say. Although I don't condone everything about Dolly, I don't condemn her either. I am not her judge; God is. One thing I know for sure: God has had His hand on Dolly, and I am excited to see what He does with her life. That night at the Dove Awards, Dolly Parton sang like an angel.

One "country friend" of ours who was more controversial than most was the governor of Alabama, George Wallace. Always a highly respected politician in my home state, George attracted national attention when the 1960s Civil Rights movement confronted long-held prejudices in America. George was considered a racist by some and a hero by others.

My connection to George had nothing to do with politics or race.

We were "family," distant cousins because Grandma Freeman and George Wallace's grandmother were second cousins. I had met Governor Wallace in Birmingham when we were there for an "all-night-singin'." Howard and I had just checked into the Tuttwiler Hotel and had started down the hall toward our room when we were stopped by security guards. They wanted to see our room keys before they'd allow us to pass.

"What's going on down there?" I nodded toward one of the hotel ballrooms.

"Governor Wallace will be having a press conference," one of the men said.

As we passed the room where the press conference was to be held, I noticed the door was open. Although I had never been formally introduced to him, I had heard that Governor Wallace was a big gospel-music fan, so I said to the security guard at the door, "Go in there and tell George that I need to see him."

The governor heard me speaking and recognized my voice. He called out, "Is that Vestal Goodman?"

"Yeah it is, George," I called back. "Tell these boys that I need to come in there to see you."

"Bring her in here," the governor directed the security guards. The security men quickly ushered me into the room where I met the governor face to face.

We talked a bit, laughed, and discussed Goodman music and our family connection. "I just figured I needed to stop by to check on you. We cousins need to see after one another."

The governor nodded, "Yes, we have to take care of each other."

In May 1972 as George Wallace was campaigning for president in Maryland—one of his three bids for the presidency—a gunman attempted to assassinate him. The bullet wounded him seriously and ended his presidential campaign and nearly his life. Although George Wallace survived the assassination attempt, he was confined to a wheelchair as a result.

Later that summer I was hospitalized in Nashville with gall-bladder problems that required surgery and put me out of commission for several weeks. A week after the operation I was recuperating in the hospital when one morning Howard called me from Madisonville. He told me that he would be coming through town about ten o'clock on his way to Montgomery, Alabama. He and Rusty and Sam had been invited by some businessmen to visit with Gov. George Wallace.

For some reason, Howard's words struck a chord in my heart. I felt strongly that the Lord wanted me along on this trip. "Howard, I want to go too."

"Now, honey, you know you can't do that. The doctor says it will be another week or so before you are able to come home, let alone travel."

"No, Howard. I believe God wants me to go with you."

I called our daughter, Vicki, and told her to bring me my clothes and to come to the hospital to pick me up. Then I called my doctor, Dr. John C. Birch, and said, "I'm going to leave the hospital today about ten thirty, but I'll be back this afternoon around four or five o' clock."

Dr. Birch said, "I can't sign a release for something like that."

"Okay, fine," I said. "Then I'll go without your permission. I'll just slide my hospital name band up under my sleeve, and nobody will know the difference." There was no talking me out of it because I knew that I was to go. To keep my stitches from popping, the nurses wrapped my entire chest and stomach, from shoulders to waist, with heavy, four-inch tape. I looked like a mummy.

I felt awful and looked even worse—tired, pale, and sickly, but with Vicki's help, I did my best to dress up and appear respectable for our visit with the governor. Vicki drove me to the airport where I met Howard and the boys and then flew on to Montgomery.

When we landed in Alabama, a governor's staff limousine was waiting to whisk us to the state capitol where we were ushered immediately into Governor Wallace's office. He greeted us warmly, and we talked for a while, and of course, the Happy Goodman Family stood around George's desk and sang a cappella for the governor. I sensed from our conversation that Governor Wallace was uncertain whether he would be able to continue his political career, and I realized then why I had felt so impressed to get up from my hospital bed to come visit him. I walked over to where he was sitting and hugged him. I said, "George, I don't approve of everything you've done or everything you've said, but God is not through with you. You are going to be governor again."

I wasn't simply making a political prediction; I knew this was the message God had sent me to deliver.

Tears filled the governor's eyes as he looked up at me from his wheelchair. "Just keep prayin'," he said.

I leaned over him and prayed. When I was done, I felt impressed to deliver another message to him. "You need to make a public confession of your faith in Jesus Christ."

George Wallace nodded in understanding.

Following our visit, we flew back to Nashville. Vicki met me at the airport, and I kissed Howard good-bye as he and the boys continued on to Madisonville. Vicki drove me back to the hospital where I tried my best to be inconspicuous as I passed the nurses' station on the way to my room. I hurried inside, shut the door, changed back into my hospital clothes, and climbed back into bed. It wasn't quite five o'clock.

Whew! All in a day's work!

The following Sunday, Governor Wallace attended morning worship services in Montgomery. When the invitation was given at the close of the service, George Wallace had a staff member wheel him to the front of the sanctuary, where the governor publicly acknowledged Jesus Christ as his Savior and Lord. Governor Wallace became a licensed Methodist minister and expressed deep regret concerning the racial hatred and violence that had characterized his earlier years in office. In 1974 George not only won a third term in office, but he was reelected later for a fourth term. His personal reformation was so apparent following his public confession of faith that in the next election the majority of black voters in Alabama voted for George Wallace.

CHAPTER 18

HEART TROUBLE

As the congregation of Life Temple grew, it became apparent that we needed a larger building if we intended to expand the church's ministry. Howard and I began searching all over town for potential property on which to build a new church. Nearly everything we liked was out of our price range, and the properties we felt we could afford were extremely unattractive. We believed that God wanted us to have a good location for the new church, so we continued to pray for His guidance.

One day my friend Hannah Jackson came to see me. Hannah and her husband, E. W., were members of our church, and she was the one who had fasted and prayed with me concerning our new bus and whether I should continue singing.

She said to me, "Vestal, the property that we need to build the church on is over on Park Avenue. It overlooks the park, and E. W. and I own it. I'd like you to take a look at it with me. It's one of the prettiest pieces of property in town."

When Hannah and I drove up to the property, I wasn't so sure. The land was covered with trees and underbrush, plus it had ditches and ravines big enough to hide automobiles. We walked to the top of the hill and looked out across the scenic valley below us.

"It will fit right here," Hannah said, "right on top of this hill." Hannah and I stood out in the open air on the hillside and designed a church that would seat at least one thousand people. It was our plan that eventually was used by the contractors to build the new Life Temple. Hannah and E. W. donated the property, and we broke ground late in the summer of 1965.

Building the church was a difficult experience—it seemed to take forever—but it was also a time of great spiritual growth for our congregation. We moved into the new church and dedicated it to the Lord in September of 1967. The church cost $150,000 to build, a huge figure in those days. With our expanded seating capacity and more comfortable worship facilities, more people began showing up at our services. Not only did more local folks from Madisonville attend, but frequently we'd have visitors from hundreds of miles away stop by to worship at the home church of the Happy Goodman Family.

I was glad that the church was growing rapidly, and I threw myself into doing all that I could to ensure that our congregation was growing spiritually as well. I had already been burning the candle at both ends, but now I started burning it in the middle too! Every week I was on the road singing in concerts around the country and then racing back to sing and preach at Life Temple on Sunday mornings.

As a result of the Happy Goodman Family's popularity, we were inundated with demo tapes from songwriters wanting us to record their material. Large sacks filled with cassette tapes showed up in our mail regularly. Many of the songs we received were wonderful, even if they were not songs the Goodmans chose to sing. Others were . . . let's just say not so wonderful. Of course, all songwriters believe that their song is special; to them it is, especially if they feel the Lord inspired the song. But that doesn't mean the song is for everybody or that we should feel obligated to sing it.

Rusty and I spent hours every week going through the demo tapes, listening to as many as we could, searching for just the right songs for the Happy Goodman Family. One day I was in the office when Rusty called for me. "Vestal, I think I found something. We better listen to this one."

"Okay, let me hear it," I replied.

"First, let me read you the letter that is with it," Rusty said. The letter identified the songwriter as Audra Zarnaco, a preacher lady who felt she had written a song I could sing. The song was titled "God Walks the Dark Hills." Her demo tape was not elaborate, just a vocal with piano accompaniment done on what sounded like a home tape recorder, but the words of the song captured my attention.

> *God walks the dark hills, the ways, the byways.*
> *He walks on the billows, life's troubled sea;*
> *He walks in the cold dark night, the shadows of midnight.*
> *God walks the dark hills, just to guide you and me.*
> *God walks in the storm, the rain or the sunshine.*
> *He walks in the shadows or just through glimmering light.*
> *He helps me walk up the mountain so high,*
> *Cross my rivers, through my valleys.*
> *He really loves you and me.*
> *God walks the dark hills*
> *To guide my footsteps.*
> *He walks everywhere, by night and by day;*
> *He walks in silence, right on down my highway;*
> *God walks the dark hills to show me the way.*

Rusty wrote out the chords to the song, and we went straight into the recording studio. As soon as I started singing it, we knew there really was something special about this song. When we later recorded it on an album and started singing it in concerts, the song received fabulous accolades. "God Walks the Dark Hills" would become a favorite of Goodman audiences for nearly three decades. To this day, people relate to the song's lyrics and find encouragement to face the obstacles in their lives.

For me, the song came just in the nick of time. I was about to walk through some dark hills and valleys of my own.

By 1974 the exhausting pace of working with the church, singing on the road, and trying to be a good wife and mother began to take a physical toll on me. Our hectic schedule was causing too much stress on my system, and I began to have heart trouble. Dr. Bill West, my doctor in Madisonville, explained, "Vestal, you are like the man who had a great farm, but he didn't give it a chance to rest and recoup. Instead, he just kept planting and planting and planting. After a while, the land had no more nutrients and could no longer bear the burden of producing crops. The land needed to lie fallow for a season just to replenish itself and regain its ability to bear fruit. Your body is like that. You have been working so hard for so long that you are depleting your resources; you need to let yourself be still for a while."

I agreed with the doctor's diagnosis—he had described me to a tee—but I wasn't sure about his prognosis. It wasn't that I didn't *want* to slow down; I didn't know *how* to slow down. I was so accustomed to working I honestly didn't know how to rest properly.

By October of that year I didn't have much choice.

About that time I started to have severe chest pains, which forced me to breathe in short, painful gasps. With each breath, it felt as though a knife was ripping through my heart. My chest hurt worse when I would lie down, so I sat in a chair most of the time, simply so I could breathe more easily. When I couldn't stand the pain any longer, I knew I had to see a doctor.

When Dr. Baker examined me at St. Thomas Hospital in Nashville, he immediately told me I had too much stress on my heart. He suggested I have an angiogram, which revealed blockages in the arteries leading to my heart. The doctors said they would have to operate.

In his kindly manner, Dr. Baker said, "We are going to send you home, Vestal, and let you rest for two weeks. Then we will bring you back to the hospital and do open-heart surgery."

I looked back at the doctor and said, "No, Dr. Baker, you won't.

That would be like Mama saying she was going to give me a whippin', but that she was going to put it off for two weeks. If you're going to do it, let's do the operation now while I'm here."

Dr. Baker looked back at me and laughed. "Okay, Vestal, let me take a look at my schedule. If I have an opening and the operating rooms are available, we'll do your surgery tomorrow."

"Thank you, Doctor," I replied sincerely. It was bad enough to find out that I had to have heart surgery. I sure didn't want to put it off any longer than necessary. Besides, I felt like I would be wasting time to go home and sit around for two weeks, when I could be doing something constructive.

The next morning Dr. Baker and Dr. Stanley Owenby and their expert staff performed open-heart surgery on me, doing a double bypass of the arteries leading to my heart. Today such surgeries have become almost commonplace, but in the early 1970s such an operation was considered extremely delicate and potentially life-threatening. The operation was a success, but it was not without complications. I continued to have severe angina and inflammation around the wall of my heart, which medication could not bring under control. Despite the double-bypass surgery, I continued to be in constant, excruciating pain.

While I was still in the recovery room, Lucille Wells, one of my dearest friends in the world, came to visit me. She had been my hairdresser for more than a decade and was also a registered nurse who had traveled with me to hundreds of concerts around the country. Lucille knew me as well as she knew her own family. But when she came into the recovery room to see me, she was shocked.

She hurried to the nurses' station and declared, "I can't find Vestal. Where is she?"

"She's right over there," the nurse on duty replied, as she pointed in the direction of my bed.

Lucille whirled around, walked into my room, and promptly marched back to the nurses' station. She approached the same nurse and repeated her question, this time more emphatically. "I can't find Vestal Goodman. What have you done with her?"

This time the nurse walked with Lucille to the recovery room and pointed me out.

"Oh no," cried Lucille. "That's not her. Vestal is a white lady." Apparently my body had been so traumatized by the operation that my skin had turned a deathly blue-black color, so much so that as I lay in recovery, Lucille literally thought that she was looking at a black person.

She was not alone in her shock over my condition. When my baby sister, Bobbie, came to visit me, she took one look and fainted dead away. She later said that I looked as though somebody had beaten me with a lead pipe.

Somebody once asked me, "Vestal, if you were serving God with all your might, why do you think He allowed you to go through heart surgery and all the pain that went with it?"

That's easy to figure out. I believe God has a purpose for everything that happens to His children. He does not necessarily cause bad things to happen to us, but sometimes when Satan attacks us, God allows it and uses it to make us stronger, to help other people, and to bring honor to His name. Satan is not free to do anything he pleases to God's child. He is like an angry dog on a leash; he may make a lot of noise, but he can only go as far as the leash allows. That's what I mean when I say the devil can attack us, but only if God allows it. In the Old Testament, Satan attacked Job because God allowed it. Job was a good man who loved God before the time of testing came; he was one of the best men of his day, upright in all of his ways. Yet God allowed Satan to sift Job like wheat.

In a similar way, Satan attacked Moses because God allowed it. Moses wound up on the backside of the desert for forty years, but when that time of sifting was finished, God said, "Now, Moses, go to work."

I believe that is what happened to me. I am not immune from the devil's devices; I am not too good to be attacked, if God allows it. If the

Lord allowed Job to go through such trials and the Lord allowed His man Moses to be hounded to the backside of a desert, it certainly is not outside the realm of possibility that I might have to go through tough times too. But He never left me during those hard times; He went through those difficult days with me. In fact, during one of the worst periods after my heart surgery, the Lord permitted me to have one of the most dramatic experiences of my life.

Because of the complications from my heart surgery, I remained in intensive care for thirty days. My condition was stable but not improving, and the severe, constant pain remained. I couldn't understand what was happening to my body, but even more disconcerting to me, I couldn't understand what God was doing through all of this. Why was He allowing this condition to continue? I knew He could heal me with just a word—just a thought for that matter—but here I was still suffering in the hospital. I couldn't see how God was going to get any glory out of this situation.

One night I was lying awake in horrendous pain, asking God to help me make some sense of things. I said, "Lord, I am to the point now where I don't understand what is going on. So please either heal me, let me die and go home to be with You, or let me know what is happening here. If You will just let me know what is going on, I can handle it."

By way of response, the Lord used a special desire of mine to help me understand. All of my life I have loved music. Of course, my favorite music is Christian music, but I'm also a big opera fan! I especially love the harp, that gorgeous stringed instrument that produces sounds so beautiful a person can almost imagine being in heaven. I have never learned to play an instrument, but if there is an instrument I would want to play, it's the harp.

Not surprisingly then in my prayers, and when I'd read Psalms, I'd often say, "Lord, tell David to keep the harp tuned up for when I get to heaven. I want to play the harp when I get there."

As I was praying in the hospital that night, asking the Lord to let me know what was going on, suddenly my room lit up in brilliant, almost blinding light. It was so bright I had to shield my eyes, while I tried to peek through my fingers to catch a glimpse of this awesome sight. It was like trying to look directly at the sun in a cloudless sky. I knew that I was the only patient in that room, but I quickly began to sense that I was not alone. Another presence was in that room with me!

To this day I don't know if what occurred next was a vision, a dream, or something else; all I can tell you is that it happened.

As I lay there mesmerized by the brilliant light that filled the room, the Lord Jesus appeared and walked toward my bed. I could see Him as clearly as I had ever seen anyone before—better actually, because He was awash in bright light.

He looked to be a medium-sized man, with nothing spectacular about His build, but His face . . . oh, His face! He had such an expression of kindness and peacefulness on His face. Of course, I was drawn immediately to His eyes. I've always had a tendency to "read" people by their eyes. When I talk to someone, I like to look in their eyes. I've always prayed, "Let people see Jesus in me through my eyes." On the other hand, I've rarely trusted someone who didn't look me in the eyes when speaking to me. But when I looked into Jesus' eyes, He looked directly into mine, and His eyes told me, "You can trust me. You're safe. I am with you." Words fail me in trying to describe Him. All I can say is that He looked more magnificent than the most beautiful pictures of Jesus I had seen. I wanted to simply bask in His presence.

Although I was in awe, I felt no fear as Jesus walked over to my bed, put His hand on my shoulder, and said, "Daughter, I brought a visitor to see you."

I instinctively looked in the direction He seemed to be indicating, and there at the foot of my bed David was playing the harp! I could hear the exquisite sounds as he gently plucked the strings. Oh, it was music such as I had never heard before! The Lord didn't say anything while David played, and neither did the great psalmist. For an undetermined amount of time, I simply basked in sounds so rapturous I thought I was in heaven.

When David finally stopped playing, the thought struck me that they had come for me, that it was my time to leave this world. *That's fine*, I thought. *I'm ready to go.*

In an almost childlike manner, I looked up at Jesus and asked, "Can I have the harp now?"

He patted me on my shoulder and softly said, "Not yet, daughter, but just any day we will come back for you."

Then as suddenly as the Presence had come, He was gone, and I was alone in the room, but the brilliant light continued.

A telephone sat on a table near my bed. I had two new grandbabies, Rick and Dianne's handsome son, Travis, and Vicki's beautiful girl, Nicki, and I wanted to hear the voices of "my dolls" while I was in the hospital. Family members who visited me during my hospital stay often put the receiver up to my ear so I could hear the grandbabies, but I was in too much pain to reach over the rail and get the phone myself.

The moment Jesus and David vanished from my room all the pain left my body! Immediately I reached over the rail, picked up the telephone, and dialed Rusty's number. I couldn't wait to tell him about my experience; I sensed that this vision was not for me alone, and I knew that Rusty could put it into a song. I was so excited I never gave it a thought that it was three o'clock in the morning!

Rusty answered the phone. "Hello," he growled groggily.

"Rusty! It's me, Vestal!" I nearly shouted.

When Rusty heard my voice, he panicked, thinking there was an emergency, that something had to be extremely urgent for me to call him in the middle of the night.

"What's wrong, Auntie?" he cried. "What's going on? What's wrong?"

I said, "Nothing is wrong; everything is right! I am not going to die; I am going to live, and I want you to write me a song. If I were going to die, I would be gone right now, but I am going to live. The Lord said He would come back for me later." As best I could, I described to Rusty every detail of what I had just seen. "Write me a song about this, Rusty," I repeated, "because soon I will be back on the road singing."

Rusty listened intently, and I could tell he was scribbling.

Just as suddenly as the brilliant light had appeared, it was gone. My body began throbbing with horrendous pain, while simultaneously the monitors in the nurses' station began screaming their alerts. Apparently throughout the entire time the light had permeated my room, before and after the Lord Jesus and David had appeared, my monitors had shown no unusual activity. Not even my stretching for the phone had caused any fluctuation on the nurses' screens.

But the instant the bright light disappeared, my monitors went wild. My body was so wracked with pain I couldn't even hang up the telephone. I faintly heard Rusty's panic-stricken voice shouting into the phone, "Auntie, Auntie! What's going on? Are you okay? What's happening?"

But I could not respond. From the nurses' frenzied actions and comments, it was clear they thought I was delirious. One of them peeled the telephone from my fingers, and then they laid me back on the bed. I tried to tell them, "I am okay. I'm fine, really I am." But they were busily attending to me and disregarded my mumblings.

Most of my nurses had become good friends during my hospital stay, and several of them knew me from my music. They had grown accustomed to my usually upbeat attitude, but they were still surprised when I told them, "No matter what anybody tells you, I am not going to die. I am going to live."

CHAPTER 19

GOD CAN HEAL A HEART

After a prolonged stay in the hospital, I recovered sufficiently that the doctors agreed to discharge me, but still I was not well. Although I was convinced I was going to live, I felt as though I were going to die at any moment. Pain seared my body almost constantly—intense pain, from the time of my surgery in October throughout the winter and into the springtime of the following year. Nothing the doctors did helped. During that time I was rushed back to the hospital by ambulance five times. Frequently the pain in my chest became so severe I couldn't speak; I couldn't call out to anyone, move my body, or communicate in any way. Occasionally the pain became so excruciating I lost consciousness. Sometimes I keeled over on the floor. At other times I blacked out in bed and remained that way until Howard happened to come in and find me lying there unconscious.

When Howard or someone else would find me in that condition, we always made a mad dash for the hospital. Each time I was readmitted the hospital personnel thought I was done for, that I was not going to pull through. During one relapse I was in St. Thomas Hospital in Nashville for thirty straight days. When they could do no more for me, the doctors let me go home.

I had severe angina and a lot of other physical problems that the physicians could not get regulated. All they could do was give me more and more pain medication—so much that I became addicted. Not only did I get hooked on the medications that eased my physical pain, I became hooked on medications that eased my emotional stress—drugs such as Valium, which today I consider to be one of the most dangerous little drugs in the world. It's no wonder I have a great compassion for drug addicts. I can empathize with them; I know how easy it is to become dependent on something that temporarily takes away the pains of life. I also know how difficult it is to break the power of addictions.

Near the end of March 1975 once again I was rushed to St. Thomas Hospital in Nashville. On three previous occasions I had been taken to a hospital near our home in Madisonville, Kentucky, but when the pains came throbbing back this time, the doctors immediately sent me to the larger facility two hours away in Nashville. I knew I was in bad shape.

John Travis drove me to Tennessee in a hearse owned by the local funeral home. Madisonville didn't have any emergency vehicles or paramedics or other convenient medical care like we have today. Back then if someone needed to be transported to the hospital, the funeral directors allowed their hearse to be used as an ambulance. When we saw a hearse going through town, we never knew whether the person in the back was dead or alive.

John Travis returned to Madisonville after delivering me to the hospital and went to the funeral home and quit his job that very night.

The owner, Miss Artie Mae Stroffer, a dear friend of mine, was flabbergasted. "John, why? Why are you quitting your job?"

John replied sadly, "When they took Mrs. Goodman out of my vehicle in Nashville, she was in bad shape. She looked like she was just about dead. I don't think she's going to make it. I know somebody will have to go back after her body, and I can't do it. I love her too much."

John wasn't too far wrong. When the doctors in Nashville saw me, they, too, thought I was nearly dead. They did all they could do to bring me back, to start my heart functioning again. Finally they were able to stabilize my pulmonary system.

When the anxiety level lowered enough that the doctors could carry on a conversation with my family members, they confessed their consternation in trying to treat me. The doctors suggested that Howard take me to the highly esteemed Mayo Clinic in Rochester, Minnesota. He readily agreed.

The doctors in Nashville made the necessary medical arrangements and shipped my medical records to Mayo. Before they discharged me, however, their final instructions to Howard betrayed their lack of confidence that the physicians at Mayo Clinic would be any more successful in helping me than they had been. The doctors told Howard, "Take your wife home for a few days, and let her friends and family members be around her. Then Sunday fly to Minnesota, and have her at the clinic by eight o'clock Monday morning." I was later told by some nurses that they suggested this because they thought I was going to die; they had done all they could do for me.

That Sunday morning before I was to fly to Minnesota, people crammed into every available space in our home. Heavily sedated and with oxygen tubes in my nose, I rested in my bed as a virtual parade of friends and family members trooped through to greet me. Looking back, I now realize they were all coming to tell me good-bye, because they didn't think I would ever return from the Mayo Clinic alive.

All except Willodean.

Sister Willodean Vaughn was one of the most saintly and sophisticated women I had ever met. A strong, slender woman of color, her beautiful light brown complexion was highlighted by her bright eyes and constant smile. Never married, Willodean had given her life totally to the Lord. She had sold out to God. More than anyone else I had ever known, Sister Willodean was the kind of Christian I wanted to be.

Her denomination had tapped her as a "home missionary," assigned to holding evangelistic tent meetings in the hills of Kentucky. Out of those meetings, Willodean became the "mother" of at least five new churches.

Always dressed impeccably, Willodean had a penchant for gorgeous hats, one of which adorned her head nearly everywhere she went. Her very presence evoked a sense of peace in whoever happened to be near her. In fact, it was impossible to be around Willodean for long without feeling the presence of God. More important than her dignified physical deportment, however, Sister Willodean was a true prayer warrior in the kingdom of God. Everyone for miles around our community knew that whenever Sister Willodean prayed, God answered.

Once while Willodean was conducting a live radio broadcast during a revival service, a woman who was singing in the choir suddenly collapsed and died. Members of the audience rushed to the woman. Several nurses in the congregation tried to revive the woman, but she was gone. Almost immediately, her skin faded to a dull gray. All over the church people were either too stunned to move, or they were sobbing uncontrollably. Meanwhile the dead choir member slumped further down in the seat where she had fallen.

About that time Willodean felt that the Lord was instructing her to pray . . . to pray that the dead woman would be raised to life!

Obediently Willodean boldly ordered, "Everybody in here who does not believe that God wants to do a miracle can just go. And go now! Hurry, we don't have a lot of time. You that believe gather 'round."

Willodean waited while most of the congregation filed out of the sanctuary, leaving a group of about ten believers. Willodean began to pray, rebuking death itself in the name of Jesus, saying, "Death, you've got to get away from this woman and leave the building. Don't even hang around."

Then Willodean spoke to the dead woman, "Open your eyes. In the name of Jesus, I tell you to open your eyes."

The woman suddenly revived and opened her eyes. She looked around and then slumped again. Willodean and the group prayed a second time, even more fervently. Soon the woman opened her eyes, lifted her head as if in a daze, and then slumped over again.

One member of the group said, "We better call the undertaker."

"No!" Willodean said firmly. "God's gonna work a miracle."

A woman in the group placed a mirror below the dead woman's mouth to see if she was breathing. She was not. But Willodean was undaunted. She prayed the third time.

Once again the woman revived. Only this time she let out a whoop! and jumped out of the seat and took off dancing around the church. The woman lived for five or six years after that.

I was well aware of Willodean's prayer life. I had often said, "Willodean is in such close communion with the Lord that when she prays, she goes directly into God's throne room." Many times I had called upon Willodean to pray for me, and I had often been the beneficiary of her prayers. On only one occasion had I known Sister Willodean's prayers to be ineffective . . . and it led to a humorous incident I will never forget.

Early in my battle with heart disease, Willodean had come to our home to pray for me. As we sat in our family room, Willodean prayed, but she felt stymied in her efforts.

She looked at me and asked plaintively, "Sister Goodman, are you holding on to anything?"

I thought she was implying that I was holding on to a secret sin or harboring some lack of faith, so I replied, "No, Willodean. Not that I know of."

"Are you sure you're not holding on to anything?" Willodean asked again with a baffled expression on her face. "For some reason, my prayers are not getting through."

"No," I repeated, "not that I know of."

Willodean paused for a moment and put her hand on her chin as though she were pondering some great theological truth. She nodded slightly as understanding dawned on her. At that, without a word of warning, Willodean reached inside my robe, right into my bra, and pulled out the Valium and nitroglycerin that I had concealed there in some facial tissues. She grabbed that medication and threw it across the room against the refrigerator!

"You don't need that medicine," Willodean declared.

Willodean was not being presumptuous. She knew I had been

placing too much faith in my doctors and the medication they were giving me, and she wanted my faith to be solely in the Lord. Even so, Willodean surprised herself by her boldness. She later confided to me that when she arrived home, she told Mother Vaughn, "Oh, Mama, I'm so ashamed. I can't believe that I reached right inside Sister Goodman's bosom and threw her pills away!"

Now nearly a year later, I heard Willodean's voice the moment she stepped inside our front door, even though my bedroom was way down the hall in the back of our house. Willodean marched into our home and down the hallway as though she were a soldier on a mission. She seemed oblivious to the other people, who hastily moved out of her way, much the way people do when a distinguished government official passes by.

As she swept through the crowd, Willodean was loudly rebuking Satan, the enemy. "Satan, you can't have her!" Willodean nearly shouted. "You are not getting Sister Vestal."

When Willodean arrived in my bedroom, at least fifteen people were already by my bedside, standing around trying to encourage me. At first Willodean didn't say anything to anyone; she simply stood inside the doorway and continued praying. Almost immediately, a hush fell over the well-wishers as every eye turned toward the woman in the doorway.

Willodean didn't waste any time on chitchat or idle conversations. Quietly but firmly she asked, "How many in here believe that God is going to heal Sister Goodman?"

The crowd of well-wishers was stunned. Of course they were praying that God would heal me. Most of the people in the room were devout Christians who believed that God *could* heal me if He wanted to. But nobody was bold enough to ask the question that Sister Willodean did. An awkward silence fell over the room. Hesitantly the men and women at my bedside began saying things such as, "Well, Sister Willodean, we are really trying."

I will never forget Willodean's words. She said curtly, "Well, go in yonder and try." She motioned for all the well-wishers to go into the living areas of our home. She didn't speak loudly or forcefully, but there was such a spirit about her—actually it was *the Spirit* within her—that burly men and godly women alike shuffled quietly out of the room without a word of protest.

By the time all the doubters were gone, nobody was left in the room but Willodean, Howard, and me. Tears were streaming down Howard's face. Willodean turned and looked at Howard and said, "Elder Goodman, do you believe God is going to heal Sister Goodman?"

Ever gracious, Howard replied, "Sister Willodean, I am really trying to believe, honey."

Trying to believe wasn't good enough for Willodean. She looked directly at Howard, my husband and the senior pastor of our church, as she said, "Well, you go in yonder with the rest of them and try."

And she put Howard out of the room too!

After Howard left the room, Willodean shut the bedroom door. She turned around and, as only a precious saint like she could do, she stomped her foot and said, "Lucifer, you and me are going to war!"

I lay on my bed in a semistupor, too tired, too sick, and too stunned to say or do much as I watched Willodean walk over by my bed and open her purse. Then to my surprise she reached inside the handbag and pulled out a large bottle of olive oil. Not merely a tiny flask of oil or a pretty, little container such as pastors often keep somewhere around their pulpits or in their pockets. Willodean's anointing oil came in a cooking-oil sized bottle!

With one hand she picked up that oil, and with the other she reached her arm around my neck and lifted my head off the pillow. Willodean pulled my chin down and opened my mouth with her hand. I was so sick I didn't care what she did. I was half-unconscious anyway from the pain medicine. Willodean didn't mind. She continued about her mission. She opened my mouth and turned that bottle of olive oil upside down and poured its contents down my throat!

All the while Willodean was saying, "Oil of the Holy Ghost, go through my sister! Oil of the Holy Ghost, go through my sister."

Then Willodean prayed. Oh! How she prayed!

When Willodean prayed, she wasn't much for form or theology or fancy-sounding words. When a person is in that big of a spiritual fight, you don't say, "Our Father, which art in heaven," or, "Now I lay me down to sleep." You say, "Jesus! Please come to my rescue. Satan, be bound and be cast away!" At least, that's the way Sister Willodean prayed for me.

And when Sister Willodean finished praying, I knew I had been prayed for!

Following her prayer, with no pretense or fanfare, Willodean leaned down, hugged me, and kissed my forehead. She smiled serenely as she said, "Honey, go on to Mayo. They're expecting you. I'll see you in a few days."

A few days? *A few days!*

Nobody outside of my immediate family was talking about seeing me in a few days. Of all the people who had passed through our home that day, Willodean was the only one who dared suggest that we would see each other again. Everyone else was saying sweet, well-intentioned things, such as, "Good-bye, Sister Goodman; we love you. We'll be prayin' for you." They were precious people, good church people, but they didn't have the kind of faith and intimate communication with God that Willodean had.

Nor could I blame them. They had seen me suffer for so long that they were beginning to lose hope that I really would be healed. No doubt some of them felt I would be better off just to die and go to heaven and be out of my misery.

But not Willodean. She was not about to give up without a fight.

The following day Howard and I, along with my good friend Lucille Wells, flew to Minnesota. I was taking so much pain medication that I don't even remember leaving my house. I don't remember getting to the airport in Evansville. I don't remember flying to Chicago and changing planes and going on to Minnesota. I don't remember any of it.

The next morning Lucille and Howard dressed me, and Lucille

fixed my hair so I could look decent and feel better about myself. We arrived at the clinic at eight o'clock, just as the doctors in Nashville had instructed us. Nurses quickly emerged from the clinic to assist me in getting out of the car. During the past seven months of dealing with my heart surgery and the subsequent problems surrounding it, I had developed severe cases of phlebitis in both legs. I couldn't walk and could stand for only a few moments before the pain became intolerable. Consequently when we arrived at Mayo, the nurses transferred me from the car to a wheelchair and propped my feet up on pillows atop the wheelchair leg braces. My legs were so swollen they looked like tree trunks! The nurses wheeled me into the receiving area where Lucille and I waited while Howard filled out the paperwork required for admission.

Sitting in the wheelchair that morning, I suddenly felt Willodean's "oil of the Holy Ghost" kick in. A warm sensation flowed over my forehead and down through my body, and as it went down through my head, it was the sweetest feeling, just a wonderful massaging sensation, similar to the feeling of standing in the shower with warm water cascading gently over your head. But this warm sensation was not only on the surface of my body; I could feel it flowing inside me too!

For the first time in days, I could think clearly. It was as though the grogginess caused by medication had been washed right out of my system. My eyes began to focus better, and I saw Howard standing at the registrar's counter. I saw Lucille standing by me.

But the warm sensation didn't stop when it passed through my head; it went on down through my body; I felt it gently flow through my neck and shoulders, and I felt it go through my chest and my heart. Immediately I felt my heart begin beating normally, something I had not experienced in many months. All the while, as the warm sensation flowed through me, I just sat there in that wheelchair, watching, never saying a word, just basking in the warmth of the Spirit of God. I felt the sensation pass through my feet and legs.

That's when I saw something that nearly made me shout right there in the foyer of the prestigious Mayo Clinic. Sitting in the wheelchair, with my legs propped out in front of me, I watched in amazement as the swelling in my legs and feet disappeared! As it did, my legs and feet were reduced to their normal size in a matter of moments!

That's also when I noticed I could breathe normally again. For months, because of the angina, I had been breathing in short, painful gasps, afraid to take a deep breath because every time I did, pain shot through my chest cavity. Now I started taking wonderful, deep breaths. Oooh! Stale hospital air never felt so fresh!

I looked up at Lucille and quietly tried to get her attention. She was watching Howard over at the admissions desk, waiting for a sign from him that she should wheel me to our next stop in the admissions process. "Lucille," I said softly, "I have been healed."

Lucille had heard me say many times before, "I am going to be healed." She would always agree with me, but then later on I'd catch her crying.

"Lucille, don't cry," I'd tell her. "I am not going to die. I'm going to be healed."

"I know, honey," she'd always say, turning her face away quickly so I wouldn't see the tears beginning to well in her eyes again.

Now sitting in the admissions area of the Mayo Clinic, Lucille didn't quite hear me correctly. I said, "Lucille, I have been healed!"

Dear Lucille thought I was simply expressing my faith again. She leaned over, patted me on the shoulder, and said, "I know it, hon."

I grabbed her dress and shook her as I said, "Lucille! I didn't say I am gonna be healed; I said, 'I *have* been healed.' Watch this." She looked around at me, as I leaned back and sucked in a huge breath and then slowly exhaled.

Lucille's face froze. "Oh, please don't do that, honey; don't do that." She was afraid I was going to pass out.

I said, "Lucille, please go over there and tell Howard that I don't need to stay, and I am ready to go home. I have been healed!"

Poor Lucille must have thought I was delirious again, so she tried to placate me as best she could. "Just wait," she consoled me. "Elder Goodman will be through in a minute."

I spoke up louder, "No, go tell him now that I am ready to go home."

Lucille ignored my urgings. Now she *knew* I was delirious.

I wasn't delirious. In fact, I was more aware of my faculties than I had been in months. I was frustrated that I couldn't make Lucille understand, so I had no other choice. With dozens of other patients in the waiting room, I yelled at Howard all the way across the lobby, "Howard, come here, quickly! I've been healed."

People who had been idly thumbing through magazines suddenly lifted their eyes and fixed their gazes on me. Nurses and other hospital personnel stopped abruptly and turned to see who had the audacity to make such a claim in the lobby of the Mayo Clinic. All in all, my outburst caused quite a stir. I didn't care; I knew God had touched my body.

Howard bounded across the room to where Lucille and I were waiting. "What are you talking about?" he asked excitedly.

As best I could explain it, I told him what had happened. Howard has always been a man of great faith, but like most men, he likes to see things in black and white. He believed me when I told him I had been healed, but he added, "Well, honey, let's just stay here and make sure."

"All right," I agreed reluctantly. I knew the doctors would be wasting their time.

The hospital staff admitted me—the admissions people sped up the process after my announcement that I had been healed—and instructed Howard and Lucille to follow a nurse back to an examination room. Immediately the doctors started running tests on my heart.

The doctors in Nashville had instructed me to take all my medicines with me to Mayo, so Howard and Lucille presented the paper sack of medications to Dr. James Maloney, the cardiologist at Mayo who initially examined me.

After Dr. Maloney finished his exam, he called for Howard and Lucille to come into the examination room along with me.

When we were all seated, the doctor held up my sack of medicine and pulled every prescription out, one by one. "Why are you taking this medication?" he asked, looking quizzically at another bottle of pills.

I answered, "Well, the doctors in Nashville said I needed this." I added quickly, "And Dr. Maloney, *then* I did need it."

The doctor replied, "Well, you don't need it now." Dr. Maloney looked puzzled as he said softly, "This has to be miraculous."

That got my attention, and I saw Howard's and Lucille's eyes widen, but we didn't have time to ask what the doctor meant. He continued speaking slowly but emphatically, "I have your records from the hospital in Nashville, and I have studied their charts, even their X-rays, but when I look at ours, they look like they are from two different human beings."

I smiled slightly. I really wanted to shout, but I wasn't sure how the good doctor might respond. I knew it was time to bear witness to what God had done in my body. "Dr. Maloney, let me tell you what just happened out in the admissions area. I have had a miracle." I made the doctor listen, and I told him exactly what I had experienced. I even told him about Sister Willodean and her "oil of the Holy Ghost," and then I told him about my healing Monday morning around eight o'clock. "It's a miracle, Doctor."

"It has to be . . . ," the doctor answered as much to himself as to us.

Dr. Maloney was fascinated. He was not cynical or mocking in any way. Quite the contrary. Oh, he was precious; he was wonderful. He believed me.

I stayed at the Mayo Clinic from Monday morning until Friday morning when they discharged me. My medical records say that the doctors at Mayo could find no phlebitis, nor could they detect any signs of a heart problem. It was gone!

Howard returned home after the first few days of my stay at the Mayo Clinic. He had numerous responsibilities at the church that required his attention. Besides, I was doing fine. Lucille stayed to help me, just in case I needed anything. On Friday morning, before Dr. Maloney released me, he stopped by to visit me. We both knew I was okay, but out of respect for the doctor, I asked him if there was anything I should do once I left Mayo.

Dr. Maloney smiled and said, "You don't need any medication. You can take a vitamin if you want to, but you really don't need even that. It would be wise if you gave yourself some time to rest for a few weeks, just to regain your strength. After that, you can do whatever you want to. I'm not placing any restrictions on you."

I thanked the doctor for his kindness, and Lucille and I prepared to leave the Mayo Clinic. When we got to the airport, Lucille said, "Vestal, you can't walk to the airplane. I am going to ask the ticketing agent if he can get you a wheelchair."

"Oh, Lucille," I answered. "I don't need any wheelchair. I can walk just fine."

"I know, I know. But if you fell, I would never forgive myself."

"All right, Lucille," I conceded. "If it makes you feel better, I'll ride in the wheelchair down to our gate."

Lucille spoke to the agent, and they arranged for me to use a wheelchair in Rochester. They also called ahead so a wheelchair would be available for me when we arrived in Saint Louis, where we were to catch another flight to Evansville, Indiana, which was the closest airport to our home. Sure enough, when we deplaned in Saint Louis, an airline attendant was waiting for us with a wheelchair just inside the gate. I compliantly sat down in the chair, and Lucille began pushing me down the long, narrow airport corridor. When we got to the end of the corridor, we realized that our gate was still a good distance away. I stopped the wheelchair, turned to Lucille, and said, "Lucille, I don't need this chair."

She said, "Oh, Vestal, please stay in the chair until we get home."

Too late. To Lucille's great dismay, I had already gotten out of the chair and had stood up. I pushed the wheelchair over to the wall, out of the way, and said, "Thank you, chair, for taking care of me, but I don't need you anymore."

Lucille said, "Vestal, just walk real slow . . ."

No way! I started *running* down that corridor, with Lucille hurrying along behind me, trying to keep pace! We were half-laughing, half-crying as we two, supposedly sophisticated women, raced like schoolgirls through the airport corridor.

I had strength, *strength,* and more strength! And to think that less than a week earlier, I could barely raise my head off the pillow without awful pain. God had indeed done a miracle.

When Lucille and I arrived home that night, one of the first things I wanted to do was go to church. Can you imagine how surprised the members of our congregation were when I walked in and sat down in my usual spot? They had been praying for a miracle, but now they could actually see one right before their eyes. I could hardly wait to stand up and tell everyone what God had done for me! And then to top things off, I sang a song that night! The congregation just about raised the roof with their praises to God when I sang, "There's Nothing My God Can't Do." Honey, we had church!

About midway through the service, I sat down in one of the chairs behind the pulpit as Howard was speaking. Suddenly through the doors at the rear of the sanctuary, I saw her. It was Sister Willodean!

As Willodean made her way down the center aisle, I leaped out of my chair, jumped off the platform, and ran down the aisle to meet her. Howard lost his train of thought and simply began to praise the Lord, as did the entire congregation when they saw what was going on. Spontaneously the crowd stood to their feet and began clapping, shouting, and praising God. It was jubilee time!

Willodean and I met in the center of the church, and when we did, I was so thrilled I literally lifted her off the floor and swung her around in a bear hug! We laughed and cried and praised God for His healing power. "It happened! It happened, Willodean," I practically shouted in her ear above the bedlam that had erupted in the church.

"We asked for it; we got it, so let's praise Him for it," Willodean said matter-of-factly. So praise Him we did!

The following week I went back out on the road with the Happy

Goodman Family and never looked back. The great tenor Johnny Cook had been taking my place with the group for the months I had been incapacitated, and he had been doing a fantastic job. But I told him, "Johnny, you can get back to singing solo again, because I'm feeling better than ever!"

For the next twenty-some years, I never had another problem with my heart. But God still wanted to teach me a lot more about trusting Him.

CHAPTER 20

ON THE ROAD AGAIN

Mark Lowry, baritone singer with the Gaither Vocal Band, loves to tease me about how I used to wear "that foot-high hair." Occasionally people come to me after concerts and ask, "Why do you let him talk about you that way?"

I reply, "He says my name right, and the truth is, I did wear a foot-high wig." For people born after the late 1960s, it might be difficult to believe that the huge "beehive" hairdo was actually the style for a while, especially in my church and music circles. The idea was to pile as much hair as possible high on your head turban-style, or for those women with poor balance or bone structure (that hair was heavy!), like the leaning tower of Pisa. Few women I knew, however, had hair enough to pull it up that high. I certainly didn't. I had a wig (two of them, in fact), so I fixed my own hair around the edges, pulled it up as high as it would go, plopped the wig on top of my head, stuck about a dozen hairpins in it, and I was ready to go.

It still surprises me how many people actually believed all that hair was mine.

After I experienced the healing of my heart, however, I really didn't care to mess with the wig any longer. I decided to work with what hair I had, and Richard Sorells, a young stylist in our church, offered to style my hair for me, using my own hair.

Richard did a fabulous job, too, but when I went back out on the road with the group, I was shocked at the negative mail I received concerning my new "do." Some older Christians were quick to remind me (often in rather unloving terms) that my long hair was a glory to the Lord. Was my hair really a glory to the Lord if it was fake?

Some letters said, "Oh, we can't believe that Vestal cut off all that beautiful long hair."

Others said, "We can't believe that you have backslidden so far as to cut your hair. We thought you were going to remain faithful to the Lord." Most of those letters I ignored, but they still caused me to wince a bit.

Not long after I was out of the hospital and on the road again, we were in concert in Monroe, Louisiana. I had my hair styled without the huge hairpiece I had worn in years past. After the concert I was walking out of the auditorium when I saw a group of eight women standing in my path. "Hey, Vestal, we need to talk to you," one of them called to me as I approached.

I stopped, and as I did, the women completely encircled me so I couldn't get out. Then those women began talking to me about my hair, and they were not offering compliments. Quite the contrary, they were saying all sorts of ugly things to me. Their demeanor and their words were downright cruel and mean-spirited. "All of these years we've prayed for you and believed in you," they whined. "We thought sure we could depend on you. Dottie Rambo had all that long hair, but then she brought a reproach upon us by cutting it off. Now you've gone and brought a reproach upon us, too, by cutting off all your long hair."

I was about to cry, and I wanted to say, "No, no, girls; I didn't cut it off. I still have it. It was a wig." But I was so taken back by their nastiness, I never said a word. In my spirit, I felt as though the Lord wanted me simply to keep quiet.

These women were not interested in the testimony I had given an hour or so earlier from the stage. They were not concerned about my health; they didn't want to hear about my healing. They didn't care whether I was doing okay now. The only thing they were concerned about was the fact that I had cut my long hair and brought a reproach upon Christian women from their denomination.

They wanted to lay hands on me and pray for me. I didn't say anything, but in my spirit I was screaming, "Lord, don't let them touch me." With attitudes such as theirs, I didn't want them praying for me, because I knew that these women were not operating under the direction of God's Spirit. God's Spirit isn't ignorant; He knew I was wearing a wig all those years. But these women didn't, so they were clearly not being led by the Spirit of Truth. Nor did they have a gift of discernment—so whatever spirit they were operating under, I didn't want any part of it. At the first opportunity I pushed my way through two of the women and literally ran out of the auditorium.

When I got to the bus, all the group members were already aboard. They had loaded the equipment, instruments, and albums while I had been inside. Several of the fellows were about to come looking for me.

I hurried up the steps and tried to swish past the fellows sitting in the front of the bus, hoping to get to my room in the back without having to talk to anyone. I almost made it, too, as the fellows were absorbed in the usual, relaxed, after-concert banter. But as I passed Rusty, he grabbed my arm and asked, "Hey, are you okay?"

I shook my head yes. I couldn't speak.

"No, you're not. What's wrong with you?" Rusty probed.

"Nothing, nothing," I said.

"Yes there is," said Rusty. "Now you tell me what's wrong."

At that, the dam broke, and the flood of tears let loose. I started boohooing like a baby. "Oh, those women in there have just broken my heart," I said through my tears. "They just talked awful to me."

"What about?"

"They said I had cut my hair, and they were just eatin' me up for it!"

Rusty wanted to go back into the auditorium and find the women and "give them some scriptures," but I wouldn't let him.

My women accusers' attitude was so foolish and legalistic, not to mention, unbiblical. Yes, the Bible talks about a woman's hair being her glory and that it is wrong for a man to have long hair, but even those statements must be read in light of what they meant to the original readers. Most men who have long hair today would have been considered well-groomed in Jesus' day. Don't get me wrong; I believe a man should look like a male and a woman should look like a female. When we purposely try to blur those distinctions, I believe we are going against God's plan. But to arbitrarily place our cultural definitions on the length of someone's hair, or almost any other aspect of outward adornment, will get us in trouble every time.

I was much more concerned about the attitude of those women's hearts. Where was love and compassion? Even if I had sinned horribly, which of course I hadn't, where was their desire to restore me to fellowship? I learned a good lesson that night. For years, Howard and I were rather conservative; okay, to put it bluntly we were straight-laced.

Someone asked Howard not long ago, "After all the years you have served the Lord and been in the ministry, what would you do differently if you could?"

Howard replied simply, "I'd let a lot more people into heaven." He was admitting that we, too, had been narrow-minded in some of our external definitions of how Christians should look.

Maybe that's why when the Oak Ridge Boys let their hair grow longer—no small scandal in gospel music circles of the mid-1970s—and started using new sounds in their stage performance and on their records, I was one of their strongest supporters. I had known them all for years. Nora Lee Allen, Duane Allen's wife, had sung at Life Temple many times. Richard Sterban and Joe Bonsall were two of the church's best soul winners and evangelistic workers during their younger days. We had worked hundreds of concerts together, and I felt I knew the fellows' hearts. Even when they left gospel music to pursue a career as a country group, I still believed in those boys. I refused to judge them on the length of their hair. I knew well what it felt like to be judged unfairly by legalistic Christians.

When the Oaks "went country" and started working Las Vegas and other secular venues, many people in the gospel community hung them out to dry, especially when Bill Golden adopted his mountain-man look, allowing his hair and beard to grow longer than my hair. I didn't see Bill for a long time after that, not until Howard and I attended the funeral of a mutual friend—Smitty Gatlin, one of the early members of the Oak Ridge Boys.

After the service Howard and I had started down the sidewalk when we saw Bill Golden coming toward us. When Bill got about a hundred feet away, he purposely turned and went across the street to avoid bumping into us. I immediately turned and went across the street after him, yelling, "Bill. Bill Golden. Bill Golden, you stop right now!"

What was he going to do? He could keep on walking and allow me to make a big scene, or he could stop and confront me. Bill stopped and shuffled back in my direction.

I caught up with him and hugged his neck and told him how much I loved him. I said, "Bill Golden, why did you cross that street to avoid us?"

"Well, Vestal, I know a lot of people in the gospel industry are upset with us, and I was afraid you felt the same way."

"Bill, you know better than that," I said. "Don't you ever be guilty of doing that again. I love you. And I love all the Oak Ridge Boys. Now the only gripe I've got with you—and I'll tell you to your face—is that you've gone out there and given the devil a lot of ammunition to shoot you with. I don't mind how you wear your hair or what kind of music you do, but you gotta keep your life right with the Lord. You gotta watch where your steps take you and be careful what comes out of your mouth, because you're gonna need God."

Bill and I have been big buddies ever since.

Funny thing about some of our traditions—many of them get started for reasons that have nothing to do with Jesus, the Bible, or anything spiritual. For instance, over the years people have associated a white lace handkerchief with me. It's gotten to the point that I carry one with me every time I walk onto a stage or a church platform. Some folks figure the lacy white handkerchief must have a deep spiritual significance. Some imagine the mystical material has supernatural healing benefits. Actually the reason I carry that white handkerchief is quite simple: I need it.

I started carrying a small white handkerchief with me into the pulpit or on stage simply because my body's metabolism causes me to perspire heavily around my head and face. A woman named Inez Brown, from Austin, Texas, drove a motor home to Madisonville every year to attend our church homecoming. Inez noticed that I frequently blotted my face with a small white handkerchief. As a special gift, she made me several, large, cotton handkerchiefs, with lots of pretty lace on them. She's been making them for me ever since. I don't know how spiritual they are, but they do a great job of blotting perspiration.

Recently I was on stage at a Gaither *Homecoming* concert, along with dozens of other artists. Sitting nearby was Janet Paschal, who had just sung one of her beautiful, deeply moving songs, which had literally moved her to tears. The tears were trickling down Janet's face and dripping onto the stage as she tried to regain her composure. Her makeup was running, and she had mascara on her cheek.

I had been crying, too, and had smeared makeup on my lace handkerchief, but it looked as though poor Janet needed it more than I did. I passed my handkerchief over to Janet. She nodded her appreciation to me and gratefully used the lace handkerchief. Rick and Dianne noticed what I had done and quickly retrieved another clean handkerchief for me.

When the concert was over, I said to Janet, "Here, darlin'. Take this clean handkerchief and give me that dirty one back."

"No!" Janet pulled the hanky away and clutched it closely to her body. "I want this one. It was yours, and you gave it to me, and I'm keepin' it forever. How many people can say they have a handkerchief actually used by Vestal Goodman?"

"Not many," I said as we laughed and hugged. "Well, if that's what you want, just keep it."

The next time I saw Janet, I asked, "Did you ever get all the makeup out of that handkerchief?"

"No," she said sweetly, "but it's mine and I'm keeping it."

In September 1979 President Jimmy Carter hosted an "old-fashioned gospel singing" on the lawn at the White House, and as lifetime members of the GMA, the Happy Goodman Family was invited to attend. Although we had never met the president, we were well aware of his Christian commitment, and we had heard that he was a fan of gospel music. We knew of at least one occasion where he had been in our audience. In the mid-1970s, when Jimmy Carter was still governor of Georgia and just beginning his campaign for president, the Happy Goodman Family had sung at a large outdoor concert in Bonifay, Florida, which Governor Carter attended.

Several years later when the White House concert was being arranged, someone at the Gospel Music Association put together a list of the president's favorite gospel singers, and the Goodmans were on it. When the invitation came for us to sing at the White House, we could hardly believe our eyes.

The president and his wife, Rosalynn, made us feel right at home. During the reception on the White House lawn, Mrs. Carter came over and sat down with me. We talked as though we were old friends. "Vestal, will you sing my favorite song when you perform later on?" she asked.

"Why sure I will, if I know it," I replied. "What is it?"

"My favorite song is 'Jesus Is the Sweetest Name I Know,'" the first lady answered.

"Oh, sure. I know that song. I'll be glad to sing it for you," I said.

Several other gospel singing groups were on the program that day. The Blackwood Brothers Quartet was there, as were the Speer Family, and Francis Preston, head of the music licensing group Broadcast Music, Inc. (BMI). When it was our turn to sing, I sang Mrs. Carter's song and dedicated it to her. Not many months after that, I recorded the song and dedicated that recording to Rosalynn Carter too.

When President Carter came around, I expected him to shake hands with me. He didn't. Instead he put his arms around me and hugged me. Just then, I went against White House protocol. If I had taken time to think about, I might not have done it. But as the president of the United States was hugging my neck, I suddenly felt an overwhelming urge to pray for him, so I did . . . out loud, with everybody—Secret Service agents and all—watching us. For a few seconds, the president allowed me to cradle his head on my shoulder as I prayed for him.

When I finished praying, President Carter took a step backward, put his hand on my shoulder, and looked me right in the eyes. "Vestal," he said, "don't ever stop doing that."

We chatted briefly, and he noticed a pendant I was wearing. The pendant was in the shape of a piano and was a special gift that Howard had had made for me. President Carter picked up the pendant and looked at it. "That is simply beautiful," he said. He turned the pendant over and read the inscription on the back: "A Special Howard Goodman Girl."

"That is one of the most beautiful pendants I have ever seen," the president said. Both Howard and I were beaming.

Back home, it was time to get ready for our annual homecoming at Life Temple, held each year over Labor Day weekend as a time to celebrate what God had done in our church and through the Goodman family. Lots of good singing and preaching and eating characterized the Goodman Homecoming. The first few years we held the event we limited it to one day and held it in the church. Great gospel singing groups such as the Bill Gaither Trio, the Florida Boys, the Speer Family, and a host of others provided the music, along with the Happy Goodman Family. Howard or I preached, and we all had a family-style picnic dinner.

The response was so overwhelming that for three years we moved to the high school gymnasium and expanded homecoming to several days. Maude Aimee and Rex Humbard came to do the preaching. The Humbards were pioneers in Christian television and in using gospel music on their programs, broadcasting their services from the Cathedral of Tomorrow in Akron, Ohio. Henry and Hazel Slaughter appeared regularly on their show, as did the Weatherford Quartet, featuring a young singer with a great voice and a deep love for God, Glen Payne, who went on to great success with the Cathedrals. The Humbards and their featured music teams were a favorite among our homecoming crowds.

Unfortunately the Madisonville High School gym was not air-conditioned. The heat became unbearable, and the crowds soon became too large for the school to handle, so we obtained permission from the city to hold our homecoming in the park across from Life Temple. The boys bought lumber and built an outdoor staging area with a roof over it.

The last few years we held the event more than forty thousand people attended the Goodman Homecoming. Every hotel and motel within one hundred miles of Madisonville was filled to capacity. Nearly all the billboards in town bore messages of congratulations or welcome to the Happy Goodman Family Homecoming. People came from all across the United States, and many came from as far away as Canada. The interstate highway was backed up for miles with people taking the exit to our tiny town. Since we were holding a giant festival and picnic in the park, the Goodman family provided free barbecue sandwiches for all those people attending—all forty thousand of them!

Homecoming was always one of the highlights of our year. But it was also hectic and exhausting. As Howard often said, "Thank God homecoming don't come but once a year. I just don't think I could stand it more often."

CHAPTER 21

THE UNHAPPY GOODMANS

With a name like the Happy Goodman Family, you might assume we were always a happy-go-lucky bunch, just praising the Lord up and down the highways of America, with never a problem or a conflict. You might assume that . . . but you'd be wrong.

Like most families, and especially those that work together in close quarters the way we did, we had our fair amount of family squabbles and spats. A few of those familial fights nearly spelled the end of the Happy Goodman Family as a gospel singing group.

On one occasion we traveled all night in our bus to Alexandria, Louisiana, to arrive in time for the following evening's concert. Bobby, Howard's youngest brother, had just joined our group to play bass guitar. Bobby had driven the bus through most of the night, so that morning we let him sleep while one of the other members of the group drove.

About three hours away from the concert location, Sam and Rusty began discussing how they might more easily label the many boxes of records we were hauling into churches and concert halls each night. In those days, most gospel groups carried their recordings in the bus, right with them in black or brown fiber cases, each box holding about one hundred records. Record racks were set up in the lobbies of auditoriums or the foyers of churches, and during the intermission and following the concert, people could purchase the recordings and other related merchandise directly from the artists. Extra records were carried in the luggage bays of the bus, and each night before the concert the supplies of albums in the record boxes were replenished so they would be readily available if there was a rush of people wanting records at the concert.

Early in our recording career it was easy to figure out which boxes contained which recordings. We had only a few titles, so it was no problem to keep up the record supply, even on a busy evening at the concert. With each album we made, however, it became increasingly hectic and confusing as we tried to find and retrieve the correct record from the right fiber case while a patient fan waited. Sam and Rusty recognized the problem, and they were discussing various solutions as we drove toward Louisiana that day.

Rusty suggested that we put stick-on numbers on the lid of each fiber case to identify which albums were located in which boxes. That way, a person could quickly spot the location of a record without having to search through all the cases. It was a good idea and seemed to make sense. Only one problem: Sam didn't like the idea.

"That will never work," Sam said bluntly. "If we do that, the letters will come off, and it will be the same mess. I'm in charge of merchandise, and I don't want to do that." Sam had been a sergeant in the air force, and if he didn't agree with someone, often he could be pretty bullheaded. Trying to tell Sam how to do much of anything was usually futile. He loved to argue and would pick a fight over the slightest issue. He especially enjoyed a heated debate and at one point even thought of going into politics. He probably would have done well at that, too, because Sam never saw an issue he didn't have a staunch opinion about.

Rusty, on the other hand, was a peacemaker. He hated to argue about anything. He was rather even tempered, more analytical, and logical. But as brothers or sisters will often do, Rusty was much more willing to get in a fray with a family member, and usually that family member was Sam. In the discussion of the record boxes, Sam and Rusty went back and forth for about fifteen minutes, arguing the pluses and minuses of the labeling.

Finally Sam became defensive, and then he simply blew up. "Fine, do it your way," he declared. "I quit!"

"You what?" Rusty recoiled in surprise.

"You heard me. I quit."

Looking back, it seems ludicrous that Sam was going to quit the Happy Goodman Family because of a dispute over how to label the record boxes. But that was Sam.

Rusty, however, was not about to back down. "Well, fine. We'll just quit. The Goodman Family will go off the road, and you can do whatever you want."

"Well fine," answered Sam. "But don't think I'm singing tonight either. I quit!"

"All right, fine!" Rusty retorted.

We pulled our bus into our hotel, checked in, and everyone went their separate ways. Nobody planned on going to the auditorium that night.

Fortunately Sam's wife, Barbara, was with us on that trip. Barbara did not often travel with us, but on this occasion the Lord had her in the right place at the right time. Barbara became the peacemaker. She brought Sam to Howard's and my room to apologize. Then we all went to Rusty's room to apologize. The brothers apologized to each other and to Howard and me.

"Okay, fine, it's over," Howard announced. "Now let's get to work." As quickly as the argument had flared, it dissipated. Everyone hugged, and we were off to another concert by the again *Happy* Goodman Family.

Still asleep in his bunk on the bus, Bobby had missed the entire incident. Later as he and Rick were fine-tuning their instruments right before the concert, Rick said, "Whew! For a while there, I didn't think we were going to sing tonight."

"What do you mean?" Bobby asked.

"Do you mean to tell me that you didn't hear what happened?" Rick asked him.

"Hear what?" Bobby replied innocently. Rick went on to tell Bobby about the dispute over the record boxes and how close the Happy Goodman Family had come to breaking up.

"Well, how about that?" Bobby said with a whistle. "I was hired and fired and rehired all in the same day, and I didn't even know it!"

In many ways Bobby naturally gravitated toward his brother Rusty. The two youngest of the Goodman boys, they had many of the same interests, and they enjoyed working together. One of the things they loved to work on was our bus. Early in our career we traveled to concerts in an old 1947 GMC 4104 bus. It was a clunker the day we bought it, and it was still a clunker when we sold it. During that time, Rusty and Bobby spent most of their spare time trying to keep that bus on the road. Having been a professional truck driver during his younger days, Bobby knew a good deal about bus engines. As a young man, Bobby had gotten away from the Lord for a while and had played rock 'n roll music in nightclubs. After that, he went into military service, and when he was discharged, he took a job in Dallas driving a truck. When we bought the old bus, we invited Bobby to come and drive for us. Eventually he played bass guitar with the Goodmans for several years, but his first love was that old bus.

One day Bobby and Rusty were working together on the bus's water line, which was beneath the center aisle of the bus. They crawled under the vehicle and were using a workman's trouble light to see.

Bobby's dog—a combination pit-bull-Chinese-pug-junkyard mutt that ironically Bobby had named *Sam*—was playing nearby.

As Rusty and Bobby were working, Rusty noticed that Sam was chewing on the cord to the light. "Look over there, Bobby," Rusty said. "He's chewin' on the cord to that electric light, and he needs to quit it. He's gonna get hurt."

Bobby answered nonchalantly, "Oh, don't worry about ol' Sam. He'll be all right. If he chews through the cord, the moment his teeth touch that wire, he'll quit."

Rusty laughed and said, "Yeah, but he's liable to get fried."

"Naw, he'll be okay. Don't worry about it," Bobby replied. "Let him go."

Rusty and Bobby continued working, Rusty under one end of the bus and Bobby under the other. Suddenly the trouble light began to flicker. About that time, the boys heard a bone-chilling howl from Sam. Sure enough, the dog had bitten through the rubber coating and into the electric wire. Worse yet, the wire had gotten stuck in Sam's mouth. The poor dog was yelping to high heaven and rearing up and down, shaking his head ferociously, trying to rid himself of the wire. With every move, he was receiving more shock.

Rusty was closest to Sam, so he scrambled out from beneath the bus to help. In his haste, he banged his head against the bus frame and opened a gash that immediately began to gush blood. With blood spewing from his head, Rusty grabbed the electric cord and began pulling on the wire, trying to get it out of Sam's mouth.

Meanwhile from beneath the other end of the bus, Bobby heard all the commotion and thought perhaps Sam had attacked Rusty. Bobby grabbed his wrench and started crawling back down the narrow area under the bus, calling out, "Hold him, Rusty. I'm coming! I'll get him off ya!"

About that time Sam finally was able to shake loose of the wire, and he streaked under the bus and kept on running, yelping all the way.

"Rusty, are you okay?" Bobby asked with genuine concern for his brother. "Where did he bite you?"

"I'm fine," Rusty replied. "I just hit my head under the bus. But I'm not so sure about your dog. He took off that way."

The brothers searched all over Madisonville for ol' Sam, but he was nowhere to be found. About two weeks later Sam returned, his eyes still bloodshot from the shock. From that time on, if anyone waved a string, or a cord, or anything resembling a wire in front of Sam, that dog would take off running.

On more than one occasion Bobby was oblivious to what was happening around him. One trip Bobby was driving the bus on rough, bumpy roads through some of Mississippi's most rugged terrain. When at last Bobby pulled the bus onto a main highway, he floored it. Sailing along, he was as happy as could be.

About an hour later, Howard got up and went to the front of the bus. He looked out the window and saw nothing familiar. Howard said, "Bobby, where are we?"

"I don't know, Howard," Bobby said with a smile. "I just found me a good road here, and we're making good time."

Howard picked up a map and began studying it. His brow wrinkled as he compared some of the road signs we were passing and the lines on the map. "Bobby, you're on the wrong road, boy. You missed it somehow. Did you pass a junction that intersects with the interstate awhile ago?"

"Yeah, I sure did. I passed that a long time ago."

"Well, didn't you know you were supposed to take that?"

Without blinking an eye, Bobby replied, "Well, it didn't look like it was as good a road as this one."

"Bobby!" Howard nearly shrieked. Howard made Bobby stop the bus, turn around, and go back. Bobby had gone fifty miles past our junction—one hundred miles out of the way.

"Bobby, what in the world were you thinkin' about?" Howard wanted to know.

"I don't know. I'd been on bad roads all night long, so when I found me a good piece of road, I decided to stick with it," Bobby answered with a straight face. It was so funny there was no need to say any more about it, but the rest of the family never let Bobby live it down.

Some people think that traveling the country by tour bus and singing is a glamorous lifestyle. They see the musicians and singers pull into town in their big coaches, and they watch their favorites onstage dressed in their fancy suits or dresses, and the average music fan says, "Wow, talk about the lifestyles of the rich and famous." Of course, the only people who say such things are those who have never tried it. They have no idea what it took for us to get to their town to sing.

Once we were on our way to a concert in Red Jacket, West Virginia, traveling through the mountains on some of the most twisting, turning roads imaginable. On some of those turns we felt as though we were meeting ourselves comin' and goin'. By the time the back end of the bus cleared a curve, the front end of the bus was heading into another corkscrew turn. Up and down, back and forth, we felt like we were riding a roller coaster. Making matters worse, unlike tractor trailers, buses don't bend in the middle. So as we climbed the mountain, when the front end of the bus started up a grade, the incline caused the back of the bus to drag on the road, making a horrible screeching noise and causing sparks to fly right beneath our engine. Then as the bus pulled off that obstacle, the front of the bus scraped the pavement as it moved into the next turn, up a little higher. At one point the middle set of tires—the drive wheels of a bus, the wheels on which the bulk of the weight is carried—actually lifted off the ground, and our bus stood suspended on a mountain curve, the front end stuck on the curve ahead of us, the back end stuck on the incline behind us, with our drive wheels spinning helplessly in the air.

"What are we going to do?" Howard asked. We knew the high school auditorium where we were to sing that evening would already be filling up. We were expecting a capacity crowd, probably with more people than the room could safely contain. They would be waiting on us, and here we were, stuck on a mountain curve.

"I have an idea," Sam offered. "If we take some air out of the back tires, that might cause the back of the bus to lower a bit and the weight to shift back onto the drive wheels."

"It's worth a try," said Rusty. In a flash, Rusty, Bobby, and Sam were outside on their knees, purposely letting air out of our back tires. Sure enough, just as Sam had suggested, the back of the bus lowered, the weight shifted, and the drive wheels touched the road just enough for us to keep going.

"Whew, sure glad that is over," said Sam as he flopped down on a seat in the front of the bus. "Wait a minute! What's that awful smell?"

By now everyone on the bus was coughing and sputtering, our eyes were watering, and we could barely breathe. Rick ran to the back of the bus, where the rest room was located, and he quickly found the problem. In all the herky-jerky movement of the bus, a bottle of liquid blue toilet chemicals—similar to those used in airplanes to suppress odors from waste products—had spilled all over the floor of the rest room and was seeping out into the carpeted area of the bus. Apparently one of the main ingredients in the blue stuff was formaldehyde, and although Rick could clean up the liquid, the horrendous aroma was literally suffocating.

The men quickly opened as many windows on the bus as they could. The bus had emergency windows only and a line of four-inch windows at the top. Because of the way the bunks were built into the back of the bus, some windows would not open at all. Others opened only by inches. We opened every window as far as it would go, but that hardly made a difference as the formaldehyde wafted through the vehicle. We even opened the front door, trying to get some air into the bus as we drove.

Like people in a burning, smoke-filled building, we wrapped wet towels around our faces to help filter the awful gas. When the Happy Goodman Family arrived in Red Jacket, West Virginia, that night, we all got off the bus, wearing towels around our faces. No doubt, the folks who greeted us wondered what they were in store for with "An Evening with the Happy Goodmans"!

On another occasion a booking agent (with whom we had a short-lived relationship) had booked us in a twenty-five-hundred-seat high school auditorium in Texas. We arrived early in the day—a rarity for most traveling music groups and especially for us. Nobody was around, but the doors to the school were open, so we went ahead and unloaded all of our sound equipment, instruments, and merchandise and proceeded to set everything up. "This is great," Sam said. "For once we have more time than we need."

"I'll say," Rusty agreed. "I've been wanting to solder some of those speaker cables. We've had a loose connection the last few concerts, and that buzz in the system has been driving me nuts."

We finished our load-in chores, did our sound check, and went to our hotel where we checked in, washed up, and had a meal. It was about three o'clock in the afternoon when we returned to the school. To our surprise, the parking lot was empty. We looked inside the school, and nobody was there yet, not even the usual complement of school custodians or stagehands.

Four o'clock . . . same thing. The parking lot remained empty except for our bus. "Boy, we're not going to have a crowd here at all tonight," Sam lamented. Normally, by late afternoon people began showing up for our concerts, some wanting to help us unload, others simply wanting the best seats. Inevitably the concert location was bustling with activity several hours before the music was scheduled to begin. But not tonight.

Howard went inside and started making phone calls, hoping to find out what the problem was. Soon he came back out, wagging his head. He stepped into the bus and announced, "Boys, we done set up in the wrong schoolhouse." It seems our agency had given us directions to the wrong high school! (Now you know why we had such a short-lived relationship with them.) Hurriedly the boys tore down all the equipment and virtually threw it back into the bus. We raced across town and began the unloading process all over again, this time in much more of a rush. The concert that night was billed as "An Evening with the Happy Goodman Family." We were the only group on the program, so we couldn't use anyone else's sound system. We had to set up all the equipment, haul in all the records and merchandise, and hurry to the bus to wipe the sweat off our faces, change clothes, and run back into the school in time for the master of ceremonies to introduce us. So much for our early arrival.

We rarely missed a concert, but one time we came mighty close. Ironically the incident occurred while everyone, including the audience, was already at the auditorium. We were in a high school auditorium in Rome, Georgia, when the Goodman brothers had another spat. Once again, the boys' argument resulted in someone quitting. This time, however, Barbara was not along to initiate the peace process.

The backstage dressing areas were divided into three individual dressing rooms. Sam was stubbornly ensconced in one room, Rusty in another, and Howard and I were in the other. Five minutes before the concert was scheduled to begin, neither Sam, Rusty, nor Howard was about to budge.

"Aren't you folks coming out?" one of the band members asked.

"No," came a chorus of replies, the closest thing to harmony that had come out of the Goodman mouths that night. "We're not going on."

"Well, what should we tell the people?"

"Tell them what you want to. We're not singing tonight."

I was being uncharacteristically quiet about the matter. Ordinarily I would tolerate the boys bickering for a while, after which I would step in and say, "All right, that's enough." But for some reason, this time I remained with Howard and made no effort to make peace with the others.

Eight o'clock came, and the Happy Goodmans were still in the dressing rooms, not speaking to each other.

"What are we going to do?" Johnny Minick, our keyboard player, asked Rick.

"I don't know," Rick replied, "but it's time to go on, so let's go play a song." At that time we were carrying a six-piece band with us, and in most concerts, the band was featured on an instrumental rendition of "I Wouldn't Take Nothin' for My Journey Now." So on this night, with most of the Goodmans secluded in their dressing rooms, when the master of ceremonies introduced the Happy Goodman Family, the band took the stage and performed a rousing—and somewhat extended—version of "Journey." The audience, most likely thinking this was the preshow warmup, applauded.

The band members had been rehearsing another song, one in which two of the fellows sang a duet. The band performed that song, too, after which Johnny Minick announced, "Folks, I'll tell you what we're going to do. We're gonna take a short intermission, and we'll be right back."

An intermission? After only two songs! The crowd applauded kindly once again, even if they were a bit confused about what "An Evening with the Happy Goodmans" entailed. Meanwhile the band members exited the stage and scurried back to the dressing room area, wondering what they were going to do next.

They needn't have worried. When Howard, Rusty, and Sam heard the music on stage, something clicked inside. Call it professionalism or spiritual responsibility, I don't know. All I know is that within moments of hearing the band onstage, all three dressing-room doors opened almost simultaneously. The men came out and apologized to one another, and in no time at all they were crying and hugging each other's necks. The Unhappy Goodmans had once again become the Happy Goodman Family. What can I tell you but that our family has been pretty much like yours. We have had our share of fussin', fightin', and feudin,' but in the end, our love for each other always wins out.

In one situation our family's love and ability to bear a wrong was severely tested—when my daughter, Vicki, and her husband divorced. Howard and I had been aware for some time that their marriage was in trouble. Nevertheless, I was stunned when I received a telephone call from Vicki, frantically begging for help. "Mom, please come quickly," she cried. "I need you."

Without even waiting for Howard, I jumped in the car and raced from Madisonville to Nashville, where Vicki, her husband, and their six-year-old daughter, Nicole, and their newborn baby, Donny, were living. When I arrived at their home, Vicki's husband was out. I consoled Vicki for a while, then I called her husband. It was late when he came home, but I was still waiting for him. He wanted to go straight to bed, but I was not about to let him. I kept him awake all night long, talking about his life, his relationship with the Lord, and, of course, his relationship with our daughter and grandbabies.

I tried to encourage him. I offered Howard's and my help to do anything necessary to salvage the marriage and get them back on track. At several points our son-in-law broke down in tears. At other times, he'd get angry and want to go to bed.

"No, we're going to talk," I said. "I am not going to turn loose of this marriage easily. You belong to God; you belong to our family; we've treated you like our own son, and I am not going to give up unless there is no hope."

I had prayed for healing in their marriage, and for more than three years I had believed and fully expected that God would work a miracle in their relationship. I desperately wanted my baby's marriage to be happy. After all, both Vicki and her husband were Christians. Surely God could restore their relationship. But I had not realized the extent to which the marriage had deteriorated. Not even God will hold two people together if one of them is determined to leave.

By seven o'clock the following morning, I knew it was hopeless; I was convinced that nothing else could be done to save their marriage. With a heavy heart, the last thing I said to our son-in-law before he went to bed that morning was, "You can be sure that I will always love you."

Divorce is one of the most traumatic things any couple or family can experience. Howard and I were devastated because we had preached for years that divorce was wrong. But what grieved us even more was knowing that our daughter had stayed in her destructive marriage for several years longer than she might have otherwise because she was concerned about disappointing her Christian parents.

Howard and I arranged for Vicki and the children to move back to Madisonville, and the entire Goodman family rallied around her to make the transition easier. Vicki went to work in our office, and most important, she became involved in the church. Rather than avoiding the family of God out of a sense of failure or embarrassment, she sought strength and support from God's people. And they responded fabulously, with acceptance and love. I believe Vicki's choice to plunge back into the church and the church's response were major factors in her emotional healing.

Nicole and Donny grew up right alongside their cousins, Travis and Leslie. As you might imagine, Howard's and my countryside home was constantly buzzing with activity, and we loved having all the grandchildren about. At one point, when the kids were a little older, we bought them three-wheel Hondas, and the kids raced through our yard until the grass was worn bare.

Some of our neighbors said, "Why do you let those kids tear up your lawn like that?"

I replied, "We can always plant more grass, but we'll only have this time with our grandbabies right now."

One of the joys of Howard's and my life was to sit in our swing out back and watch our grandchildren romp and play and, yes, tear up the grass. We enjoyed it almost as much as they did.

Eventually Vicki remarried, and her husband, Clark Meadows, happily took on the parenting responsibilities of Nicole and Donny. Today, the kids are all grown up and are serving the Lord in various ways. God turned what the devil intended for evil—some of the darkest, most difficult days in our lives—into good.

CHAPTER 22

THE END OF THE LINE

By 1980 it seemed that we were Unhappy Goodmans more often than we were the Happy Goodman Family. A major part of our frustration stemmed from the music industry itself. In the late 1970s, a large part of Christian music was changing radically, moving away from a "southern gospel," country sound toward a rock 'n roll or pop sound. Rusty and Sam wanted to update the Goodman sound. None of us had any illusions about competing with Amy Grant or Michael W. Smith, but the boys felt that if we could make our music more contemporary, we could broaden our audience. They had numerous heated discussions about the direction we should take.

Adding to our dilemma, in 1977 Marvin Norcross, our musical "Rock of Gibraltar," died suddenly of a heart attack while talking on the phone to his dear wife, Chic. Marvin had always been the glue that helped hold our differing musical tastes and opinions together. If Marvin had still been alive, he might have been able to pull us back together again, but Marvin was gone.

Howard and I had no desire to change our sound. We weren't opposed to progress, but we certainly didn't want to sing contemporary Christian music. I was glad for the many new contemporary artists, but that sort of music simply didn't fit the Happy Goodman Family. I didn't even know how to sing that kind of music. We finally came to an impasse with the other fellows, and we all decided it was time to go our separate ways. We had threatened to disband many times before, but this was the real thing. The breakup was amicable but not comfortable. We said things back and forth that we later regretted. Rusty, especially, was offended at Howard and me because of our refusal to change. Some of his comments seared our hearts.

Howard and I continued with the church, but it was never the same. It was no longer the home church of the Happy Goodmans. The group's assets were liquidated and distributed. It was the end of an era: The Happy Goodman Family was gone forever.

But as the popular singer-songwriter Dallas Holm has said, when God closes a door, He always opens a window. Almost immediately Howard and I began receiving invitations to minister in churches, as did the other fellows. Rusty established a strong solo ministry, going out with a piano player and performing in churches. Sam, however, was never able to put anything together musically, so he went back into the business world until he retired.

Johnny Minick, who had been with the family group, stayed on to sing and play piano with Howard and me. Johnny was great, but of course we missed Sam and Rusty and the rest of the band, even if we were half-aggravated at them. Their absence was especially apparent when it came time for Howard and me to record a new album.

We had always relied on Rusty's songwriting as the primary source for our material. Certainly we recorded other people's songs, too, but nobody could express what the Goodmans wanted to say quite like Rusty. If we wanted a song about a certain subject, we'd go to Rusty and he'd write it. Whether Sam, Howard, or I sang the song, it came across onstage and on the album as though it were an expression straight from our hearts, because in a real sense, it was. Rusty was able to tap into our heart cries and put those feelings into song.

Now Rusty was gone, and we were searching frantically for new material from other songwriters. We found several great songs, but as our recording date drew closer and closer, we could not settle on the final songs for the album.

I called Dottie Rambo, one of the most prolific songwriters in the history of gospel music. "Dottie, we're about to record, and I have to have a song that describes what we are experiencing."

Dottie said, "Vestal, I've just written one that will be perfect for you. I didn't know what it was all about, but now I do. The song is called 'Oh, Blessed Hope.'"

When Dottie read the words to me, I knew I had to sing "Oh, Blessed Hope."

In November, about a month after we had left "the Family," Howard and I were in Oklahoma City singing on a live television show. Rick came into the studio during a break and sat down next to me. "Mother," he whispered, "have you thought of any more songs for our new album?"

"No, and right now is not a good time for me to think about it, since we're right in the middle of this television program," I whispered back.

"I know, I know. But we have to have some new songs ready to record by the time we get home, and I can't seem to find anything that says what we want to say right now."

"Okay," I said, "go in yonder in that room and write one."

Rick looked at me as though I had hit him with a baseball bat. Rick had never written a song in his life.

"I'm serious, Rick. Go in there and write. I'll pray."

Rick and Johnny Minick went into one of the back rooms at the television studio and wrote these words:

> *I was facing decisions with answers unknown,*
> *A battle with no end in sight;*
> *But I stepped out in faith believing*
> *That I soon would be receiving*
> *What He promised to make of my life.*
> *He lifts us higher,*
> *And promises we'll not be alone.*
> *He keeps lifting me higher, higher, higher;*
> *So high; soon we'll be home.*

There's troubles on every hand,
But we're not distressed.
Perplexed but not in despair,
Sometimes persecuted, but not forsaken,
Even cast down, but never destroyed,
Because He keeps lifting me higher.

Howard and I recorded Dottie's song "Oh, Blessed Hope" and Rick's song "He Keeps Lifting Me" on our new album. To this day, both songs remain among the most requested numbers we have ever recorded.

The breakup of the Happy Goodman Family was devastating to me, but it could not compare to the hurt I was about to experience. In a way, the group's demise almost helped me to prepare for what was coming.

In May of 1983 Howard and I were in Texas for a concert on a Saturday night. Ordinarily we would have been flying home that night, as we had done throughout the years, but we trusted our associate pastor and felt that the church was in good hands, so occasionally we felt it was all right to be gone on a Sunday morning.

This occasion, however, was not one of those. Although we were not scheduled to be in our home church that Sunday, I felt strongly that Howard needed to be there.

"Howard, tomorrow is Mother's Day, and you need to be home at the church," I told him.

"Well, I don't want to go home and leave you here," he protested.

"I'll be fine," I told him. "Don't worry about me. Something is happening, and you need to be there."

Howard acquiesced and caught an early-morning flight on Sunday. He flew into Evansville, and our daughter picked him up and drove him to the church.

When the associate pastor saw Howard walk in the door, he was flabbergasted. "What are you doing here?" he asked Howard.

"Well, I just felt like I wanted to be here," Howard replied.

"Well, I hope you understand what I'm doing today." He stepped up to the pulpit and said, "Those of you who want to go with me, I'm leaving this church, and I'm going across town to start a new one." With that, he walked down from the platform and out the center aisle.

Pandemonium broke loose in the sanctuary. People were shouting, "I want to say something! Let me talk. I want the floor!"

Howard bounded onto the platform, stepped behind the pulpit, and said loudly, "I am the senior pastor here. Have a seat. There will be no outbursts." Howard calmed the congregation by assuring them that he and I were still committed to the church and that we would be there until the Lord moved us out, no matter who else wanted to leave. Howard's words, soothing as they were to the people who remained, could not bring back the large portion of the congregation that had left with the associate pastor. We later learned that the Mother's Day coup was merely the outward expression of an insurrection the associate pastor and some of his friends had been planning for some time.

Howard and I tried valiantly to keep pressing on, but the one-two punch of the group's dissolving and the church splitting was almost more than we could take. Not surprisingly, our enthusiasm began to wane. Despite the fact that the board voted to give Howard and me a salary, something we had never before accepted from the church, we sensed that our remaining time there would be limited. In late August 1984 Howard and I resigned our positions in the church. We continued to attend church and live in Madisonville for another year, although we were not there very often.

Long before the church's problems arose, Howard and I had been making regular trips from Madisonville to Heritage USA in Fort Mill,

South Carolina, to appear on the popular Christian television program *The PTL Club,* hosted by Jim and Tammy Faye Bakker. In no time at all, we fell in love with the Bakkers, and they sort of adopted us as their surrogate parents. Jim and Tammy referred to Howard and me as Papa and Mama Goodman, and we thought of them as our kids. Almost every Sunday that we were all in town, we had a cookout at Jim and Tammy's house after church. When they caught a cold, I was always quick to make homemade chicken soup for them. We truly were just like family.

Since the Happy Goodman Family was no longer on the road, many of our friends were unaware that Howard and I were still conducting concerts, so appearing on the Inspirational Network provided us with much-needed publicity. Soon our phones began ringing off the hooks again with invitations to churches around the country.

Jim was happy about our rejuvenated career, but he enjoyed having us around PTL and wanted us to become part of his regular staff. Howard and I had confided to Jim what had happened in our church, and he seemed to perceive—even before we did—that our ministry there was drawing to a close. "Why don't you move to Heritage USA and work with us?" he and Tammy often asked.

By July 1985 their invitation sounded mighty good. In one of the most difficult moves Howard and I ever made, we sold almost everything we owned, said good-bye to our church family, and moved to Tega Cay, a subdivision a few miles from Heritage USA. Rick and Dianne and their children moved along with us. Although we moved our office to South Carolina and moved into a home provided for us by PTL, we took no salary or any other compensation from that ministry.

Not that it wasn't offered. But as much as Howard and I enjoyed appearing on Jim and Tammy's programs, ministering on the air, we still wanted to maintain our freedom to go where we felt God wanted us to go. We loved the ministry of Heritage USA, but we felt that if we received a salary and were on staff at PTL, we would feel obligated to be there more often, rather than doing what we knew we were called to do—sing and minister in concerts around the country.

Only once during the three years we lived at Tega Cay did we take any money from PTL. Howard and I were scheduled to do a series of concerts, and I got deathly sick with the flu. Jim Bakker found out that I was sick and was deeply concerned.

"Mama Goodman, you can't go out there and sing and minister this weekend. You can hardly stand up," he said. "Please stay home and get better. Stay in bed, have some hot tea, and recuperate."

"No no, we have to go. We have several concerts scheduled. I don't want to disappoint our friends. Besides, we need to pay bills, and if we don't sing, we don't get paid. We can't just cancel."

Jim got Rick on the phone and asked, "How much would you likely take in this weekend?"

"With three concerts, we hope to take in close to eight thousand dollars, and we really do need the money right now to pay some bills," Rick told him.

A short while later a representative from PTL showed up at our door with a check for ten thousand dollars and a note from Jim Bakker saying, "Stay home, stay in bed, and get better."

That was so typical of Jim Bakker—always kind and considerate, always quick to help others by giving beyond what was needed.

While appearing regularly on PTL, I began to understand more than ever before the awesome power of Christian television and why the devil works so hard to destroy it. We were reaching literally millions of people with the Good News. In fact, we could reach more people in an hour than we could in a lifetime of traveling across the country from town to town.

I must admit, though, that I was surprised at the large number of unusual requests I received from people who had seen me on television. Apparently some of our viewers figured that anyone who appeared on TV was rich. Consequently I received letters asking me for everything from my jewelry to the clothes I wore.

As often as I could, I tried to comply with viewers' requests. I gave away so many clothes that at several points my closet was nearly bare.

Once I received a letter from a woman who said, "Vestal, you look to be about my size, and I don't have a decent dress to wear to church. If you ever get rid of any of your clothes, would you please consider sending them to me?"

I'd get letters saying, "I need a robe," or "I need some underwear," or "I need a coat." I was astounded. I didn't know that people would identify with the personalities on Christian television to the extent that they would feel free to ask for such things.

One day as Howard started out the door, I handed him a box and said, "Please mail this, hon."

"What are you doing now?" Howard wanted to know.

"Oh, a lady wrote to me and said she didn't have a good dress, so I'm sending her one. But, baby, you gotta really help me pray. I can't send any more clothes until I replenish my closet, because I've given away everything I can."

The next day a delivery service rang my doorbell. The man carried a box about four feet long, two feet wide, and six inches deep. It was from a dress shop in Cocoa Beach, Florida, a place I had never been. A letter was attached to the box. I opened it and read, "Dear Vestal, I see you on the TV programs and I enjoy them so much. You really minister to me. I own a dress shop, and I was in my shop the other day when the Lord told me that you needed some dresses. I trust these will work."

I opened the box to discover eight gorgeous dresses that looked as though they had been designed especially for me.

Later I told Howard, "Honey, if I hadn't given that last batch of dresses, these wouldn't have come. But God knew my heart. He knew days before that I would give away those dresses, and He had this woman in Florida send the dresses to replenish my supply. Ain't God good? He knows exactly what we need and when we need it."

CHAPTER 23

THIS CAN'T BE HAPPENING!

Like many Christians, I was devastated in March 1987 when I heard that Jim Bakker had had a one-time sexual encounter with Jessica Hahn seven years earlier. I understood moral failure; Jim was not the first, nor unfortunately will he be the last, minister to make a foolish mistake.

What I did not understand, however, was how Jerry Falwell could suddenly become a friend to PTL and posture himself as the hero who could save PTL from destruction. For those of us living at PTL during that time, nothing could have been further from the truth. Virtually overnight the picturesque Heritage USA became a police state. The spirit of the place changed immediately from one of freedom and serenity, a carefree, peaceable attitude, to an atmosphere of fear, intrigue, and duplicity.

Jim and Tammy Bakker were in California completing Tammy's over-the-counter-drug rehabilitation program when word of Jim's sin and Jerry Falwell's "help" hit the news services. Falwell's regime was cleaning house—anyone who had been associated with Jim and Tammy in any way and was not willing to sign a loyalty oath pledging allegiance to the new leadership had to go. That included Howard and me. Although we were not on staff at Heritage USA, we were living in property owned by the ministry. In short order, we received a letter demanding that we vacate the premises within two weeks.

At first, Howard, Rick, Dianne, and I debated whether we should go or stay. One night while we were deliberating, Howard woke me up, and he was crying. Howard said, "Vestal, I dreamed that we came upon a bad wreck, and there were lots of people standing around watching these cars that were all mangled and bent. I could hear people hollering and saying, 'Help us get out, help us get out,' but nobody would go and help them. I went over and started pulling on the metal of the car, trying to get a door open, and when I finally got it open, I was shocked."

Howard wiped the tears from his eyes as he said, "Vestal, it was Jim and Tammy, and they were bloody and mangled, and they were saying, 'Help us, help us!' I was trying to pull them out of the wreckage. I know that dream was from God; we can't leave Jim and Tammy. We must do whatever we can to help them."

When Howard told Rick and Dianne about his dream, Rick said, "Okay, you and Mom stay here. Dianne and I will go out to California and stay with Jim and Tammy through this mess." We put our own ministry on hold, while Rick and Dianne went to Palm Springs to be with Jim and Tammy Bakker. They spent the next three months trying to help the Bakkers hold their lives together.

Meanwhile back at Heritage, after the Falwell regime had taken over PTL, I went over to the television studio one day to watch the show. The studio was supposed to be open to the public, and anyone was welcome to attend the TV tapings as long as space was available. But as I neared the entrance to the studio, a security guard hastily approached me. I recognized the guard from my many visits to the set to appear on the program. The guard took me aside and whispered, "Vestal, you need to get out of here. Get off the grounds as quickly as you can. If they find out that I told you this, I will be fired, but I just heard on my radio that the man in charge has ordered that you be arrested if you try to get into the studio. The head of security has already called the Fort Mill police, and they are on their way to arrest you for causing a disturbance on the grounds."

Reporters were crawling the grounds of Heritage USA, searching for some new angle on the Jim and Tammy saga. The place that had once seemed permeated by the Spirit of the Lord had been turned into a media circus. Whenever I went anywhere near the PTL property, I tried to avoid the press, but inevitably someone would ask me what I thought about the way things were being handled. I was never bashful about giving my opinion. I guess the new management considered that to be a disruption.

I could tell that the security guard was not joking. I thanked him for the tip and headed for the car. Sure enough, just as I exited the grounds, the police pulled through the gates.

When it became obvious that Jim and Tammy were not going to be able to return to PTL, they retreated to their hideaway mountain home in Gatlinburg, Tennessee. Their children, Jamie Charles and Tammy Sue, were still in the Charlotte area. Tammy Faye and Jim knew it would be a fiasco if they attempted to pick up their children, so they asked if somehow Howard and I could get the kids past the press and bring them to Gatlinburg. We said, "No problem."

That's how little we knew.

We packed up the Bakker children—Jamie was barely eleven, and Tammy Sue was no more than sixteen—and along with Rick and Dianne's children, Leslie and Travis, we started up the interstate. I was driving the car, and Howard was sitting in the front passenger seat. No sooner had we pulled out of Heritage USA than I looked in the mirror, and to my surprise, I noticed that we were being followed. A bevy of press vehicles surrounded us, trying to photograph the children and trying to get us to stop. "Duck down, kids!" I told them as I stepped on the gas. "And hang on!"

The car roared up the highway, faster and faster, but the press vehicles were still on our tail. They careened dangerously in front of us, around us, behind us, cutting from one lane to the other, trying to get a photo of the kids. Several times I nearly lost control of our car as I swerved violently trying to avoid one of the press cars. For their part, the kids were having a ball. From their secluded spot on the backseat floor, they were yelling, "Go, Granny! Go, Granny! Go, Granny, go!"

Suddenly a horrible thought struck me. *If I keep going, I am going to lead this slew of vultures right to Jim and Tammy!* They had gone to Gatlinburg to get away from the media. I knew I needed to contact the Bakkers, but I didn't have a car phone. I decided to risk stopping at a pay phone to make the call. I steered our car off an exit, and the media entourage followed right behind me. I saw a telephone booth outside a restaurant and whipped the car to a stop in front of it. The kids covered up with a blanket as I hurried to make a call to Jim and Tammy.

As soon as we stopped, the press vehicles surrounded us, literally pinning our car in on all sides. The reporters swarmed around me to see what number I had dialed, but they were too late. I already had the Bakkers on the line. "Just keep coming, Mama Goodman," Jim told me. "If the press follows you, we'll deal with that when you get here. We'll be watching for you."

I hung up the phone and faced the press. "Where are you going?" they screamed. "Where are Jim and Tammy?" "Whose children are you carrying?" Hundreds of questions flew at me in a moment. I didn't answer any of them. Howard stepped out of the car and bellowed, "Get out of the way, or we will call the state police!"

Reluctantly the press vehicles allowed us to exit the parking lot, only to fall in line behind us once again on the highway.

"Howard, this isn't going to work," I said. "We've got to come up with an idea." We motored up the highway, the cameramen still pressed against our side windows. An eighteen-wheeler loomed in front of us, and again I nearly lost control as I tried to avoid scraping the press car next to me as I pulled out to pass. But that big truck sparked an idea. "I've got it!" I cried.

During all those years traveling with the Happy Goodman Family, we had spent a lot of time at truck stops. That's where we fueled our bus, and often after a late-night concert that's where we ate our meals. We could identify with the truck drivers' lifestyle, being on the road as much as we were, and truckers had always been friends to the Goodmans. Now it was time to call in some chips.

Racing up the highway I watched for anything that looked like a truck stop. Finally I saw a sign advertising a large auto-truck center. It was worth a try. I waited until the last second before exiting, hoping that some of those reporters in hot pursuit would miss the exit and blow on by. One or two cars did just that, but most of the press was sucking our exhaust fumes.

I screeched to a stop and hurried into the truck stop while the kids covered up and Howard stood guard. It was obviously busy. White-outfitted waitresses scurried around the room, hastily carrying trays of food. A horseshoe-shaped bar was in the center of the room lined with truckers. Booths lined the outside walls, and they, too, were mostly filled. The place seemed enveloped in cigarette smoke and noise.

For a moment I stood in the entryway and wondered if my idea was such a good one. *Oh, well; what do I have to lose?* I thought.

I raised my voice and said, "Fellas, I'm Vestal Goodman of the Happy Goodman Family."

A buzz went through the restaurant. "Oh, I know you!" a bearded truck driver called. "The wife and I have been to a bunch of your shows."

"Me too," someone else called.

"Same here," I heard from behind me.

"Well, I've got a problem, and I need your help," I told the truckers. "I have Jim and Tammy Bakker's kids in my car, and I'm trying to get to Gatlinburg, but there's a whole passel of press behind me, and they won't let me alone. Can you guys help me out?"

"Why sure, Vestal. Anything at all."

In a matter of minutes several truck drivers had lined up in front of our car, gunning their engines and moving ominously close to the press vehicles as if to say, "I want to be where you are parked." One by one the press cars backed off.

Other trucks fell in line behind our car. We rolled out of the truck-stop parking lot with a virtual wall of trucks all around us. The press vehicles couldn't get near us.

"Just keep it in the rocking chair, Vestal," the truckers had told me, which meant that I was to make sure a truck was in front of me and behind me at all times. "We'll get you out Interstate 40 and then you're on your own into Gatlinburg."

We zoomed out I-40, and the kids once again took up their chant, "Go, Granny! Go, Granny! Go, Granny, go!" As we went along, more trucks joined the parade, forming a convoy that C. W. McCall could only have dreamed about. Not a single press vehicle was within miles of us as we honked loudly to our benefactors when we took the Sevierville exit and raced the remaining fifteen miles or so to Gatlinburg. We roared up the side of the mountain, and the gate at Jim and Tammy's home swung open. We flew inside, and the gate shut behind us. It wasn't until we were safely inside the house that I realized the audacity of what had just happened.

People have often asked me since those days, "Were Jim and Tammy Bakker for real? Or were they charlatans ripping off little old Christian ladies?"

I always tell them, "Jim and Tammy were two of the kindest, most sincere Christians I ever met." Jim Bakker was not concerned about having a bunch of money. He didn't really care so much about the property at Heritage USA; he was concerned about the body of Christ—the people who went to PTL looking for fellowship with other believers.

After staying through the darkest days of the PTL debacle in 1987 and 1988 and stonewalling requests from the new management that we move out, Howard and I finally felt that we couldn't take any more. We needed to move. We had not complied earlier with the Falwell camp's requests because we were still hoping that someone would find a document stating that the board of directors of PTL had given us the house at Tega Cay in which to retire. Under Jim Bakker's presidency, Richard Dortch, then executive vice president of the ministry, repeatedly had promised that he would see to it that the house's deed was put in our name. It never was. When the new leadership took over PTL, it was only natural that they would lay claim to all the property owned by the ministry. That included the house in which Howard and I were living.

It was not a dream house. Like most of the homes in that Tega Cay complex, it had not been well built. Only after PTL's extensive refurbishing were any of the ministry homes there improved. Furthermore, the house was three stories high. Howard had bad knees, and even after surgery he could hardly get from one level to another. But the house was all we had, and it had been promised to us. Now even that was gone, and we had nowhere to live. Yes, we could have stayed and fought for what was supposed to be ours, but it wasn't worth it. Besides, by that time, our financial resources were totally depleted.

When we had moved to PTL in 1985 we had money in the bank, enough to retire on, and we were doing okay financially. By the time we moved out in April 1988, we were flat broke. We had to borrow five thousand dollars from a friend simply to be able to move our belongings to a little two-bedroom cabin that fortunately we still owned on Kentucky Lake near Madisonville. It was cramped and crowded, but at least we had a place to lay our heads.

Howard and I continued doing concerts and revivals, and Rick and Dianne commuted from Charlotte to Nashville to meet us. We knew that we needed to find a better living situation, but how? We had no savings; we had nothing left to sell except our little cabin.

Some friends offered to loan us money to make a down payment on a house, so Howard and I began hunting a house in Nashville. We searched for days and could find nothing in our price range. Exhausted, we returned to our little cabin in Kentucky. "Lord, You know I'm perfectly willing to live in this little cabin for the rest of my life, but if You have something else in mind for us, You'll have to show us."

Rick and Dianne drove to Nashville from Charlotte, where they were still living, to take up the search on our behalf. It was a Thursday afternoon when they arrived. Our real-estate agent took them through houses all day Friday and Saturday, but they could not find anything they liked.

Saturday night in their hotel room Rick and Dianne prayed, "Now, Lord, You know where the house is that Mother and Dad are supposed to have. We're not going to talk about it or worry about it anymore, but we're asking that tomorrow You show us the house You want them to have."

The next day Rick and Dianne told the real-estate agent that they did not need any assistance, that they were going to do some scouting on their own. They got in the car and sat there. Dianne said, "Rick, which way should we go?"

"I think we need to go toward the south part of town," Rick replied.

"That's exactly what I was thinking too," said Dianne.

They pulled out of the hotel parking lot and pointed the car south on Interstate 65. They got off the highway on Old Hickory Boulevard, and Rick said, "Which way should we go?"

"I feel like we ought to go west," said Dianne.

With no particular location in mind, they headed west, looking for the house God had for us. They pulled into a subdivision where they saw a sign with an arrow, announcing an "open house" that afternoon. They followed the signs and found the house. Several cars were already parked in the driveway, indicating that other prospective buyers were viewing the property. Dianne got out of the car and walked toward the house, while Rick parked the car.

When Dianne stepped inside the foyer, she froze. A few seconds later Rick walked in, and he, too, stopped short. Tears began to trickle from their eyes. "Dianne, this is Mom and Dad's house!" Rick whispered excitedly.

The house was built on the exact floor plan as our home in Madisonville. It looked as though someone had picked up the home we had designed and built in Kentucky and had transported it to Nashville! As Rick and Dianne walked through the rest of the house, they felt right at home, as though they were walking through the home in which we had lived from 1972 to 1985. It was as though God was giving us back everything we had lost. We continued living by faith, trusting God to bring in the concert dates and the money we needed to survive.

Then in 1991 we did the first of the *Homecoming* videos with Bill Gaither, which jump-started our singing careers once again. We were back on the road, singing all across the country. But I was about to encounter a terror that threatened to put an end to my journey of faith.

CHAPTER 24

NO PROBLEM IS TOO BIG

*I*n January 1992 Howard and I were conducting a series of evangelistic services with Pastor "Happy" Darnell at North Side Faith Assembly in Houston. I had been feeling extremely fatigued and had to spend most of each day in bed at our hotel. I got up just long enough to do the service, and then I was right back in bed. I thought perhaps I had been overdoing it, but no matter how much I rested, I couldn't catch up. One night at the conclusion of the service, I asked our hosts to take me back to our hotel as quickly as possible. I was totally exhausted, fatigued to the point of almost passing out; I had a lot of pain in my stomach, I was nauseous, and my entire body ached horribly. I knew something had to be done.

"Howard, I don't think I can go on with these meetings," I said. The concerned look on Howard's face told me that he understood. He had seen me sick before, but he had never before heard me say that I couldn't go on.

"That's all right. We'll just close the meeting and fly home."

When we got home, Rick took me to the doctor. By now, my stomach had become extremely swollen. The doctor briefly examined me and said that I needed to be in the hospital immediately so he could perform exploratory surgery. I checked into Centennial Hospital in Nashville the following day.

Somehow Bill Gaither found out that I was in the hospital and made a beeline to see me. Bill came into the room and in his usual upbeat manner said, "Well, Vestal. Are you going to make it?"

I smiled at Bill and said weakly, "Yeah, I'll make it."

"You have a lot of folks who love you and are praying for you."

I took Bill's hand and said, "Bill, you pray for me."

Bill hesitated for a moment. "This is kinda tough, Vestal," he said. "Because you're the person we usually ask to pray for us."

"No, you pray for me," I asked. Bill squeezed my hand, and with just the two of us in the room, Bill Gaither prayed one of the kindest, most heartfelt prayers I have ever heard, asking God to touch me and make me well. When he finished praying, I looked up at him from my vulnerable, prone position and said, "Sing me a song."

"Are you serious?"

"Sing me a song, Bill, please."

Bill gulped hard, and the composer of multitudes of songs that have blessed the world began to sing a classic written by another songwriter, Stuart Hamblen. Bill sang for me "Until Then":

> *The things of earth will dim and lose their value*
> *If we recall they're [just] borrowed for a while;*
> *And things of earth that cause a heart to tremble,*
> *Remembered there, will only bring a smile.*
> *But until then, my heart will go on singing. . . .*

I gripped Bill's hand and drew much-needed strength from his faith in God, as well as my own. It was a special moment for both of us.

Later I asked the nurses to call for Dr. Marvin Gregory, my gynecologist. Dr. Gregory is one of the sweetest men I know and is a dedicated Christian. When he came to visit me, I told him, "They said I have to go to surgery, but I told them that I won't go unless you promise to go with me."

Dr. Gregory smiled and said, "I will be right there."

True to his word, when they wheeled me into the operating room on January 29, 1992, Dr. Gregory was there. He held my hand until the anesthetic took effect and I fell into a deep sleep.

Dr. William D. Johnston performed my surgery, and when it was over, while I was still in the recovery room, Dr. Gregory went out to the waiting room to speak with Howard, Vicki, Rick, and Dianne. Dr. Gregory had tears in his eyes. The doctor explained that the problem was in my spleen. He told them that ordinarily a human spleen should be no larger than an orange, but mine was about the size of a football and weighed twelve pounds. Worse yet, the spleen was full of lymphoma . . . I had cancer.

Howard, Vicki, Rick, and Dianne were surprisingly upbeat. "Okay, we can whip that," Howard said.

In the intensive-care unit, I was barely conscious. Dr. Gregory came in and patted my face. I came to just long enough to look up at him and smile. I said, "I love you, Dr. Gregory," and then I was out again. I could hear him, but I could not respond. But while I was drifting in and out of consciousness, I heard Dr. Gregory praying, "Lord, please take care of Vestal, and please don't let her die." He said, "The world needs her and I need her." The last thing I remembered as I slipped back into unconsciousness was the sound of Dr. Marvin Gregory crying.

When I awakened, Rick, Dianne, and Howard were in my room. I could tell that the news was not good because of the way they were trying to protect me. They were not letting anyone see me, as the word had already gotten out that I had cancer. My family didn't want anybody to talk to me about it or to plant any negative thoughts in my mind.

A new doctor, Dr. Charles McKay, an oncologist, soon joined them at my bedside. Dr. McKay explained that the doctors had removed my spleen, because I had lymphoma. Dr. McKay didn't pull any punches as he described the severity of the disease. He said, "I think it is something we can beat, but you have some spots on your stomach and on your liver that we are going to have to watch closely."

"Okay, Doctor," I said, "but how long before I can go back to work?"

Dr. McKay looked at me as if to say, *You poor, naive woman. You don't realize what we're talking about.*

I said, "Howard and I have a lot of bookings, and I have to hurry and get back on the road."

"Oh, Vestal," Dr. McKay said softly. "I don't think that you will have that kind of energy again."

"Oh, but you don't know me; you don't know where my trust is."

"Vestal, you don't understand. You will have to face reality."

I looked back at the brilliant doctor, smiled, and said, "No, *you* don't understand. You're not understanding in Whom I have placed my trust, and I am persuaded that He is able to keep everything that I have committed to Him. And I committed my body to Him long before you ever saw me."

The doctor just smiled.

Dr. McKay suggested that I begin chemotherapy as soon as I was strong enough to do so.

"How long can we wait?" I asked him.

"Until you regain your strength," Dr. McKay replied. "We could wait as much as three months. But no longer."

"Let's wait," I said. "And then let's test again to see if I still need it."

Dr. McKay smiled and said, "All right, Vestal. Three months."

I had heard a multitude of horror stories about cancer, but I believed that God would heal me, not just *could* heal me, but *would* do it. Consequently I never felt one twinge of fear. I was aggravated at the pain from the eighteen-inch incision stretching from the middle of my stomach all the way around my side. But I never experienced fear.

The doctors allowed me to go home, and my precious son and daughter-in-law helped Howard take care of me as though I were a baby. Of course, we had people everywhere praying that God would touch and heal my body. Sue Tripp Smith, a young woman who had lived with us in Kentucky and whom Howard and I regarded as our goddaughter, received a revelation from the Lord. The Lord confirmed to her heart, "Vestal Goodman will not die. She is going to live and will cause the devil even more trouble in the years to come."

Three months later I was feeling fine. I was still wearing bandages all the way around me, but other than that, I felt great. When I went back to the hospital so the doctors could check me and see what kind of therapy I would need, they were amazed. They could not find any cancer in my body!

Dr. McKay was astounded, but as an oncologist he wanted to be cautious. He said, "Let's take some medication for six months as a precaution." He showed me some small pills that he wanted to prescribe.

I said, "Okay, what kind of damage will it do?"

"It won't do any damage," the doctor answered, "but if there is any cancer remaining in there, the medication will help destroy it."

"Will it make me sick?" I asked.

"Not likely."

"Will I lose my hair?

"No. This is not the kind of medication that will cause you to lose your hair. You may have a few side effects, but they won't be anything serious."

I was confident I didn't need the pills, but for my family's peace of mind, I took that medication for six months. Please understand the balance here. I have a great faith in God, and I have experienced His healing power. I know God can heal my body, but I'm also convinced that it is not a sin to take medication. In fact, I think we ought to take advantage of the medical resources available to us. To do so doesn't lessen my faith in God whatsoever. If God wants to use the medicine to make me well, that's okay with me. If He chooses to heal me without the use of doctors, hospitals, or medicine, that's even better. That's why I decided to take whatever medication the doctors prescribed, even though the record said I was healed.

Dr. McKay was right; I never had any serious side effects from the medication. I did have a few small bouts of nausea, but it was never debilitating. Just a temporary inconvenience.

During the first year following the discovery of the cancer, my doctors checked my blood every three months. The second year, they checked it every six months; the following year, only once. To this day,

I still go once a year for a checkup. The report has been the same every time: Vestal Goodman is cancer free.

Satan is not nearly as bright as he thinks he is. If Satan had any wisdom—which he doesn't—he would know better than to attack a child of God. Once a believer goes through a satanic attack, he or she comes out better, stronger, and more committed to the Lord. His or her faith is increased. Look at Job. When he came through the devil's attack, he was twice as wealthy with twice as many cattle. God gives back in abundance.

When I was healed of heart disease, I came out of that ordeal with mega-faith in what God would do. Something similar happened after my bout with cancer. My focus was not on the attack Satan had thrown against me; it was on the God who had healed me. I said, "Thank you, Lord. I never knew what James meant when he said to 'Count it all joy when you're going through diverse trials.' Now I understand."

Now I have a personal vengeance against heart disease and cancer, because I know that the same God who heals me, heals others. He rescued me from two of the most dreaded diseases in our society, and if He will do that for me, He will do it for somebody else. He doesn't love me more than He loves others. He wants them delivered too.

The key is to "come boldly to the throne of grace and make your petitions known," and when you are attacked physically with disease, or emotionally with a broken heart, or mentally with stress, if you are a child of God and you know the Scriptures, come boldly to the throne of God in prayer and make your petitions known to Him. He not only will hear you, He can fix the problem.

Contrary to some Christians who believe in healing, I encourage people who are suffering from an ailment to listen carefully to their doctors and follow their instructions. But remember, doctors are merely well-educated human beings. God is your Creator, and God is your healer.

Frequently someone comes to me and says, "Vestal, my doctor just told me I have cancer. What should I do?"

I say, "First, we are going to pray. The doctor said you have cancer, but we believe in the Great Physician, Jesus Christ. We are going to pray, and we are going to 'cover you with the blood of Jesus.' Satan is afraid of the blood of Jesus and the Word of God. We are going to pray and believe. You go ahead and do what your doctors tell you, but every time they say you have to have more treatments, before you get your treatment, say, 'Let's do some blood work to see if I still have it.'"

During my bout with cancer, whenever Dr. McKay asked me to submit to any treatment or medication, I said, "Okay, you can do this, but every step of the way I want you to do blood work and tell me if I still need it."

I have lot of faith, but I pray daily to increase my faith. Hebrews 11:1 says, "Now faith *is* . . ." That word *is* doesn't refer to last week's faith, but it encourages us to have faith *now*. Yes, faith is the substance of things I hope for, but it also produces the evidence of things I can't see. I base my faith on what Jesus has done for others—the lepers and cripples who were healed, the blind men He healed—and the promises of His Word. Jesus said, "If you ask Me anything in My name, I will do it" (John 14:14, NASB). In fact, just before that, He said, "Truly, truly, I say to you, he who believes in Me, the works that I do shall he do also; and greater works than these shall he do; because I go to the Father" (John 14:12, NASB).

Because I know what God has done for me, I always assume that it is God's will to heal His child, unless God shows me otherwise. I refuse to entertain thoughts that God cannot or will not heal someone who trusts Him. Sometimes, it takes persistence though.

In 1995 Lynnette Hart, a friend of our family, was diagnosed with cancer that had already spread throughout her stomach and other areas of her body. The doctors did everything they could for her; they gave her all the treatments they could, but they finally said nothing else could be done. They told her she should make plans for her death.

One of her family members telephoned me and told me, "Lynnette has cancer, and it is very serious."

I got on the phone with Lynnette and reminded her how God had healed me of cancer. Then I said, "Lynnette, get your scriptures and say continuously like David in Psalm 118, 'I shall not die, but live, and declare the works of the LORD.'" I said, "Lynnette, whatever you do, don't turn it loose; confess your healing daily."

Lynnette's faith was weak, but it was genuine. She believed that God *could* heal her, and gradually she mustered the faith to believe that God *would* heal her. The doctors sent her to the Mayo Clinic, but unfortunately the best experts at Mayo told her there was nothing they could do. They, too, sent her home to die.

Despite the bad report, Lynnette was determined. She said, "I am not going to die, I am going to live."

Admittedly she looked like death. She had lost all her hair, her liver was swollen, and she looked frail and sickly. Still she said, "I am not going to die."

Her husband, Jimmy, encouraged her over and over every day, "Lynnette, say it: 'I shall not die, but live, and declare the works of the Lord.'"

At Lynnette's lowest stage she was so weak and in so much pain that she wanted to die. Jimmy got up on her bed and put his knees on both sides of her, straddling her emaciated body. He laid over Lynnette's face and said, "Lynnette, say out loud, 'I shall not die but live.'"

She said, "Okay, okay, I believe."

Jimmy said, "No! You can't just believe me. Say it!"

Lynnette weakly said, "I shall not die . . ." and her voice trailed off.

But Jimmy was adamant. "Finish it! Finish it, Lynnette!"

"Jimmy, just let me go. I'm too tired."

"No, God told us from the beginning that you're gonna live, and we are not going to give up."

One day when she was begging him to let her go, Jimmy said, "Say it, Lynnette, say it."

Lynnette said, "I shall not die."

Jimmy said, "Finish the rest of it."

She said, "Well, you said it; that's good enough."

"No," Jimmy replied. "You are the one who has to say it."

He kept after her until she said, "I shall not die, but live, and declare the works of the Lord."

Lynnette later told me, "Jimmy was so determined that if I had not finished it, I think he might have slapped me!"

One day, it was over. Just like that, she was healed.

In no time at all Lynnette was back in church, playing the organ and singing. Her hair grew back even more beautiful than it was before, and her energy returned abundantly.

Today, several years later, Lynnette continues to be cancer free; she looks and feels wonderful. To me, Lynnette is a perfect example of a person who did all that she could do—she took all the horrible pain medicines and did everything her doctors asked her to do—but in the end, it came down to her faith in God. The Scripture says that God will never allow us to be tempted or tested beyond what we are able to stand (1 Corinthians 10:13). When God said, "Okay, that's enough," Lynnette was healed.

CHAPTER 25

MIRACLES STILL HAPPEN

God continues to perform miracles today. But He does not intervene in our lives merely for show or for our spiritual titillation. On the contrary, as far as I can see, God does miracles for three reasons: to bring people into a relationship with Him; to meet a need that cannot be met otherwise; (and this is the most important) to cause His great name to be honored on earth.

One night not long after I was healed of cancer, I was standing on the stage in Birmingham, Alabama, in front of five thousand people, along with Howard and Johnny Minick, who was now singing with us regularly. I was singing one of my favorite songs, "What Heaven Means to Me," and as I sang the second verse, I became totally immersed in the sweet presence of God's Spirit, so much so that I had no idea what words I was singing. It was as though the Spirit of God was singing right through me. I picked up the chorus and went back into the song with the trio, thinking nobody had noticed.

After the concert a woman came to me and said, "Well, it happened just like you said it would."

"What's that, hon?" I asked. "What happened like I said?"

The woman looked at me as if she had seen an angel. She said, "Don't you remember when you were on the stage awhile ago, singing about heaven? As you sang, you looked right at me in the balcony; you pointed at me and said, 'Joyce, if you will give your heart to the Lord right now, I will save you and deliver you from drugs.'"

She said, "And so I did. I gave my life to Christ, and I believe He has delivered me from drugs. I don't even have a desire for drugs anymore."

I loved on Joyce for a while and rejoiced with her, but when I got back to the bus, I asked Howard and Johnny, "Do you fellas remember me saying anything about somebody being delivered from drugs tonight?" Neither of them did. I realized that it was not me speaking to Joyce at all; it was the Holy Spirit speaking to her through me as I was singing.

I later learned that Joyce had been a nurse and had been on drugs for years, but that night she was totally delivered and set free. To me, that is a miracle.

As a result of my own healings, my faith has increased, and I am now even more bold to trust God to touch others when they ask me to pray for them. Once we were in a revival in Bell Garden, California, and I had spoken that night on the subject of healing. At the end of the message, I sang "Rise and Be Healed"; then I suddenly stopped. I knew, I *knew*, I *KNEW* that the Lord was going to heal somebody who had an eye problem. It was not my usual way of doing things, but I said from the platform, "Is there someone in the service who has a serious eye problem? God wants to heal you."

A woman stood up in the back of the church and said that she was legally blind as the result of an explosion that had sprayed her eyes with tiny specks of glass. She could see enough to get around, but she could not see to read, write, or drive. The doctors had told her that there was nothing they could do for her eyes, that her sight would continue to dwindle, and that eventually she would be totally blind.

I walked off the platform and met her in the aisle. I had the congregation join me and stretch their hands toward her. We prayed for her and believed with her, asking God to touch her eyes.

And God instantly healed her!

From where we were standing way back in the church, the woman looked up at Brother Coleman McDuff on the platform and told him what color his tie was. She could see perfectly. I rejoiced with her, as did the congregation. Before she left though, I encouraged the woman to go to her doctor and let him examine her eyes.

She came back the next night, carrying a written note from her doctor saying that her eyesight was twenty-twenty.

She didn't need the doctor to tell her that she could see, but I have learned over the years that the devil tries to refute it when a genuine healing takes place. That's why I encourage people who have been healed to go to their doctors; let them confirm and document their healing. I believe the medical verification of a healing increases faith. And that is often why God performs miracles for His children, to increase their faith and trust in Him. When people have documented proof of their healing, and their faith increases, they are going to tell everyone about what God has done for them. That, in turn, will cause someone else to believe. And the Lord's great name will be honored.

One night, during the days when *Jubilee* was still airing, fourteen-year-old Becky Douglas and her mother came to see me backstage after our concert in the Dallas–Fort Worth area. Becky was deaf and could barely talk. She communicated mostly by reading lips and signing with her hands.

That night Becky's mother told me, "She says that when she sees you on TV, she sees Jesus in your face."

That just broke my heart; it tore me up and filled my eyes with tears.

I asked Becky's mother to tell her, "If Jesus loves me enough that He would show through my face, and He loves her enough to allow her to see Jesus in me, then He loves both of us enough to heal her." I looked at Becky and said, "I want you to hear me, and I want you to talk to me."

We prayed, and I asked God to let Becky hear me. After we prayed, I said, "Becky, tell your mother if you can hear me."

Becky opened her mouth and repeated my words, "Tell . . . your . . . mother . . . if you . . . can hear me."

Her mother got powerfully excited, and both she and I started asking Becky all sorts of things, trying to make sure she was actually hearing us and not simply reading our lips. Becky's speech was broken at first, but little by little it got better as she answered our questions.

By the time she left there, she was speaking fluently and hearing everything that was going on. As Becky and her mama prepared to leave the auditorium, I reminded her, "Becky, I don't want you just to see Jesus in me, I want you to hear me singing about Him."

When the Goodmans returned to Fort Worth, Becky and her mother came to our Saturday night concert. She could hear me perfectly. After the concert I told her, "Becky, tomorrow at church, before the service starts, I want you to tell your pastor what has happened to you. If he allows you, give your testimony in church. If he doesn't want you to tell what God has done for you, or if he doesn't accept your healing, find another church. You must have the Word continuously in you to hold on to this healing."

The next time I saw Becky I asked her how her church had responded to her healing. She said that she had gone to her church and had told the pastor what God had done for her. "And he hugged me and said, 'That's wonderful!' And when he went to the pulpit, he had me come to the platform, and he told the whole congregation what had happened to me." The last time I saw Becky she had established a sign-language ministry in her church. God had blessed Becky so she could be a vessel He could use to bless other people.

Not all of God's healing miracles are physical; some are emotional, and those healings are just as significant. David and Renee Byerly are a couple for whom God has done such a work. The Goodman family first met David when he was a young boy in Texas. He and his mama came to our bus after a concert, and he made quite an impression on the family because he knew every song we had recorded. We became good friends almost instantly. Beyond that, David looked and acted so much like our son, Rick, they could have passed as brothers. In fact, over the years David and Rick became as close as brothers.

David's mama had been in poor health and had told me, "Vestal, if anything happens to me, please take care of David." She must have known that she didn't have long to live. David's mama died when he was in his early twenties, so Howard and I took him under our wing as our godson and invited him to come work for us and manage our office.

About the same time, another friend of ours, Renee Crabtree, was also going through some traumatic experiences. We invited Renee to come live and work with us too.

God filled the void in David's life left by his mama's death, and He healed the hurt in Renee's life as well. David and Renee fell in love and married within six months of coming to work for us. Today they are back in Texas, serving the Lord with four precious children of their own: Blake, Brittany, and twins, Brandon and Brady.

God seems to delight in taking what the devil intends for evil and turning it around for good. Karen Lynch is such a case. I first met Karen in Texas in the early 1970s. Not long after that, I received a phone call from her. She wanted to know if she and her husband could visit us in Madisonville. I gladly consented. When Karen and her husband arrived at our home in Kentucky, she asked me to pray that they might have a child. They had been trying to have a baby for quite a while without success, but they believed God could perform a miracle for them.

I prayed for the couple and then, almost to my surprise, I heard myself saying, "Karen, within a year you are going to have a son." I had no doubt that the message was from the Lord.

Eleven months later Karen gave birth to a strong, healthy "miracle baby," a baby boy whom she named Kyle. Three years later the couple had another child, a daughter they named Kerri. Howard and I rejoiced with them and over the years came to love Karen's family as our own. Eventually Karen came to work with us as our secretary. Kyle and Kerri grew up to be sweet, model children.

In high school Kyle became an outstanding football player, and I was one of his most enthusiastic fans, next to his mother of course. I went with Karen to as many of Kyle's games as I could. By the time he began his senior year, he had received several scholarship offers because of his athletic prowess.

In March of that year, Kyle and three of his friends went out to a party. The boy who was driving the car that night started drinking. On the way home he lost control of the car and hit a tree head-on. The impact of the crash threw Kyle out the back window of the car.

The police called Karen about two o'clock in the morning to inform her of the accident. She immediately called us, and we began to pray. Rick raced to the hospital and arrived in time to hear the doctor tell Karen, "Your son didn't make it."

Karen went wild with grief. "No, that can't happen!" she screamed over and over. "Kyle is okay. He'll be out in a few minutes." But Kyle was not okay. A few days later, Kyle was buried in his varsity letter jacket, which he had received that very day.

For the next six months, Karen was a basket case. She tried to come to work, but more often than not, she could only stay a few hours. Some days she could not function well enough to come at all. Nevertheless, whether Karen worked part-time, full-time, or not at all, we were determined to keep her on our payroll and help her deal with her grief.

During that time, Karen became extremely involved with MADD, Mothers Against Drunk Driving. Howard and I went with her to several MADD meetings to sing for the group. Through it all, Karen became a tremendous ambassador for MADD. Today she works tirelessly as the director of Mothers Against Drunk Driving for the state of Tennessee. She travels the country with a message of warning and a message of hope, born out of the death of her "miracle baby." Even in that situation, God has brought good out of what the devil intended for evil.

As I said before, I always assume it is God's will to heal someone until the Lord shows me otherwise, but sometimes we can have great faith, we can pray and believe and do everything else we know to do . . . and God does not heal the person. A situation such as that in 1990 shook me to my spiritual core.

CHAPTER 26

LIFE OUT OF DEATH

For nearly ten years following the breakup of the Happy Goodman Family in 1980, Howard and I had not seen or heard much from Rusty. Although we had all asked for each other's forgiveness, the many hurtful things that were said at that time had created an awkwardness between us; at least it seemed to linger with Rusty.

Since leaving the group, Rusty had established a successful solo ministry. He and his wife, Billie, and their two children, Tanya and April, had moved to Hendersonville, Tennessee, and their family was thriving. Tanya and April had both married, and Rusty and Billie were enjoying their roles as grandparents to Mallory and Allison. Howard and I didn't think it odd that we didn't hear from Rusty quite as often. He had a full and busy life apart from us.

But then one night Rusty called us from Chicago. "The doctors up here say I have cancer," Rusty said through his tears. "I gotta have you with me through this thing."

"We'll be there, Rusty," we assured him.

As soon as Rusty got home, Howard and I drove over to Hendersonville and took Rusty and Billie out to eat. We tried to be positive and upbeat, talking about the goodness of God and reminding Rusty of how the Lord had healed me. But nothing we could say lifted Rusty's spirits. "You're gonna make it just fine, Rusty," Howard told him.

Rusty shoved the food around his plate with his fork, hardly eating a bite. He shook his head and said, "I don't know if I am going to make it or not."

"Yes, you are Rusty," I said emphatically. "You are going to make it."

"I don't know," he replied. "I have not lived good." He sat in the restaurant that day and just cried and cried.

Rusty said, "I repent for everything that I have said about you all and everything I have done wrong. I want you to forgive me."

"Rusty, how many times have you repented for that?" I asked.

"Oh, Lord," he sighed, "over and over and over."

"Well then, God doesn't know what you are talking about. He has forgotten it," I said. "So why don't you forget it too?"

Rusty received what I was saying, but his heart was really broken for the things he had said and done.

I told him again and again, "You can't go back and erase things that have happened, but after you repent, then the accusations about those things are not from God; they are from Satan. The Scriptures say that Satan is the accuser of the brethren. Not God. He doesn't accuse you of anything. When you repented of it, He put it in the sea of forgetfulness and never remembers it again. That is what He says."

Rusty looked at me intently, and I could tell he was carefully considering my words.

"Leave it behind you, Rusty." I continued. "You've asked Howard and me to forgive you, and we've done that. I don't need to hear anything else. All that junk is in the past. It's over. God has forgotten it, and I choose to forget it too. You don't need to bring it up anymore."

Throughout the summer of 1990, Rusty was in and out of the hospital. He underwent all the treatments the doctors recommended. The chemotherapy caused his hair to fall out, and the treatments sapped his energy. He looked awful. Beyond that, the medical expenses ate up his life savings and any money he and Billie had set aside. The financial pressures weighed heavily on Rusty and exacerbated an already difficult situation. After being self-sufficient all his life, the enormous medical bills threatened to bankrupt him.

After several months in critical condition, Rusty told the Lord he was ready to die. He confided to me that he really didn't want to die, but he didn't think that he deserved to live because of some of the things he had said and done. Rusty always felt unworthy. Even though he understood the forgiveness of God, Rusty was a perfectionist, and he said, "I will never be perfect enough."

"None of us are good enough, Rusty," I tried to tell him. "That's what God's grace is all about. That's why Jesus had to pay the price for us. You know that. You said it yourself in a song: 'Had it not been for an old rugged cross, then forever my soul would be lost.'" Rusty nodded, but I could tell he was still having a hard time forgiving himself.

In early September 1990, Michael English, who was singing with the Gaither Vocal Band at the time, had a conversation with Bill about Rusty. Michael had grown up listening to Rusty's music; he regarded Rusty as a hero. Michael said to Bill, "Our buddy Rusty Goodman is in trouble. He's hurting. What can we do for him?"

Bill was already aware that Rusty was battling a serious case of cancer. Because of their mutual songwriting interests, Rusty and Bill had stayed in contact over the years, so it was not unusual when one day Rusty called Bill. During the course of their conversation, Rusty casually mentioned that the medical bills were eating him up faster than the cancer. Bill understood the toll a prolonged illness could take on a family's financial resources. Always sensitive to the needs of others, Bill pumped Rusty a bit further concerning his financial needs.

"Let me see if I can get some people together to do a concert," Bill suggested.

"Do you mean a benefit concert?" Rusty asked.

"Yeah, let me make some phone calls, and we'll see what happens."

Rusty was a bit uncomfortable with the idea of a benefit concert, but he was the only one who voiced any reticence. When Bill Gaither put the word out that he wanted to do a concert to help pay some of Rusty's medical bills that insurance had not covered, within minutes his telephone began to ring. Amy Grant, Gary Chapman, and Michael W. Smith were among the first to answer the call. Amy said, "Sure, I'd be happy to help."

Ricky Scaggs and Larry Gatlin said, "We'll be there and we'll help."

Sandy Patty, Larnell Harris, the Talleys, Steven Curtis Chapman, Russ Taff, Gold City Quartet, Geoff Moore, and Eddie DeGarmo quickly answered the call. In all, more than thirty artists from across the musical spectrum volunteered to perform in a concert at Christ Church in Nashville. The Imperials, First Call, J. D. Sumner and the Stamps, the Christ Church Choir, Bebe and Cece Winans, and a host of other artists, including, of course, Michael English and the Gaither Vocal Band, all offered to participate. The concert card read like a Who's Who of the Christian music industry.

The event was scheduled for September 18, 1990, at seven o'clock. By six thirty, more than forty-five hundred people were crammed into Christ Church, and another two thousand had to be turned away because of fire codes. Traffic was at a standstill as people tried to get anywhere near the church parking lot.

Throughout the concert, one artist after another paid tribute to Rusty, noting his influence and contribution to their careers. Rusty sat with tears trickling down his face most of the evening. One of the most poignant segments of the evening was provided by a series of video clips featuring Rusty singing some of his most beloved songs, such as "Who Am I?" "Had It Not Been," and the almost prophetic, "I've Got Leavin' on My Mind."

Lately all I've got is leavin' on my mind.
It seems it's all I think about most of the time.
How that soon and very soon, I'll leave my troubles so far behind,
Lately, I've got leavin', leavin' on my mind.

Gloria Gaither summed up the feelings of most of us in the room that night with a dramatic reading she had prepared in Rusty's honor. Weaving lines from Rusty's songs throughout her prose, Gloria read:

> Rusty Goodman is a poet; he sees and helps us to see what we might have missed. He notices a grin in an elevator and puts value in a handshake. He reminds the breaking heart that there is a promise of a new dawn and points out to us battle-weary soldiers that we are almost home.
>
> When we've lost someone that we love, Rusty, you've told us of a greater love that we can never lose, a love of our very own.
>
> When we were tempted to put too much store in what we have or what we know, you've reminded us that we really know nothing until we've known the love of God.
>
> When we focused on our failures, you've pointed us to the Potter who doesn't patch up a broken vessel, but puts it back on the wheel and remolds it into something brand-new.
>
> When we struggled for some sense of worth, when we'd feel insignificant, you'd sing to us of a God who cares about robins that fall, lilies of the field, wind-ravaged trees, and frightened sailors in a storm, and assure us that He will speak peace to the storms in us, because He loves us infinitely more.
>
> We found ourselves more than once, because of you, singing at the top of our lungs, *if I could still I wouldn't take nothin' for my journey now*.
>
> And even though we know that for a long time now you've had *leavin' on your mind*, we're asking you to stay, because we need—and this sick old world needs—what you are to us: a lover, a visionary, a dreamer, a poet. We need you here to walk with us and sing your pilgrim's song.

Tears streamed down Rusty's face, and he shook his head slightly as if to say, "Surely, Gloria, you can't be saying those things about me." But she was. Everyone else in that room was saying something similar in their hearts.

At the close of the concert, Rusty wanted to sing one more song with the family. Howard, Sam, and I stood on the platform while Rusty sang from the chair in which he was sitting. We sang a song Rusty had written, "I Believe He's Coming Back Like He Said."

The concert was officially over, but Bill Gaither grabbed a microphone and launched into the hand-clapping "I'll Fly Away."

It was a fitting way to close out Rusty's career.

Howard and I were scheduled for a Sunday-through-Wednesday revival in Jacksonville, Florida, so on Thursday night before we left, we visited Rusty and Billie in their home. He was lying in the den in his recliner, wearing his robe and pajamas. We sat there and talked to him for a while, and we had a wonderful time. Just before Howard and I left, I got down on my knees next to Rusty's recliner and prayed with him. I said, "Rusty, don't give up. I am not turning you loose. You are gonna be healed."

Rusty looked at me with a worried expression and said, "Auntie, I don't know if I am going to be healed or not."

I said, "Well, I am not turnin' you loose."

Rusty chuckled through his pain and said, "Don't turn me loose."

When I got to the door, I turned around and looked back at Rusty to wave good-bye. He looked back at me sadly and tried to wave as I heard him say, "Auntie, don't turn me loose."

Sunday morning Howard and I ministered in Jacksonville at Bro. Danny Drake's church. We had a good service and went to rest in our hotel. Sunday night we returned to the church shortly before service time. Brother Drake was waiting for us and asked us to go with him into his office. That was not unusual; it was our practice to pray with the pastor before each service.

Once inside Pastor Drake's office, however, he said, "I have some very uncomfortable news for you." The pastor paused, and tears welled in his eyes as he said softly, "Brother Rusty went home to be with the Lord this morning."

I thought my heart was going to stop. Everything within me wanted to scream, *No! This can't be true.* I was so shaken I couldn't cry. I was in shock; I simply could not believe that Rusty had died. I said, "Brother Drake, I can't handle this. God was supposed to heal Rusty."

"He did," the pastor said. "There is healing through doctors, healing through faith, the healing of miracles in which there is an instantaneous healing, and there is an ultimate healing in which your body is instantly changed, and you are with the Lord. Rusty got the ultimate healing."

Brother Drake's explanation made sense, but I didn't want to accept it. I hadn't been praying for Rusty's "ultimate healing." I understood that when a Christian dies or when Jesus comes we will have a new body in our eternal state in heaven. But I hadn't been praying for Rusty to go to heaven. I had been praying for, believing, and expecting Rusty to get up out of that recliner and start shouting the praises of God. I expected him to be healed here and now, in this life, not in some ultimate, heavenly way. The idea of an "ultimate healing" sounded hollow as I thought of my brother-in-law's cancer-ridden, lifeless body.

NO! It is not supposed to happen this way. God's Word is true. Jesus said ask anything. And I've been asking, begging almost, believing against the odds that God would heal Rusty. Don't tell me that one of these days we'll all be with Jesus. I know that, but what about Rusty right now? A million questions and emotions pummeled my mind and body all at once.

Brother Drake reviewed some wonderful scriptures with Howard and me in an attempt to comfort us, and I genuinely appreciated his kindness. But in my heart I grieved.

It was about five-thirty, and the service was scheduled to begin at six. The pastor compassionately said, "You folks go back to the hotel, and we'll schedule you for flights the first thing in the morning to fly back to Nashville."

"What are you going to do about the service?" I asked.

He said, "Oh, we will go ahead and have church, and I'll explain to the people."

I said, "No, that won't be God. Satan may be whipping me by telling me that he wanted Rusty home . . . "

Brother Drake interrupted me. "You can't look at it that way, Vestal. You have to believe that Rusty won. You may have lost, but Rusty won. He has no pain and won't have any more, so he won. You may feel like you lost, because Rusty is no longer with you, but you really haven't. You will see down the road."

"Okay, if that's the case, I am not going back to the hotel," I said. "I am going into that service, and I'm going to do everything we had planned to do before we got this news."

At six o'clock Howard and I walked onto the platform, and we sang, and I preached, and we had church. One of the songs I sang was a song that Rusty had recently written just for me. Earlier that year we recorded an album called *Reunion* in which, for the first time in ten years, Rusty, Sam, Howard, and I sang together. It had really been a venture of faith, since Rusty's cancer had already advanced, and Sam had serious lung problems due to emphysema. But we were believing that God was going to heal them both, and who knows? Maybe we could even do a reunion tour.

In preparing the material for that album, I had gone to Rusty's house and had spent a great deal of time with him, talking about the album and the songs but also about what was most meaningful in life to us. Rusty asked, "What do you want me to write for you?"

"The Lord is going to give you a song, Rusty," I replied. "You know me and all my failures and faults. And you know how much I enjoy being with my husband and family, with my grandchildren, with singers and with friends, but the ultimate happiness for me is when I know that I am pleasing the Lord . . . when I am in a service or concert and the Spirit of God is using me to bring honor to Christ. Now that is ultimate happiness to me. When I stand in the pulpit or on the concert platform, singing and ministering, and I can watch people's expressions change from sad to happy, that is ultimate happiness to me. That is the Spirit of God flowing through me out to them, and I love it."

Rusty nodded in understanding. Although we were near the same age, he was almost like a son to me as I shared my thoughts with him. I said, "Rusty, please write me a song about being in the presence of God, because you know how much I love being with the King."

"Okay, Auntie, I'll do it.

A few days later I went back to Rusty's, and he had written a new song just for me: "Standing in the Presence of the King." As I read the lyrics, I realized that Rusty had expressed my heart in song:

> *The world just slips away beneath my feet,*
> *When I'm standing in the presence of the King.*
> *Mortal man could never write*
> *The song that my heart sings,*
> *When I'm standing in the presence of the King.*

That Sunday night I informed the audience of Rusty's death and told them, "I had planned to sing this song, 'Standing in the Presence of the King,' during this service even before I learned of Rusty's death. I could not have imagined, though, that it would be the last song Rusty would ever write for me. I want you to hear it."

I sang all the way through the song, and the people in that church sensed God's presence. It was almost as though the Spirit of the Lord covered the audience like a blanket, as the Holy Spirit poured over that crowd. People stood to their feet and raised their hands and worshiped the King. It was truly wonderful; I knew that Rusty, looking down from heaven, must have been smiling.

When Howard and I got home on Monday morning, funeral preparations were already well taken care of. Nevertheless, I couldn't sit down. I had to keep busy, greeting people who came to offer their condolences, trying to encourage Billie and Rusty's children, and ministering to others. I was exhausted, but I could not sleep. All I could do was pace the floors, debating with God, asking Him to give me peace.

Over and over I prayed, "God, help me to understand why You took him." I knew that God had a plan and a purpose for all this, but I just couldn't see it. I prayed, "Lord, I am not telling You that You did the wrong thing. I know that You know why You did it, but I need to understand."

It was several weeks later before I was able to work through my grief enough to see God's hand in Rusty's death. The Lord helped me realize that, like the apostle Paul, Rusty had fought a good fight. He had run the race and had finished the course. Now Rusty didn't want to fight the fight to live anymore. I believe, at that point, Rusty was so close to the Lord and he had so committed his life to the Lord, that God honored Rusty's request to die and let him go.

One of the people most impacted by Rusty's death was his brother Sam. Before Rusty had gotten sick, Sam's wife, Barbara, and I were talking one day about how close Sam and Rusty had always been. Although they weren't afraid to argue with each other, they loved each other unconditionally. In an almost offhand comment, Barbara said, "I sure hope nothing ever happens to Rusty, because if he were to die, I know Sam would go right behind him."

"Oh, Barbara, don't even say something like that," I said with a laugh.

But Barbara was right. In less than a year after Rusty's death, his brother Sam succumbed to emphysema. Howard had lost two of his brothers, and I had lost my buddies, two of the dearest relationships I will ever know on earth.

On the brighter side, one of the great blessings that came out of Rusty's benefit concert was the establishment of a new "Goodman style" church in Madisonville, Kentucky. Roger and Sue Smith traveled all the way from Madisonville to attend the benefit concert. Sue had lived with Howard and me when she had first become a Christian. She became so much a part of our family that she and Rick and Vicki were like siblings. Roger had been a rock 'n roll musician who had come to know the Lord and had moved to Madisonville to help us in our church. We hooked him up with the Hinson family, who had also come to Kentucky to work with us after Ronnie Hinson had written "The Lighthouse," a song we had recorded, which propelled the Hinsons into a far-reaching gospel music ministry of their own. Roger played piano with the Hinsons, and before long, he and Sue fell in love and married.

Nearly two decades later, after listening to the great music in an atmosphere of praise and worship at Christ Church, Roger said to Sue Baggett, another of our former church members from Madisonville, "Sue, why can't we have a church like this in Madisonville? We have a lot of musicians and other people who were attracted to our area because of the Goodmans, but we haven't had an on-fire, alive church since Life Temple closed not long after the Goodmans moved away. Why can't we have a church like this?"

Roger and Sue Smith and Sue Baggett went home, inspired to do something great for God. They rallied some friends and former members of Life Temple, and together they formed a new church in Madisonville known as Victory Fellowship, a church with the same emphasis on praise, worship, and strong biblical preaching that we had once enjoyed at Life Temple. Within a few years, Victory Fellowship grew to several thousand members. In a real way, the ministry of the Happy Goodmans continues today through the ministry of Victory Fellowship, and for that I give God praise. Once again, what the devil intended for evil—Rusty's death and the demise of Life Temple before that—God still used for good. Nothing happens by accident on the journey of faith.

For Howard and me, it was after Rusty's and Sam's deaths that the *Homecoming* video series really took off. At a time when we thought our career was over, God gave us a new start, a new vision, and a cross-cultural audience we could never have imagined reaching in years gone by. Who would have dreamed that at a time we thought we might be retiring, Howard and I would become "television stars"?

CHAPTER 27

A JOURNEY OF FAITH

I never cease to be amazed at what God is doing through the *Homecoming* video series. He is using those tapes to break down walls and reach across denominational, racial, generational, and even international lines.

In 1997 I received a letter from a fourteen-year-old girl from Ireland. She wrote to thank me for being in the videos, because she had given her life to Jesus as a result of watching us. She confessed that she had quit going to church and had not been living for God. But then she viewed one of the *Homecoming* videos and, in her words, she said she saw Jesus in me. "I want to know the Lord the way you do," she said.

A few weeks later I received another letter from Ireland, this time from a policeman. "I want to thank you for giving my fourteen-year-old daughter back to my wife and me," he wrote. He explained that because of the unrest in Ireland, he had to work long hours, and he had not been able to spend the time with his daughter that she needed. Consequently for a while they had lost her, as she rebelled against her parents. But now, she was back in church and doing well, and their family had experienced a spiritual renewal.

I wrote back to both the teenage girl and the father and encouraged them to keep trusting the Lord. I didn't think much more about it until I was at the National Quartet Convention in September of that year. An attractive young woman walked up to me, towing a man and woman behind her. They introduced themselves and I realized: This is the family from Ireland! They had come all the way to the United States just to see the Homecoming singers in person and to say thank you for what we had done.

The videos have had a profound effect on all of us who have sung on them. We had filmed dozens of videos and were nearly finished taping another when I looked across the room and noticed Jake Hess. Jake had been sick for some time, and we all knew it, and most of us had prayed for him frequently on our own. Yet for some reason, we had never taken time to pray for him as a group.

"We need to pray for Jake," I said to Bill Gaither.

"Okay, fine. Good idea, Vestal. Why don't you lead us."

We gathered around Jake and prayed that God would touch his body, heal him, and give him many more years of usefulness in the kingdom of God. We were unaware that the videotape was still rolling. After the first *Homecoming* video, the crews had learned that some of the most powerful moments in our sessions were the spontaneous events. So they were reluctant to turn off their cameras until we were completely done.

They caught the entire prayer time on film, and Bill decided to keep it in the final product. To this day, people see that tape and are inspired to pray not only for Jake Hess, but for their own friends and family members who are sick.

The videos have also spawned great new friendships among the performers. It's been especially fun to see the way the younger artists interact with those of us who are, let's say, slightly older. For example, it has been a real treat for me to work with Mark Lowry. Mark did his very first album in our studios in Madisonville before he was twelve years old. He was barely big enough to reach the microphone, but even back then, he had a mischievous, sassy way about him. Over the years

I'd see Mark at music events, but I had never worked with him. Then we began doing the *Homecoming* concerts, and we got to be great friends.

Mark loves to tease me, and the audience seems to enjoy it too. He teases me about everything from the foot-high hairdo I used to wear, to my trademark white handkerchief I carry with me when I sing, to the silk pantsuits I wear onstage nowadays. Mark tells audiences, "Vestal may have cut her hair, and she may be wearin' britches, but if she ever gets rid of that handkerchief, I'm outta here!"

One night I decided to give Mark some of his own medicine. He had been teasing me relentlessly about my foot-high hair throughout the *Homecoming* tour. I contacted Lucille Wells in Madisonville and asked, "Lucille, do you remember how to do that big hair style that you used to do for me?"

"Why sure, Vestal. How could I possibly forget that?"

"Great. I need you to do me a special wig."

Lucille styled one of my old wigs exactly as I wore it in the 1960s. I could have hidden a football in there the hair was so high. I took the wig with us to a concert at Family Fest in Gatlinburg.

The Gaither Vocal Band, of which Mark is a part, came on in their usual spot, right after Howard, Johnny Minick, and me. Mark was on a roll that night, teasing me something awful about my hair.

In the middle of the Gaither set, I carried that huge wig onto the stage (with Bill's prior knowledge). I said, "Here, Mark. I'm tired of hearin' you talk about this. I got this off the closet shelf. You've talked so much about my big hair, so here it is. Now you can have some of your own!"

Mark lost it. He was nearly rolling on the floor laughing. And believe me, you ain't seen nothin' until you've seen Mark Lowry in foot-high hair!

Guy Penrod is another young artist with whom I have forged a great friendship through the Gaither videos. With his long, gray-streaked, shoulder-length hair, Guy looks more like a rock star than a member of the Gaither Vocal Band, but one look at his face and it is obvious that the man loves the Lord. Guy is one of the most awesome singers I have ever heard. When he sings, he hits the notes right, but more important, because he strives to keep his heart right with the Lord, the Spirit of Jesus shines through his performance. Guy walks the talk and has an intense passion to know more of Jesus and live more closely to Him.

People ask me, "Of all the *Homecoming* videos you have done, which is your favorite?" It's nearly impossible for me to pick a favorite because all of the videos have special moments that have touched my heart. "The Tabernacle," a video released in 1998, is one of the most powerfully anointed projects I have ever been associated with. Bill Gaither pulled together an outstanding array of gospel singers, young and old, traditional and contemporary. We gathered in an old camp-meeting tabernacle near Anderson, Indiana, and recorded in front of a live audience.

The performers sensed something special was happening, even at the rehearsal the afternoon before the taping. The following evening, when we walked into the tabernacle, we were surprised to see fifteen hundred to two thousand people waiting for us. More important, the Spirit of the Lord was there in an unusual way.

Bill had hoped to capture the ambiance of an old-fashioned camp meeting, and that's exactly what took place. The audience responded enthusiastically, and the singers sang better than I had ever heard them. Each song seemed to get better and better!

We came to the old hymn "Rock of Ages," and Joy Gardner, Reggie Smith, and Stephen Hill sang the first verse as a trio. By the time they finished the first verse, I felt the presence of God so powerfully it was as though I wasn't even touching the floor as I picked up the second verse, "While I draw this fleeting breath . . ." An electrifying atmosphere permeated the entire tabernacle, onstage and in the audience.

Video crews from The Nashville Network (TNN) were taping the program, and when I came off the platform, Bill Carter of TNN grabbed me and hugged me and said, "I've been to a lot of these video shoots, but this is the most fabulous thing I've ever seen! I've never heard anything this great."

Later that night Bill Gaither and I talked by phone. Bill sensed it too. "There's something special about this one."

The following Friday night we did a concert together in Springfield, Illinois. Bill was exuberant. "It's the best video we've ever done," Bill gushed. He brought a "rough" copy of the tape to our bus, and as we watched it together, I had to agree with Bill. There is just something unusual about that video.

The videos have opened up doors for me that I might never have pushed on otherwise. In 1994 the country band Alabama invited me to sing at their "June Jam" concert in Fort Payne, Alabama. I have always been a big fan of Alabama, so I was honored to sing on the same program with them. It was an awesome sight to look out from backstage and see a crowd of over one hundred thousand people assembled in front of the stage. Some people sat on lawn chairs, some on blankets, and others on the bare ground as one country music superstar after another wowed them with their performances. I was the lone, strictly gospel artist on the program.

As I stood backstage, waiting for the stage crew to make their adjustments before I went on, I heard an unusual sound. It started as a rumble and increased in volume and intensity. To my surprise, I heard the crowd chanting, "Vestal. *Vestal*, VESTAL!" More and more people picked up the chant, filling the valley with my name. It was a strange feeling. I didn't really care about the crowd remembering my name—I wanted them to focus on Jesus—yet at the same time, it was an enormous honor that they even knew my name. I had grown up down the road in Fyffe, but this was an entirely new generation of music lovers out there. Many of them had never even heard of the Happy Goodman Family. The only thing I could figure was that they had seen the *Homecoming* videos. When I finally took the stage, I asked how many in the audience had seen me on one of the videos. Thousands of hands went up while thousands of others created a thunderous wave of applause.

In a much different way, the videos have found a new audience for me, one that I would never have suspected. At a concert in Atlanta, a man approached Rick and Johnny Minick in the auditorium lobby. "Can I tell you something?" the man said quietly.

"Sure, go right ahead," Rick responded casually. Rick expected the man to make a request or offer a suggestion concerning our music or our stage production. My son was totally unprepared for the man's comment.

The fellow said, "Your mom is really popular within the gay community. She is very much loved."

After Rick got over his shock, he asked, "Why do you think that is?"

"Because we feel unconditional love from her when we hear her sing."

I can't attest to the fellow's assertions, but I do know that I have a genuine concern and compassion for the men and women caught in gay and lesbian lifestyles. While I do not condone homosexual sin any more than heterosexual sin, I am often grieved by the way Christians have treated homosexuals. I believe that God hates the sin but He loves the sinner and so should I. I am especially concerned for those who are dying with AIDS. They are the walking dead, and they need to see and hear about the love of Jesus . . . soon!

That's why I accepted an invitation in 1997 to participate in a recording along with Kathy Trocoli, D. C. Talk, Carman, and other artists for the benefit of AIDS hospice services. If we refuse to reach out to the "modern-day lepers," how can we call ourselves followers of Jesus Christ?

One of my greatest blessings as a result of the *Homecoming* videos has been the resurgence of traditional gospel music among young people. For a while I seriously wondered whether my style of gospel singing was doomed to simply fade away. But thanks to the videos, we have an entirely new generation of young people singing those grand old songs. I see the young people in our concerts every night, and I'm hearing them sing around the country. How it thrills my heart to hear them!

I truly believe that God has raised up Bill and Gloria Gaither to be bridge builders between various segments of the Christian community. Something about the Gaithers' character elicits trust. I am not afraid to trust Bill and Gloria about anything. Maybe that's why when Bill suggested that Howard and I go to sing at Thomas Road Baptist Church in Lynchburg, Virginia—Jerry Falwell's church—Howard and I seriously considered it.

The Gaithers had sung at Thomas Road—in fact, they had been singing there in March 1987 on the very night the PTL scandal first erupted. A few years later when the early *Homecoming* videos first came out, Jerry Falwell promoted "Old Friends" and "Turn Your Radio On" in his television programs.

When Bill Gaither first suggested to Jerry that he should have us sing at his church, I was surprised. Bill knew that we had been asked to leave our home at PTL under the watch of Jerry Falwell. But Bill was quietly insistent. "I think you ought to go," he said. "There needs to be some healing there."

Howard and I finally consented, and a concert was scheduled for June 1995 at Thomas Road Baptist Church. On Memorial Day, two weeks before the date we were scheduled to appear at Jerry's church, I fell and broke my foot. Rick took me to Dr. Larry Laughlin, a Christian doctor who knew me very well. Larry put my foot in a cast that stretched all the way up to my knee.

When I looked at my leg and looked at our schedule, I was concerned. We were scheduled to fly to Dallas on Saturday to sing and minister at a church there on Sunday morning and evening. On Monday we were to fly to Los Angeles where we were to be with Kenneth and Gloria Copeland at their Believers' Convention in Anaheim.

Friday afternoon before we left Nashville, I said, "Wait a minute! I am not going to the Believers Convention with this cast on." The cast and the believers' convention didn't go together in my mind.

I went back to Dr. Laughlin and told him to cut off that cast.

"No, Vestal, I can't do that," Dr. Laughlin said kindly. "You don't understand. With your foot being broken the way it is, with just one little slip, we could wind up having to put pins in it. You have to wear that cast for twelve weeks, and then we will X-ray it again, and if it needs some pins, we will put them in then. If that happens," Dr. Laughlin looked at me with a serious expression, "you will have to keep another cast on your foot for another twelve weeks. But if it is healing, we will just put a regular cast back on it, and you will wear it for another twelve weeks."

I smiled as sweetly as I could at my doctor friend and said, "No, it has to come off."

Dr. Laughlin looked at me, sighed, and shook his head. Miracle of miracles, he began sawing that cast off my foot.

"Now you need this cast," he said, "so I'm going to leave it cut open, but I will put heavy tape around it." He looked at Rick, as if hoping to talk some sense into one of us, and said, "She must not walk on this foot without this cast."

The doctor also gave me a lightweight cast, which attached with Velcro. "Vestal, when you go on the platform, wear this, use your crutches, and be very careful, and the minute you come off the platform, put that heavy cast back on and tape it up tightly."

"Okay, I will do that," I promised.

As I packed to leave on Friday night, Dianne came in the bedroom and noticed that I had put some shoes in my suitcase. "Mom, don't put those shoes in there," she said. "You aren't going to be wearing shoes."

"Oh yes I will," I said. "I will be wearing these shoes before I get home."

In the service Sunday morning in Dallas, I took the cast off and went on the platform wearing only the lightweight cast. As I had promised Dr. Laughlin, after the service Rick replaced the hard cast.

When we arrived in Anaheim, Rick told Kenneth and Gloria Copeland about my foot and how I had brought my shoes along in anticipation of being healed. That night, I even took a pair of shoes in a tote bag from the hotel to the auditorium. When we went out on the platform to sing, I wore the small cast on my foot, but I didn't take my crutches on the platform.

I said, "I am not going to do it." I looked down at my foot and said, "Foot, if you want to hurt, you're just going to hurt, but I am not using those crutches."

We sang three songs, and when we finished, Howard assisted me as we started off the stage. Kenneth Copeland came onstage and said, "Wait a minute, Vestal!" He turned to the ten thousand people at the Anaheim Convention Center and told them about my foot. He even told them I had shoes backstage in a tote bag.

"Now, folks, if Vestal Goodman believed enough that she brought shoes," said Kenneth, "then let's believe with her that God will heal that broken foot." The congregation stretched their hands out toward me and prayed. As they did, I felt the Spirit of God. A warmth similar to what I felt when I was healed of heart trouble went through my body in an instant. In a moment I knew, as well as I knew my name, that my foot was healed.

I put my foot on the floor and banged it. Then I jumped up and down and did a little holy dance; I mean I was just havin' a party! And the entire audience was, too, as their faith leaped toward God.

I went backstage and put my shoes on and never put that cast on again. "Rick, whatever you do, don't call Dr. Laughlin," I said. "He will have a fit."

I knew that our good doctor friend would find out anyhow, so when we returned to Nashville, I called the doctor and told him what had happened. He understood and believed (an advantage to having a believer as a physician). "I believe you, Vestal. But you need to get it checked."

"Larry, I don't have time," I said. And I really didn't have time because that weekend we went to Jerry Falwell's church in Lynchburg.

We were scheduled at Thomas Road for both the morning and evening services on Sunday. We arrived well ahead of time and waited behind the platform in a comfortable room with a sofa and easy chairs. Several of Jerry's associates were in the room with us.

I had a queasy feeling in my stomach. Try as I might, I could not forget some of the harshness we had experienced at Jerry Falwell's hands at PTL. While the men talked and laughed all around me, I prayed so hard for the Lord to erase those thoughts from my mind. I wanted to be able to minister with a clean heart and mind, not only to Jerry Falwell, but to two thousand or so people who had gathered in the sanctuary that morning.

I prayed, "Lord fill me with Your love so these people feel Your presence and Your anointing, and they will be blessed."

When Jerry Falwell entered the room right before service time, he could not have been more gracious to us. He was kind and jovial. Maybe because of the tension, we were all trying a little harder to keep our meeting very lighthearted. As we prepared to go out to the platform, I said, "Jerry, I brought my Bible in case you need me to preach this morning."

Jerry and his underlings laughed heartily. That broke a lot of the ice. "I think I will be able to handle it," Jerry replied.

"Okay," I said, "but in case you get into any problem out there and have any lack of memory, I have my Bible."

Jerry chortled again, and we made our way onto the platform.

Rick went to the sound booth, and Dianne sat down about three rows deep in the front of the church, where she could watch everything. When it came time for us to sing, Rick had cued up a soundtrack to the old Fanny Crosby hymn "Blessed Assurance," one of my favorites.

At the time I didn't know that "Blessed Assurance" was also Jerry's favorite hymn. While I sang, Jerry kept reaching over and wiping tears from his face. Then I sang "God Walks the Dark Hills," and as Dianne later told me, Jerry seemed genuinely touched.

The service that morning was a step toward healing, just as Bill Gaither had hoped it would be. The Lord worked beautifully, and the people were blessed. The evening service was also a wonderful time of praising the Lord. The people of the church were so kind and sweet to us; they made us feel right at home.

After the Sunday night service, we were to eat with Jerry and his wife, Mazell, and several of the church people. When we stepped outside the church, Jerry said, "Vestal, I want you to ride with me."

Dianne and I climbed into Falwell's sports utility vehicle with Jerry. As we pulled out of the parking lot, Jerry said, "Vestal, the reason I wanted you to ride with me is that I wanted to ask you about this thing with your foot. They tell me that you had a real healing. Is that right?"

As we rode along, I explained to Jerry how I had fallen and broken my foot and how I had been healed.

Jerry seemed genuinely interested. "I want to tell you that I think that story about your foot being healed is awesome." Then almost as if he were speaking to himself, he said, "That is amazing; I wonder why that happened."

"Jerry, do you know why that happened?"

"Well, yes," he answered slowly, "and no."

"Okay, I am going to explain it to you," I told the world-famous preacher. "You preach John 3:16 with a fervor, and you preach it because you believe it. You believe that God loved people enough that He gave His Son to save them. You are so thoroughly convinced that you can preach it with conviction and convince other people, and they get saved. Because *you* believe it. That is wonderful. I believe it, too, and I also believe the promise in Isaiah 53 that says 'with his stripes, we are healed.' And that's why I'm healed, because I believe it."

"It would have to be that way, wouldn't it?"

"Yep," I said. "Brother Jerry, maybe you've never experienced a miraculous healing, but if you ever need one, it is available. Start telling your people that God not only heals the soul, but He heals the body as well, and that is Scripture."

He started laughing and said, "You know how to get a guy, don't you?"

"No, I am just telling you what the Word says."

I think Jerry Falwell was glad when we arrived at the restaurant, just to get away from me, but he was kind and gracious anyway.

Jerry never apologized for anything that happened at PTL; I'm convinced that he still thinks he was within his spiritual rights to do what he did. That's between him and God. As for Howard and me, we've forgiven. We don't have time to carry grudges. There's too much to do, too many people to tell about the wonderful love of Jesus. I don't want anything in my life that will interfere with God's willingness to use my life for Him.

Since I was sixteen years old and first came to truly know Christ, my prayer has been and still is: "Lord, see my future. You know my future. If there is a spot ahead of me where I might fail You, then just before I let You down and bring reproach on Your name, please take me out of this world." My concern is not simply to miss hell but to avoid ever bringing the name of my Lord into disrepute.

Although it had nothing to do with letting the Lord down, during the summer of 1997, I began to wonder if my time on earth was drawing to a close. For the first time in more than twenty years, I experienced renewed pains around my heart. I went to see Dr. Andrew F. Gaffney, a top-notch flight surgeon who flew as an astronaut on flight STS-40 aboard the space shuttle *Columbia*. After examining me, Dr. Gaffney said he felt 97 percent sure that I had some major problems with my heart, possibly a valve that wasn't functioning or a leakage around my aorta that needed to be corrected. He referred me to Dr. Greg Chapman, who suggested they do an angiogram at Vanderbilt hospital in Nashville to determine what was causing, and hopefully to alleviate, my heart pain.

On July 3, the night before surgery, as I was lying in the hospital bed, I talked straightforwardly with the Lord. I said, "Lord, we've had a good trip together. I've had fun in this life. At times it's been rough, sometimes it's been tough, but most of all it's been fun. Now if You're through with me, when the doctors operate, let's not mess around. Just shut off my heart and take me out of here. But if You're not finished with me, if there's more You want to do in and through me, when the doctors get in there, don't let them find anything. Let there be absolutely nothin' wrong with me. Let the doctors conclude that they made a mistake in their diagnosis, or better yet, let them realize that You fixed the problem before they got in there."

The next day Dr. Chapman performed the angiogram. Following my surgery, Dr. Gaffney came to visit me in my hospital room. He had a puzzled look on his face. Rick and Dianne and their children, Travis and Leslie, my daughter, Vicki, and our friends Roger and Sue Smith were in the room with me as the doctor said, "Vestal, I can't explain this. I was 97 percent sure that you had major heart problems. But, Vestal, there was nothing wrong with your heart. We found no valve problem, no problem with your aortic arteries, no leakage, nothing. I don't have an explanation."

"Okay, I do," I told the doctor. I told him what I had prayed the night before the operation.

"Well now, I'm not into all that," Dr. Gaffney said with a smile.

"Yeah you are," I replied as I smiled back at him. Since then, Dr. Gaffney and I have become great friends. My heart is still going strong, and I'm still singing.

Over the years I have sung thousands of songs, and I have always tried to sing upbeat, positive messages about the Lord. If a song had a negative feel to it, I would not sing it. Similarly, I refused to sing sad, dreary, tear-jerking numbers. On the other hand a song does not have to be a rousing, hand-clapping, foot-stomping, camp-meeting number for it to be uplifting. The song that best characterizes my life these days is a slow song, the old standard, "Sweet Hour of Prayer." The song is talking about me—"till from Mount Pisgah's lofty height, I'll view my home and take my flight"—that's where my heart and mind are these days.

> *This robe of flesh, I'm gonna drop; then I'm gonna rise,*
> *and I'm gonna grab hold, seize, that everlasting prize.*
> *And then I'll say farewell, because I will have prayed my last . . .*
> *Sweet hour of prayer.*

That is the ultimate journey of faith.

In August 1997 at the Christian Artists Seminar in Estes Park, Colorado, Howard and I were honored with a Lifetime Achievement Award for being pioneers in Christian music. I appreciated that wonderful award and all that it represented. Topping it off, on April 2, 1998, the Gospel Music Association presented us with its highest honor—The Happy Goodman Family was inducted into the GMA Hall of Fame. But the award that I really hope to win is the affirmation of Jesus, "Well done, good and faithful servant. Come on in, I have your new home ready. You have arrived at your destination. Your journey of faith is complete."

Until then, I'm going to be singin' God's praises, I'm gonna keep carryin' the gospel to the world—just like Daddy said I would.

The journey continues.

Sunday July 5
The news - Is many people Having corona
china has a high rate Virus
we didn't have church today
Because of the virus.

CPSIA information can be obtained at www.ICGtesting.com
Printed in the USA
LVOW120811210812

295223LV00001B/21/P